The Politics of Informality

THE POLITICS OF INFORMALITY

HOUSING AND PLANNING IN MEXICO CITY

EMILIO DE ANTUÑANO

University of Texas Press *Austin*

First edition, 2026

An early version of chapter 6 was first published as "From the 'Horseshoe of Slums' to Colonias Proletarias: The Transformation of Mexico City's 'Housing Problem,' 1930–1960," *Comparativ. Journal of Global History and Comparative Social Research* 30 (2020).

♾ The paper used in this book meets the minimum requirements of ANSI/NISO Z39.48-1992 (R1997) (Permanence of Paper).

Library of Congress Cataloging-in-Publication Data

Names: Antuñano, Emilio de, author
Title: The politics of informality : housing and planning in Mexico City / Emilio de Antuñano.
Description: First edition. | Austin : University of Texas Press, 2026. | Includes bibliographical references and index.
Identifiers: LCCN 2025054182 (print) | LCCN 2025054183 (ebook)
ISBN 978-1-4773-3435-5 hardcover
ISBN 978-1-4773-3573-4 paperback
ISBN 978-1-4773-3436-2 pdf
ISBN 978-1-4773-3437-9 epub
Subjects: LCSH: Municipal government—Mexico—Mexico City—History | Urban policy—Mexico—Mexico City—History | Squatter settlements—Mexico—Mexico City—History | Citizenship—Mexico—History | City planning—Mexico—Mexico City—History | Mexico City (Mexico)—History | Mexico City (Mexico)—20th century
Classification: LCC JS2128 .A58 2026 (print) | LCC JS2128 (ebook) | DDC 307.1/216097253—dc23/eng/20260212
LC record available at https://lccn.loc.gov/2025054182
LC ebook record available at https://lccn.loc.gov/2025054183

doi:10.7560/334355

Para mis papás,
y en recuerdo de Luis Fernando Granados

Contents

Abbreviations

AGA	Archivo General Agrario
AGN	Archivo General de la Nación
AHCDMX	Archivo Histórico de la Ciudad de México
AHSS	Archivo Histórico de la Secretaría de Salud
ANPRM	Asociación Nacional para la Planificación de la República Mexicana
BNHOP	Banco Nacional Hipotecario y de Obras Públicas
CIAM	Congrès Internationaux d'Architecture Moderne
CNOP	Confederación Nacional de Organizaciones Populares
CONAMUP	Coordinadora Nacional del Movimiento Urbano Popular
COPEVI	Centro Operacional de Vivienda y Poblamiento
CORETT	Comisión para la Regularización de la Tenencia de la Tierra
CSS	Consejo Superior de Salubridad
DDF	Departamento del Distrito Federal
DOP	Departamento de Obras Públicas
FDN	Frente Democrático Nacional
FOPDF	Federación de Organizaciones Proletarias del Distrito Federal
ICHP	International Congress on Housing and Planning
INV	Instituto Nacional de la Vivienda
IPN	Instituto Politécnico Nacional
ISI	import-substitution-industrialization
ISSSTE	Instituto de Seguridad y Servicios Sociales de los Trabajadores del Estado
MORENA	Movimiento de Regeneración Nacional
MRC	Movimiento Restaurador de Colonos
MUP	Movimiento Urbano Popular
PNR	Partido Nacional Revolucionario

PRD	Partido de la Revolución Democrática
PRI	Partido Revolucionario Institucional
PRM	Partido de la Revolución Mexicana
SCOP	Secretaría de Comunicaciones y Obras Públicas
UNAM	Universidad Nacional Autónoma de México

Illustrations

Figures

Tables

The Politics of Informality

INTRODUCTION

The Problem of Informality

For more than a century, Mexico City authorities have understood urban informality as a public problem, at times as an acute crisis. Yet the existence of spaces and populations at the margins of the law has allowed the same authorities to govern the city and negotiate the provision of housing for popular groups. Architect and critic Mauricio Gómez Mayorga in the 1940s described large swaths of the city peripheries as an "abnormal," "cancerous tissue," without "order and law."[1] But the neighborhoods that Gómez Mayorga viewed with alarm were already—*as he wrote*—in the midst of a process of upgrading led by city officials working in conjunction with local resident associations, a collaboration premised on the fact that these places were violating multiple planning codes. They were what we would today call "informal." In this book I describe the emergence of informality around 1900 and its evolution over the twentieth century. I historicize the ways in which policymakers have construed informal neighborhoods as a public problem, arguing that political negotiations over housing cemented the legitimacy of the postrevolutionary state as the government bent its rules for its own benefit. In a nutshell, I claim that long-standing concerns over informality conceal a mode of governance premised on the selective application of the law and the blurry and shifting demarcation between the formal and the informal city.

The informal city is the outcome of authorities defining a space or the people who occupy it as outside of the law.[2] While urban informality is associated with economic precarity, social stigma, and self-construction, the informal city has no intrinsic morphology or geography. The laws that demarcate it change over time: sanitary codes, planning ordinances, and property regimes, among others. Regardless of its legal defiance, the informal city is not the "anti-state" but rather the state's bastard child.[3] Informal neighborhoods in Mexico City have seldom been eradicated by the state. In fact, they have consistently been surveyed, mapped, and governed by state officials. Indeed, informal neighborhoods were at the center of state formation, urban governance, and local politics. In the wake of the Mexican Revolution of 1910, the opposition between formal and informal neighborhoods carved out a discursive and political arena where city officials, land developers (*fraccionadores*), political brokers, and working-class families made claims to the city. Even as authorities construed them as a public problem, informal neighborhoods bolstered the legitimacy of postrevolutionary governments, which often sanctioned their neighborhood associations, awarded property titles, and provided water, street pavements, and other municipal services. They were a rhetorical scapegoat that strengthened the authority of sanitary officials, planners, and other urban experts, but they also represented a source of profit for developers and a political bounty for populist politicians. Crucially, informal neighborhoods gave popular groups reliable access to housing, becoming the most widespread form of housing in twentieth-century Mexico City.

Informal neighborhoods, in sum, enabled the Mexican state to combine the imperatives of urban modernization with the promises of social justice derived from the Mexican Revolution. The relationship between city authorities and popular groups in informal neighborhoods was defined by the latter's paradoxical position: settlers (*colonos*) and residents stood in defiance of the law while being the beneficiaries of the revolutionary regime.[4] This contradiction produced a form of citizenship premised on access to housing within an unequal and segregated city. The phrase "problem of informality" therefore has an ironic ring and an oxymoronic quality, for the existence of urban informality was crucial for the consolidation of Mexico's postrevolutionary political arrangement.[5] The people and places that the state has defined as outside of the law were central to the political life of the capital. While elites have crafted a narrative of informal disorder to understand the city and justify their authority over it, residents of informal neighborhoods successfully negotiated with the government their integration into the city (citizenship) through access to housing. This was no utopia, but neither was it the city on the brink of collapse that planners and other experts have long decried.

Historicizing Urban Informality

Much ink has been spilled on the term "urban informality," often to denounce it as analytically unsound and politically suspect. In the process of writing, I have questioned the utility of the term, lest I infuse new life into it or succumb to simplistic dualisms, overgeneralization, and historical anachronism.[6]

But the heavy baggage that "urban informality" carries for the historian represents an opportunity as much as a pitfall. While the term was not coined until the 1970s, it contained traces of a longer history of anxieties over populations and spaces in defiance of the law and continues to do so.

"Informal" was first used by economist Keith Hart in 1973 to describe the unregulated labor sector in Ghana.[7] An artifact of the developmentalist era, the term remains suffused with dualisms: modernity and tradition, state and society, First World and Third World. Scholars have used "informal" to describe labor markets not regulated by the state, untaxed economic sectors, and illicit urban economies. In the realms of housing and the production of space, "informal" became a catch-all term describing all sorts of phenomena: self-construction; housing without property titles or municipal services and in defiance of city regulations; precarious dwellings occupied by poor residents; and patron-client relationships between settlers, political brokers, and city officials.[8] These characteristics are not intrinsic to each other: illegality is not always accompanied by precarity; wealthy dwellings often break the law. But it was the conflation of legal, architectural, and social categories and prejudices that made the term resonant. To put it bluntly, breaking the law became a problem when it was poor people doing it and when it was deemed a symptom or harbinger of other crises: sanitary, social, political, and environmental.

The invention of urban informality dovetailed with a sense of emergency in the "Third World." "Informal" was from the onset an orientalist term, inscribed within a geopolitics of knowledge production.[9] This was certainly the case in Latin America, where the category of the "Latin American city"—to borrow architectural historian Adrián Gorelik's formula—became associated with squatter settlements, demographic explosions, and revolution.[10] The Mexican state assumed that irregularity was a "problem" in the 1970s, sociologist Emilio Duhau argued, with the shantytown of Ciudad Netzahualcóyotl elevated to a national crisis.[11] In response, President Luis Echeverría Álvarez (1970–1976) made housing a cornerstone of his administration, conducting massive regularization programs for "irregular settlements" increasingly seen as the city's most urgent challenge.

But the history of informal neighborhoods as conceived by intellectuals and codified in urban regulations predates the coining of the term, warranting its anachronistic use.[12] The existence of precarious dwellings outside of the law—and their rendering as a public problem by experts—in Mexico dates to the turn of the twentieth century, when sanitary authorities viewed "irregular" and "insalubrious" shanties as a locus for disease and a broader "social threat."[13] Contrasting Mexico City with an ideal master plan, 1920s planners described large swaths of the city as anarchic and disorderly. "Mexico

City continues to expand in defiance of the inchoate and confusing actions or inactions . . . of its planning institutions," according to a 1945 editorial in an architectural journal.[14] By the postwar decades, concerns over "squatter settlements," "explosive growth," and peasant migrants saturated scholarly analyses and popular representations of Mexico's capital, with one journalist describing it as a "modern Frankenstein who would annihilate the society that created him."[15] According to a landmark 1952 housing survey, a quarter of the population lived in proletarian neighborhoods, an urban form (wrongly) described as akin to squatter settlements (*colonias paracaidistas*).[16]

These alarms reached a fever pitch in the 1970s. "No one could ever imagine that eleven million would one day live here," wrote Jorge Ibargüengoitia, the city's most ironic chronicler. "The future twenty years from now is a vision no one can dare to imagine."[17] I still remember a pervasive sense of dread in the 1990s, the certainty that demographic and environmental catastrophes were looming. I did not realize it at the time, but the place where I was growing up had come to embody the dystopic megacity.[18] But while its population has more than doubled since Ibargüengoitia penned these lines, the city lives on, rumors of its demise clearly exaggerated.

Concern over the informal city has always hidden deeper anxieties about incomplete modernization, the specters of growth and disorder, and the presence of the "urban poor."[19] In Mexico as elsewhere, these anxieties were inflected by teleological historical narratives, normative visions of an ideal city, and middle-class sensibilities. They were also premised on scientific discourses—sanitation, planning, environmentalism, among others—that changed over time but shared continuities. Among these, "informal" has always been an ethnocentric concept, describing a place as a failure measured against an archetypical "Western" city.[20] I refer to these discourses about the city and its relationship with the law as the "problem of informality," a formulation that should not be confused with the reality of people living in neighborhoods that are breaking the law. While these spaces have existed since the colonial period, the construction of informality as a public problem began in the last decades of the nineteenth century, when concerns about urban disorder, uncontrolled growth, and the place of the urban poor crystallized as an existential challenge to the modern city.

Politics in the Interstices of the Law

As a historical discourse, the problem of informality can be documented in housing surveys, urban reportages, and photographs of shanties and tenements—what historians Brodwyn Fischer and Charlotte Vorms refer to as the "intentional archive of the informal urban experience."[21] I use these sources throughout this book. But the assumption that informality is a problem obfuscates the normalcy of these neighborhoods, their routine relationship with public authorities, and the fact that they were consistently regularized and integrated into Mexico City.

Long before the federal government introduced a policy of large-scale regularization of informal settlements in the 1970s, federal and local authorities had devised written and nonwritten modes of governance to manage them, often through the selective nonapplication of the law.[22] For instance, sanitary and zoning regulations were only sporadically enforced by city officials, who instead negotiated with neighborhood associations over noncompliance with the law. Likewise, the proliferation of property claims in the city—compounded by a myriad of property regimes—gave authorities wide leeway to support some claims over others, using political tools such as expropriations to resolve legal conflicts. Authorities also used official neighborhood blueprints to allocate lots among settlers in a discretionary manner. Amid an abundance of state regulations and "spatial fixations" like cadastral plans, the law set the rules of the game whereby competing social groups negotiated their interests and visions.[23] In the case of Mexico City, this negotiation produced a fairly stable political arrangement premised, in sociologist Fernando Escalante Gonzalbo's words, on "negotiating the disobedience" of the law.[24]

The entanglement of the state, the law, and the informal city has been at the center of a thriving interdisciplinary scholarly conversation about cities in the "Global South."[25] But these ideas were already present in earlier research on Latin American "irregular settlements" (*asentamientos irregulares*) and "popular neighborhoods" (*colonias populares*), to use the terms most common in Mexico.[26] The relationship between residents of informal neighborhoods and the state has been documented at least since the 1970s (though it has existed for longer), when political scientist Wayne Cornelius studied the involvement of poor migrants with the patron-client structures of the Partido Revolucionario Institucional (Institutional Revolutionary Party, PRI).[27]

Scholars have also analyzed the built environment in informal neighborhoods, the social networks underpinning them, and their larger place within the political economy and the Mexican political system.[28] Many scholars have interpreted informal neighborhoods as "progressive" settlements characterized by their improvement over time, both through the process of self-construction (*autoconstrucción*) and through the distribution of municipal services and property titles after protracted negotiations with authorities.[29] At the same time, the informal city has also been interpreted as a locus of economic exploitation and political domination. The existence of cheap land in an irregular land market, in conjunction with self-construction, allowed the Mexican government to maintain low salaries and relieved the political pressures of the housing deficit. The politicization of this informal land market set the stage for political domination through clientelistic arrangements between settlers and the state.[30]

And yet, for all the scholarship of the last half-century, we lack histories of how informal urbanization emerged and evolved.[31] Most scholars date the significance of informality—if not always its beginnings—to Mexico City's post-1940 urban explosion.[32] This focal point follows contemporary studies that understood rural-urban migration and the housing problem as a break from the past and a challenge of modernization.[33] But the history of the informal city predates its construction as an intellectual conundrum and a public problem amenable to being solved through policy.

Revolution, Modernization, and Informality

The Politics of Informality understands informality in conjunction with the histories of modernization and revolution. The expert-led modernization of the city and the revolutionary claims to housing made by popular groups transformed Mexico City in the twentieth century. Both processes ebbed and flowed, sometimes feeding off each other and sometimes undermining each other. But the relationship between revolution and modernization was always mediated by the negotiation of the law.

At the turn of the twentieth century, public officials were bent on transforming Mexico City into a modern metropolis, in line with global models of urbanity. This modernization project was first spearheaded by a cohort of engineers and physicians, but other experts followed, including architects, planners, and environmentalists. In ways specific to their disciplines, these experts sought to craft an ideal city through public policy and legal regulations. When read against these expert visions, the history of urban informality emerges as an elite discourse. The hegemony of scientific discourses like sanitation, urban planning, and, more recently, environmentalism has been accompanied by fears of the informal city as a metonym for an unsanitary, anarchic, or environmentally degraded city. From this normative horizon, the informal city is the negative copy of the ideal city inscribed in sanitary codes, zoning ordinances, and master plans.

The visions of a modern city pursued by experts were disrupted by the Mexican Revolution and the claims-making and political organizing that it spawned. In the wake of the revolution, popular groups in Mexico City organized within a legal and spatial paradox: outside of the law, in defiance of city codes, but inspired by the revolutionary ideals codified in the Mexican Constitution of 1917, the world's first social constitution.[34] Informal neighborhoods became political arenas where working-class families—organized in neighborhood associations (*asociaciones de colonos*)—made claims to housing framed in the language of citizenship.[35] In a city with a small number of unionized workers and without elected authorities, neighborhood associations became critical means of political participation.[36] Settlers claimed a "right to the city" avant la lettre by petitioning local and federal authorities, staging protests, and occasionally invading land.[37] They were often successful, prompting city officials to expropriate land, allocate it to neighborhood associations, and provide neighborhoods with infrastructure, including drainage systems, potable water, and paved roads.

Authorities awarded these goods discretionarily, through ad hoc arrangements, with the mediation of political brokers, and in exchange for political support, enmeshing residents in webs of patronage. While settlers made claims to housing, they did not question the legitimacy of the postrevolutionary regime or ideals like homeownership and private property. The political arrangement that emerged from this relationship was remarkably stable from a Latin American perspective.

The patterns of political organization that emerged during the revolution and its aftermath structured claims to housing for the remainder of the century. From the 1910s through the 1940s, the capital was abuzz with a vibrant grassroots politics. Organized in neighborhood associations, settlers purchased lots in an irregular land market and deployed the rhetoric of the revolution to negotiate with city officials to achieve their integration into the city through titles and municipal services. A key political actor, these associations become increasingly entangled with the municipal government and officials from Mexico's hegemonic political party. At the same time, planners and other experts sought to curb anarchic growth by passing increasingly stringent laws that were seldom obeyed. Periods of political mobilization and authoritarian backlash ebbed and flowed. Through conflict and cooperation, experts and settlers set the parameters for the expansion of the city and the settlers' integration into it.

Experts set on curbing the informal expansion of the city increased their influence in the 1950s and 1960s. Mexico City was pathologized in these postwar decades, becoming a transnational urban laboratory for the study of poverty, migration, marginality, overpopulation, and other "diseases" afflicting Latin American cities.[38] These crises were real, but they were understood as symptoms of a failed modernization. Urban growth was increasingly interpreted as a disease, a diagnosis that undermined the power that popular groups had gained. As the revolutionary mobilization of the 1920s and 1930s waned, popular classes lost legitimacy and power to technocratic officials through the 1960s, the decade when my narrative ends.

Scholars of Mexico tend to analyze this political history through the lens of the PRI. Indeed, the party has become an analytical shorthand to understand the relationship between the "urban masses" and the "state." While some scholars viewed the postrevolutionary regime as a powerful mechanism of domination, others stressed the ability of the PRI to achieve modernization and stability through a deft combination of wielding carrots and sticks.[39] My intention is not to settle this debate. Rather, my main contributions lie in explaining how different branches of the city government (led by political and technical officials) and political organizations (not always subordinated to the PRI) engaged with organized settlers.

In comparison with other Latin American countries, the Mexican Revolution granted urban popular classes significant legitimacy. Informality was a problem for Mexican authorities, but it was usually managed politically, despite frequent cries from planners to raze slums. There were exceptions, including grand renewal projects and targeted eradications of squatter settlements.[40] But most of the neighborhoods established outside of the law that I discuss in this book would eventually be upgraded and integrated into the city. There was no Mexican equivalent to the Argentinean *Plan de emergencia* (1956), which sought to eradicate hundreds of working-class neighborhoods (*villas*) in Buenos Aires and was partially implemented by the dictatorship in the 1970s.[41] The Argentinean plan circulated among Mexican housing officials, but its implementation would be unthinkable.[42] "Had the Mexican Revolution created a dictatorship, [the government] would control the growth of cities," presidential candidate Luis Echeverría reassured settlers during his presidential campaign in 1969, just as fears of the informal city reached fever pitch.[43] Instead, his government attempted to solve the housing problem through the regularization of informal neighborhoods, among other policies. But many of his solutions had been tested over decades of political conflicts and policy interventions at the margins of law.

The history of informal Mexico City until the 1970s has been told—implicitly or explicitly—as the history of the PRI. But the story of the following decades is less clear. The 1970s saw an efflorescence of neighborhood associations and urban popular groups, many of which challenged the postrevolutionary regime. I survey these developments in my conclusion, but the history of this period is still to be written.[44] Whether one understands

Mexico's recent history as a transition to democracy, a process of neoliberal reform, or the violent unraveling of the postrevolutionary political arrangement, the presence of populations and spaces outside of the law remains a constant. But the promises of modernization and revolution are over, so informality no longer needs to resolve the contradictions between them.

Methodology and Chapter Outline

The Politics of Informality is structured as a historical narrative that runs from the 1900s to the 1960s. Each chapter focuses on a neighborhood, policy, or conflict that embodies an important conjuncture in the history of Mexico City. While these episodes are significant, I cannot claim that all are representative. But these histories illustrate the actors, categories, and policies that defined informality as a problem in the twentieth century. Most of the action takes place in a handful of neighborhoods in the northeast and southeast of the city: Colonia La Bolsa and Colonia El Rastro in the 1890s; Colonia Obrera and Colonia Ex-Hipódromo Peralvillo in the 1920s; Colonia Gertrudis Sánchez in the 1940s; Colonia Gabriel Ramos Millán in the 1950s; and the housing projects of Nonoalco-Tlatelolco and San Juan de Aragón in the 1960s. The neighborhoods in the northeast were located around the industrial core of the city, the heart of its working-class culture since the late nineteenth century. Those in the southeast started to grow after the revolution, sometimes encroaching on agrarian lands.

As my narrative progresses through time, the geography moves outward as I chart successive waves of urbanization farther away from the city center. Today this geography seems almost quaint. The working-class peripheries I study have become old, central, and relatively well off, at least in comparison with the entire metropolitan area. After 1950 most informal neighborhoods were established in areas designated as agrarian property (ejidos or communal lands) after the revolutionary agrarian reform. While my narrative occasionally refers to the urbanization of this land, it does not play the prominent role it would merit had I focused on the second half of the century.[45] Nor do I center on informal settlements in the State of Mexico, which became the main locus of informal urbanization in the 1960s.

Apart from Tlatelolco and (to a lesser extent) San Juan de Aragón, these neighborhoods were plagued by property conflicts, were built in defiance of city codes, and suffered from inadequate infrastructure. Yet the state played a central role in all of them by expropriating land and allocating lots, planning a neighborhood grid and facilitating the provision of municipal services, and

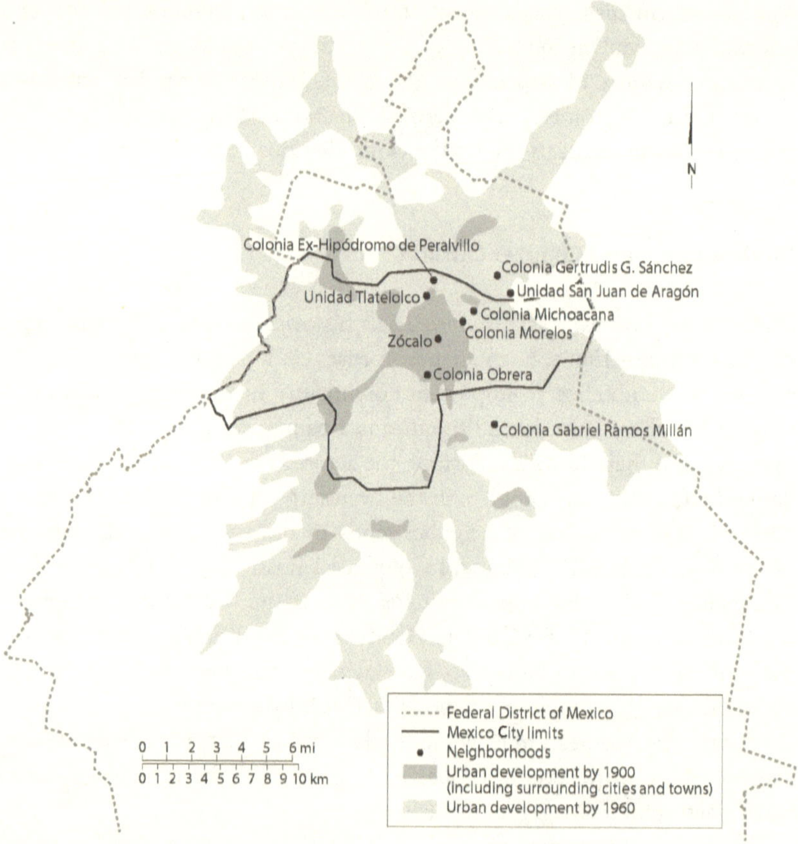

Figure 0.1. "Mexico City around 1960." © Bill Nelson. Courtesy of Bill Nelson.

acting as a broker among stakeholders with vested interests in the land: landowners, organized settlers, peasant corporations, and others. As my research illustrates, informal neighborhoods developed at the interface between government oversight and grassroots organizing, planning laws and extralegal politics, revolutionary promises of social justice and a churning real-estate market.

My archival research combines official sources—studies, reports, blueprints, and censuses created by federal and city officials—with petitions that organized residents sent to the federal government. I have also drawn from the archives of planners, architects, and anthropologists as well as printed sources such as newspapers, almanacs, and architectural and planning magazines.[46]

Documents created by the very state agents and urban experts who constructed urban informality as a public problem provide the backbone of the narrative. This is not only because the voices of nonelite groups are harder to locate in the archives. It is mainly because the questions I address involve the relationship between state officials and urban settlers. As I see it, informality arises when authorities define a space or the people occupying it as outside of the law. Accordingly, this is not an architectural, social, or economic history of the informal city; it is a history of the relationship between the state and popular groups in the city, a relationship mediated by revolutionary politics and the law.

A map of the road ahead might help readers. After providing a long-term introduction to Mexico City, chapter 1, "Sanitary Informality in the Porfirian City," focuses on the link between urban growth, public health, and the law in turn-of-the-century Mexico City. I argue that sanitary regulations codified and resignified entrenched inequalities that date back to the colonial period, specifically the seminal opposition between the Spanish grid in the city center and the Indigenous communities surrounding it. The opposition between formal and informal that crystallized in the Porfirian period mapped onto earlier geographies such as center and periphery, Spanish and Indigenous, bourgeois and plebeian.

Chapter 2, "Revolution in the Hinterland, Revolution in the City," analyzes how the Mexican Revolution transformed urban citizenship. Organized in neighborhood associations, settlers adapted modes of political organizing from the revolutionary countryside to petition for municipal services, public housing, and land. City officials were torn between two contradictory responses: controlling urban growth or placating settlers' demands by providing exemptions to city codes, negotiating the provision of waterworks, sewage disposal, and pavements, and expropriating land mired in property conflicts. Urban land, I argue, was a commodity to be sold and purchased but also a good to be distributed by state authorities. Land was at the heart of a segmented real-estate market, constitutive of state power, and the center of citizenship claims by urban settlers.

Chapter 3, "Planning and Informality," analyzes the relationship between urban planning and the law in the 1930s and 1940s. Planners drafted laws and a master plan with the goals of curbing growth, restricting land use, and connecting the city's disjointed neighborhoods. The problem of informality became the problem of the unplanned city. While planners' efforts failed to solve the problems they described, they were not inconsequential. Few projects materialized, but planning practices and laws carved out a political arena where city officials, political brokers, developers, and settlers fought to realize competing visions of the city. Planning demarcated the boundaries between formal and informal urbanization, allocated responsibilities among city officials and nongovernment actors, and disseminated a technical language that city officials and settlers alike would deploy to make claims to the city.

Chapter 4, "A Proletarian Metropolis," describes "proletarian neighborhoods" (*colonias proletarias*), a government project to make good on the right to housing codified in the Constitution of 1917. The government established these neighborhoods by expropriating land, distributing it among working-class families, and organizing these families under corporatist structures. The heyday of proletarian neighborhoods was in the 1940s, when their residents wielded considerable political leverage as they negotiated with city officials on both the provision of municipal services and the establishment of new neighborhoods. But these neighborhoods occupied an ambivalent legal and political space: although supported by the city government, they defied multiple planning and construction codes. While viewed by city officials as a means for social control, for settlers they represented a political arena where they made citizenship claims in the form of housing.

As chapter 5, "From Proletarian to Marginal Neighborhoods," argues, proletarian neighborhoods challenged the ideal of a modern city espoused by architects and planners. When measured against this vision, they were seen as marginal places defined by their infrastructural lacks and the poverty of their residents. Bent on curbing what they saw as anarchic growth, city authorities reduced their support for establishing new proletarian neighborhoods, driving Mexico City's expansion into the neighboring State of Mexico. The category "proletarian neighborhood" shifted in meaning, from a revolutionary housing mode to an urban pathology. While existing colonias proletarias continued to receive government support, references to them highlighted their illegality rather than their progressive character. Intriguingly, these references erased the long entanglements between colonias proletarias and the state, as if they were simply the outcome of the post–World War II "urban explosion."

Chapter 6, "The Housing Problem in the Era of Modernization," centers on the so-called housing problem in the 1950s and 1960s, during the regency of Ernesto P. Uruchurtu. Instead of embarking on political negotiations with organized settlers as they had in earlier years, city officials recast housing as a technical issue, amenable to expert solutions. A new generation of planners gained prominence, leading urban-renewal schemes and designing ambitious housing and infrastructure projects. Adopting the language of development and modernism, planners mapped the city through an opposition between inner-city slums and peripheral proletarian neighborhoods.

While overcrowded slums demanded demolition, proletarian neighborhoods were amenable to improvement through targeted interventions. To implement these projects, planners had to deal with overlapping government authorities, brokers, and the extralegal politics described in earlier chapters. In the end, I conclude, the boundaries between the central and outlying neighborhoods—like those between formal and informal housing—were blurry and shifting.

1

Sanitary Informality in the Porfirian City

The human density of Central Mexico, for millennia the most populated area of Mesoamerica, was the necessary condition for Mexico City's rise as one of the largest cities of the world—or, some would argue, its fall as an infamous urban dystopia.[1] Starting in the late nineteenth century, Mexico City expanded by incorporating the barrios, pueblos, and agrarian estates of the Valley of Mexico. But these settlements, in turn, exerted a profound influence over the capital, leaving an imprint on its physiognomy. The morphology of Indigenous barrios and pueblos (urban barrios adjacent to Mexico City, rural pueblos more distant), many of which predated Spanish arrival, is still palpable when walking along the city's crooked streets and small plazas. The existence of long-standing agrarian communities on the outskirts of the city impelled Mexico's postrevolutionary government to create a sui generis property regime, making these lands inalienable communal properties. Unlike other cities of the hemisphere like New York and Buenos Aires, whose demographic explosion in the twentieth century was propelled by international migration, most of Mexico City's migrants hailed from the countryside, especially from Central Mexico.[2]

Mexico's power as a capital city has always been dependent on the economic exploitation, political subjugation, and cultural hegemony over peasants, workers, Indigenous peoples, and other groups, who have often migrated from the countryside and resided in the urban periphery. But Mexico City has also provided these groups with opportunities to subvert these hierarchies and share in the riches that it has to offer, occasionally through revolt but more often through acculturation and political co-optation.[3] The city has always been a site of both "social incorporation" and "political control," a conflict that has created political, economic, and legal inequalities projected onto space.[4]

This chapter describes the beginnings of informality in Porfirian Mexico City (1876–1880, 1884–1911), which I analyze in light of these spatial inequalities. Colonial hierarchies based on class, race, and legal status in the late nineteenth century began to be structured around access to a "sanitary city" with potable water, drainage, paved streets, and green spaces, among other amenities. Public health and sanitation, I argue, became the master logics producing urban hierarchies and the division between the formal and the informal city. Following eighteenth-century Bourbon enlightened reformers and the transnational sanitary movement that emerged in nineteenth-century industrial metropoles, Mexican physicians and hygienists launched a project of hydraulic engineering with the goal of making Mexico City modern and sanitary. This project was based on an opposition between sanitary and unsanitary and authorized and unauthorized neighborhoods, reproducing and resignifying hierarchical divisions between Mexico City and the Indigenous communities surrounding it. While city officials did not use the word "informal," the ensuing formal/informal opposition was naturalized by Porfirian society as it drew from—and gave new life to—long-lasting racial, social, and cultural prejudices. Entrenched unequal geographies were thus modernized by the Porfirian elite, which reinterpreted them with the language of science, legality, and public health.[5]

The first section of this chapter introduces the relationship between Mexico City and the Indigenous communities of the Valley of Mexico during the colonial period (1521–1821) and the first decades after Independence. Then I review how urban growth and capitalist urbanization segregated Mexico City during the Porfirian era, dividing it along class lines. Finally, I analyze how class segregation was reinforced through hydraulic works and codified through sanitary regulations. The birth of urban informality under the logic of sanitation exemplifies the larger relationship of modernization, informality, and the law, which would adopt different forms throughout the remainder of the century.

City and Hinterland in the Valley of Mexico

"Bereft of limits and axes," wrote Jorge Ibargüengoitia, "it is essential that cities have, at the very least, a belly button. That belly button is Mexico City's *plaza mayor*."[6] Mexico City's belly button—also known as the *plaza mayor* (main square) or Zócalo—stands at what once was the center of Tenochtitlán, the capital of the Mexica (Aztec) Empire, founded in 1325 on a small island in Lake Texcoco. Spanish conquistadores claimed that Tenochtitlán was "destroyed and razed to the ground" in 1521, though many elements of the pre-Columbian city survived conquest.[7] The Spanish built their city atop the ruins of Tenochtitlán, refounding it as México-Tenochtitlán, capital of the viceroyalty of New Spain. Today a massive Mexican flag stands at the center of the plaza mayor, surrounded by the Metropolitan Cathedral and the National Palace. The place carries historical and symbolic weight: capital of the Mexica Empire, the viceroyalty of New Spain, and the Mexican nation-state. Political power, it seems, has always radiated from this center.

Like Ibargüengoitia, we usually understand the history of Mexico City through a "Zócalo-centric" perspective, as if the city had grown from its belly button outward.[8] The opposite is closer to the truth. Tenochtitlán was founded by upstarts from the north upon the discovery—as legend has it—of an eagle alighting on a cactus on a small island. But the Mexica made a sensible decision, founding their city in a fertile valley with a long history of human settlement, marked by centuries of cultural exchanges and dynastic conflicts. They only achieved regional prominence after decades of warring, building alliances, and brokering marriages to establish a royal lineage in the fourteenth and fifteenth centuries.[9] In 1519, the year of Spanish arrival, Tenochtitlán was the head of the Triple Alliance, which ruled over Central Mexico and reached as far as Central America. The Valley of Mexico had a population of approximately 2 million, while the population of Tenochtitlán numbered 200,000.[10] This was the heartland of the Mexica Empire.

The Spanish located their city over the capital complex of Tenochtitlán, using the debris of its monuments to build churches and palaces. They designed Mexico City following an orthogonal grid that radiated outward from the plaza mayor. This was the famous grid (*traza*) laid out by Alonso García Bravo, long interpreted by historians as a project of colonization and separation between the Spanish and the Indigenous republics.[11] The Spanish city was governed by a city council, while the Indigenous jurisdiction was politically autonomous yet subordinate. I am well aware of the double meaning of the word "city" as a human community and a physical infrastructure, a distinction that corresponds to "the city defined as *urbs*, that is, as physical unit, and the city as *civitas*, or human association," according to historian Richard Kagan.[12] The Renaissance-inspired grid was the place where Spanish "citizens" (*vecinos*) lived, engaged in public matters at the city council, and attended mass at the Metropolitan Cathedral. Beyond the grid lay the Indigenous jurisdictions of San Juan Tenochtitlán and Santiago Tlatelolco, with authority over the city's peripheral barrios and, farther away from the Spanish city, its rural *pueblos de indios*.[13]

The separation between the Spanish and Indigenous realms, if it ever existed, was subverted by the promiscuous, syncretic, and unruly colonial society. The Spanish city never had clearly defined limits and was never solely Spanish. It was always a multiethnic place, entangled with its adjacent barrios and pueblos, even though chronicles, maps, and paintings are often oblivious of the threads connecting city and hinterland. When the Spanish savant Francisco Cervantes de Salazar praised sixteenth-century Mexico, a city without "suburbs and . . . beautiful and distinguished on all sides," he implicitly erased the existence of Indian barrios beyond the traza, distinct communities that were nonetheless imbricated with the city.[14]

The relationship between Tenochtitlán and the Indigenous communities of the Valley of Mexico thus survived Spanish conquest and continued—with important adaptations—over the colonial period. Urban and rural Indigenous communities "sustained" the capitalist economy of the viceroyalty of New Spain, providing the surplus labor that gave rise to the largest city in the Americas.[15] Gargantuan public works undertaken by the Spanish Crown relied on labor drafted from Indigenous communities, a system adapted from pre-Columbian networks of tribute.[16] Pueblos like Xochimilco and Santa Anita continued to feed the city, transporting produce along waterways that predated Spanish conquest. Much closer to the city, but not fully part of it, Indigenous barrios such as Santo Tomás, Atlampa, and San Pablo Teocaltitlán were populated by shoemakers, carpenters, and masons, among other artisans and workers. As remnants of Indigenous social formations (*calpulli* and *tlaxilacalli*), barrios enjoyed a degree of autonomy under the authority of Indigenous parishes and the jurisdictions of San Juan Tenochtitlán and Santiago Tlatelolco.[17] But their "cosmopolitan" residents straddled the Indigenous and Spanish realms, crisscrossing the cultural spaces of the city.[18]

This Baroque political order—a mishmash of Indigenous and Spanish republics, religious and secular corporations—became the target of reform in the eighteenth century. Beginning in the 1720s, the Spanish Crown attempted to reorganize Mexico City into a series of homogenous districts that superseded the divisions between Indigenous and Spanish jurisdictions.[19] These efforts were part of the broader Bourbon reforms, aimed at centralizing and secularizing government, making the system of overlapping sovereignties that characterized imperial governance more efficient.[20] While not entirely successful, the reforms achieved their goal of undermining the power of Indigenous barrios, religious orders, and artisan guilds. This erosion of colonial corporations continued during the wars of independence. The liberal Constitution of 1812 dissolved the ancien régime founded on corporations, granting citizenship to Indian subjects and converting Indigenous communities into towns with their own city councils.[21] These changes were reaffirmed by the Mexican Republic, which decreed universal citizenship and instituted a municipal system that replaced colonial territorial jurisdictions.

The transformation was nothing less than revolutionary, enshrining popular sovereignty and citizenship as the unchallenged political principles of the Mexican nation-state.

For postindependence national elites, Indigenous peoples represented an obstacle to progress by virtue of their poverty, ignorance, and backwardness. In the case of Mexico City, views on the so-called Indian problem translated into elite perceptions that ascribed the features of Indigenous dwellings and neighborhoods to the people themselves. Observers understood the wretchedness that surrounded the city as a remnant of the Indigenous past. Ignacio Manuel Altamirano wrote that "the miserables of that [Aztec] time have heirs who . . . languish in [the city's] outskirts, their existence mercifully shortened by foul air, hunger, and the elements . . . the golden center of Mexico is surrounded by a ring of filth and misery."[22]

Nineteenth-century Mexico City remained divided between the original Spanish grid—the "City of Palaces" that astonished travelers—and its "horrible . . . environs," as British voyager R.W.H. Hardy described them.[23] The regularity of Mexico City, wrote geographer Antonio García Cubas, "contrasts with the irregularity of the suburbs, where a disorder of blocks and alleys reigns."[24] "Lowly barrios," according to a city almanac, "are dirty, overcrowded, characterized by poor shacks, crooked streets, and pulque taverns."[25] The contrast between the city center and its backward barrios—implicitly or explicitly Indigenous—became a common literary trope at the end of the nineteenth century, as the barrios were increasingly measured against the modern and sanitary metropolis that authorities envisioned.

The hierarchical distinction between Mexico City and these Indigenous spaces lasted for centuries and arguably continues to exist. Although the legal category "Indian" was abolished by the Mexican Republic, cultural and biological understanding of indigeneity replaced it, as the next section explains. Social and spatial inertias incubated in the colonial era lingered in the nineteenth and twentieth centuries, structuring inequalities rather than enforcing strict racial separations.[26] Mexico City's metropolitan area continues to be organized by the hierarchical opposition between center and periphery. Whereas the upper and middle classes live in wealthy central neighborhoods, most of the working classes live in the neighboring State of Mexico, commuting for hours to work near the center, far from their peripheral dwellings.

Growth and Segregation in Porfirian Mexico City

The relationship between Mexico City and the communities of the Valley of Mexico was upended in the second half of the nineteenth century when the city underwent a dramatic process of expansion. The population and physical extension of Mexico City had remained roughly static after the wars of independence, which were followed by half a century of political instability, civil wars, and foreign invasions.[27] The long rule of General Porfirio Díaz ended this period of crisis by engineering an era of "order and progress" bankrolled by an export economy. Backed by foreign investors, Díaz's *científico* (technocratic) government built a railroad network that connected Mexico with US and European markets and triggered a chain reaction of economic growth. Exports provided the state with resources that it used to pacify and modernize the country, achieving a stability that attracted further investments and loans. While the agrarian and mining sectors were the drivers of the Porfirian economy, the country experienced an urban renaissance as well. Profits from exports were invested in the modernization of cities, where a middle class expanded, national industries grew slowly yet steadily, and an urban public created by the mass media coalesced.

The Porfirian capital, as historian Mauricio Tenorio Trillo has shown, proudly embodied peace, progress, science, nationalism, and cosmopolitanism.[28] Its expansion during the closing decades of the century was identified by historians and contemporaries alike as a dramatic rupture that became comprehensible as a universal urban experience. Like fin-de-siècle cities across the world, Porfirian Mexico City came to represent a series of images then novel and now familiar: criminologists, engineers, and physicians, electric lights and railroad stations, dandies and flaneurs, neoclassic monuments and tree-lined boulevards, bucolic suburbs and bustling streets, mansions and tenements. Chronicler Jesús Galindo y Villa distinguished between his grandparents' "colonial city of palaces, suburbs, legends, and old flavor [*sabor a viejo*]" and the city built before his eyes, animated by the "speed, bustle, and agitation" of modern life.[29] Modernist poet Manuel Gutiérrez Nájera captured this vibrancy through impressionistic descriptions of tramways, electric lights, and city women that echo Charles Baudelaire and suggest intuitions by sociologist Georg Simmel. "Our customs have become more complicated," wrote Gutiérrez Nájera; "we have developed a sixth, seventh, eighth, and God knows how many more senses; we possess subtleties and refinements that are impossible to define, capricious and ephemeral as they are."[30]

Mexico City's "resurgence toward modern life" was the outcome of local, national, and global transformations.[31] Through the completion of tramways and railroads, waterworks and sewage systems, avenues and monuments, markets, parks, and prisons, the national government redesigned its capital city, turning it into a showcase, projecting to the world the image of a modern and cosmopolitan nation. The ideal of the modern city produced a series of opposing images: the atavistic, unhygienic, and criminal barrios and the bucolic, authentic, and timeless pueblos. The word *colonia*, which became increasingly common in the 1880s, captures the contours of this modern city. In nineteenth-century Mexico, the term referred to colonization, the conquest of previously unproductive, unexplored, and untaxed lands by state officials, entrepreneurs, and yeomen. In Porfirian Mexico City, colonization signified the incorporation of communal lands, ranches, and agrarian estates into a hot real-estate market where profits from the booming export economy were invested.

The consolidation of a real-estate market, a sine qua non for capitalist urbanization, was made possible by the passing of the Lerdo Law in 1856. Intended as a fix for an unproductive countryside, the Lerdo Law targeted colonial corporations—the church and Indigenous communities—in possession of inalienable lands that could not be sold, bought, taxed, or used as collateral for mortgage loans. In the case of Mexico City and its hinterland, the law untied the "juridical knot" of the ancien régime, enabling the transfer of mortmain lands to the real-estate market.[32] Starting in the 1850s, a new class of urban developers pooling national and foreign capital subdivided the city's first modern colonias on land that had belonged to the church.[33]

Mexico City's first neighborhoods, Colonia de los Arquitectos and Santa María la Ribera, were subdivided in the 1850s. Arquitectos was the brainchild of engineer Francisco Somera, who planned to sell lots to students and architects from the San Carlos Academy (hence the name). The city council distributed potable water to the neighborhood, making the venture profitable.[34] Santa María la Ribera was subdivided by Estanislao Flores and Joaquín Flores, owners of large agrarian estates surrounding the city. While its layout was inspired by the colonial grid, its houses featured new architectural trends such as front yards between the street and the house. Both neighborhoods provided a rubric for capitalist urbanization for the middle classes. Subdivided by private developers but patronized by the city government, which paid for their municipal services, Arquitectos and Santa María la Ribera were profitable investments that heralded the belle époque city that was to come.[35] The wealthiest neighborhoods were subdivided in the western part of the city alongside Reforma Avenue, toward the fertile lands of Chapultepec and Tacubaya. The first diagonal to break the colonial orthogonal grid, Reforma Avenue connected the old city with the Juárez, Cuauhtémoc, and Roma neighborhoods. According to architect Alfonso Pallares, these were the counterparts of European and US garden cities, harbingers of "urban progress."[36]

While the bourgeois city expanded westward, developers catering to working-class residents subdivided lands in the north and the northeast, close to the factories and railroad tracks mushrooming in the area near the lakebed of Lake Texcoco. Rafael Martínez de la Torre subdivided Colonia Guerrero on lands to the north of Alameda Park purchased from the Buenavista hacienda, the Indian barrio of Los Ángeles, and the San Fernando convent.[37] Martínez de la Torre sold large lots to developers who built *vecindades* (tenement houses) and rented them to workers. Colonia Guerrero followed a broader pattern: the subdivision of properties that had belonged to Indian barrios and their development as working-class neighborhoods.[38] The densification of these peripheral lands was remarkable, as overcrowded vecindades replaced the fields and individual dwellings that had previously existed in the area. By the turn of the century, vecindades had become the most widespread working-class dwellings in the city, housing around a third of its population—or 100,000 people—by 1895.[39]

A vecindad consisted of multiple single-room dwellings distributed around a central patio or corridor. Some were created in dilapidated colonial buildings: the Convent of La Merced became a well-known vecindad after the disentailment of church properties in the 1860s. But most were built in peripheral barrios. Working-class neighborhoods like Guerrero, Morelos, Peralvillo, and Valle Gómez were all established during the Porfirian era. While city officials stigmatized vecindades as disorderly and irrational, they were, in fact, a product of industrialization, rural-urban migration, and the emergence of real-estate developers eager to maximize profits. In the critical opinion of one architect, these developers understood the "difficult task of building colonias" as the "simple subdivision of a grid by calculating . . . the highest profit in the shortest time."[40] Water, drainage, pavements, and spaces for public buildings like schools and churches were neglected by developers, whose goal was simply "subdividing tiny lots [*lotecitos*], building houses, and selling" them at the largest possible profit.[41]

Consider Colonia La Bolsa, one of the city's most notorious neighborhoods, which came to symbolize the ills of the city. A lengthy exposé ("La cuna de crimen") was published in *El Imparcial*, the most successful newspaper of the Porfirian era. A reporter described the neighborhood as a cesspit of crime, vice, and disease, attracting miserable thieves, forgers, and drunkards. "The absence of planning produced a labyrinthine street system; lack of sewage created filth; lack of public lighting attracted crime."[42] But the same article provided an account, in less critical terms, of the origins of the neighborhood. La Bolsa was settled in the 1880s by railroad workers who built temporary housing near the tracks using tents and other provisional materials. The place was swarming with tenants in search of cheap housing, which landlords readily provided for a few pennies and without demanding references or a deposit. La Bolsa was located northeast of the city, far from the wealthy Porfirian neighborhoods. The federal government constructed a federal penitentiary and the Grand Drainage Canal nearby in 1900. Shortly afterward, the city council relocated the unhygienic secondhand market, El Baratillo, from the Plaza del Jardín in the city center.[43] By the turn of the century, the area had acquired a marked proletarian profile. The anonymous reporter called for La Bolsa to be razed but did not acknowledge the centrality of the neighborhood for the city economy. Neither did he consider the extent to which its inadequacies were the result of government design. The city council had not authorized Colonia La Bolsa, so it had no obligation to provide potable water, a sewage system, or pavements.[44]

Like other fin-de-siècle "penny papers," *El Imparcial* replaced the political commentary that characterized earlier newspapers with local news.[45] Halfway between amateur detectives and sociologists, penny-press reporters investigated the city and its underworld—shops and factories, barracks, jails and hospitals, theaters and bordellos, churches and cantinas, courthouses and lowly barrios—offering the public a never-ending output of stories.[46] "La Cuna del Crimen" was illustrated with a diptych that contrasted what La Bolsa was and what it ought to be: a disorderly maze of streets and tents where vagabonds drank and sang versus a neighborhood with ample streets, electric lighting, tramway lines, and solid constructions, where passersby were peacefully and circumspectly conducting their affairs. The image to the right reveals the ideal of the modern, orderly, and sanitary city that began to be disseminated in the last decade of the nineteenth century. By the 1910s, most urbanites agreed on the facilities that modern colonias ought to enjoy, including a sewage system, potable water pipelines, paved streets, planted trees, electric lighting, and access to transportation.[47] Because they lacked these amenities, La Bolsa and similar neighborhoods acquired an infamous reputation as disorderly, unsanitary, and criminal: the reverse of what a modern city ought to be.

Social inequality produced a spatial segregation that writers, reporters, criminologists, sociologists, and physicians—whose words rendered the new urban phenomena legible—observed with wonder and fear. Pre-nineteenth-century "walking cities" were congested places, with short distances separating areas of work and residence.[48] Walking cities displayed a mixture of functions in the same block or even in the same building, a condition that turn-of-the-century authorities began to describe as dysfunctional and unhygienic. Following the development of a tramway network, Mexico City experienced a fragmentation of space and class, becoming a mosaic of barrios and neighborhoods at once disjointed from each other and connected through tramway lines.

The expansion of the city, coupled with the class segregation it reproduced, led engineer Alberto J. Pani to lament that "the poor can no longer

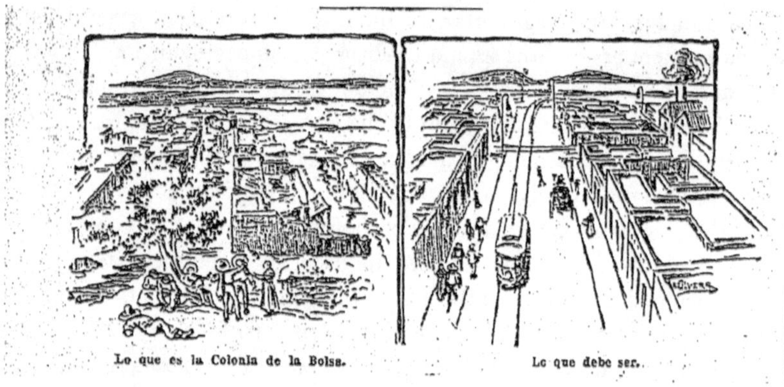

Figure 1.1. "Lo que es la Colonia de la Bolsa / Lo que debe ser" (What Colonia de la Bolsa Is / What Colonia de la Bolsa should be). *El Imparcial*, 1905. Hemeroteca Nacional Digital de México.

have recourse to their rich neighbors; they have been resettled away from us, beyond the city walls, abandoned to despair, brutality, and vice."[49] The truth is that the Mexican wealthy and middle classes decided, like their counterparts across the world, to resettle, searching for sanitary spaces and a lifestyle inspired by garden-cities and similar suburban models. Thus Friedrich Engels would accuse the wealthy classes of Manchester of abandoning the city center and condemning the "working poor to lives of misery and death in the industrial slums."[50] The "profound separation of the classes that form the social body," criminologist Miguel Macedo wrote, and their distinct "material, intellectual, moral [and ethnic] conditions" prevented any contact between them and inhibited the constitution of a community.[51]

Another criminologist, Julio Guerrero, offered a social classification capturing a city on the move in 1901. He identified men and women at the lower end of the social ladder "living in the streets, sleeping in public dorms, under overcrowded archways . . . in the rubble of houses under construction, in an inn if they can afford it." This ancient "urban rabble" (*leperaje*) was composed of beggars, ragpickers, thieves, and other unsavory characters who suffered from alcoholism and venereal diseases and frequented the city's underworld. Living alongside this group in the city barrios—albeit without intermixing—was a higher class composed of the last "descendants of the Aztec." This group displayed a superior moral sense, far from the promiscuity exhibited by the rabble and deferential to gender roles: parents were loving and wives obliging toward their husbands in their humble huts.[52]

Guerrero also identified a new class of industrial workers living in vecindades. While often violent, promiscuous, and averse to marriage, this group had been "saved by industrialism from falling into the lowest class." He described industrial workers as "illiterate . . . and ignorant of the world outside of their barrio, their factory, and a few pueblos neighboring the capital." But he also wrote approvingly of their adoption of civilization (manifest in their use of pants, shoes, electric lighting, and kitchenware), adding that the "civilizing discipline of the factory instilled in them ideas of order, decorum, philanthropy, and duty."[53] Many industrial workers were migrants in the midst of a process of acculturation, to use an anachronistic term. (Half of the city's population in 1910 had been born outside of the Federal District.) With sociological eyes influenced by positivism, Guerrero understood class as a malleable category that encompassed culture and nature, climatic conditions, race, education, customs, and residence.

Guerrero also captured changing understandings of race and the "Indian problem." His belief in racial hierarchies was representative of the Porfirian period, strongly influenced by social Darwinism and Spencerian evolutionism. Scientific racism, however, would soon be discredited by the rise of Boasian anthropology, which defended cultural relativism and contended that biological (racial) differences were, in fact, cultural. Guerrero's musings on matters such as class, indigeneity, and migration straddled scientific racism and a cultural understanding of race, which posited that "Indians" could be assimilated into the modern nation through education and access to facilities like sanitation and electricity.

Like later social scientists, Guerrero conflated geography with history, understanding pueblos in the Valley of Mexico as islands outside of history. This belief would be refined by anthropologists who argued that Mexican pueblos were examples of the ideal type that anthropologist Robert Redfield labeled a "folk society": a "small, isolated, nonliterate, and homogenous [community], endowed with a strong sense of group solidarity."[54] Redfield viewed the migration from the countryside to the city as a move in space but also in time: from a traditional to a modern society characterized by individualism, rationality, secularism, and heterogeneity. While this transition was a key paradigm of the social sciences of the first half of the twentieth century, some viewed it with trepidation—as a loss of innocence or the end of a Golden Age—while others saw it with hope, reaching a higher civilizational stage.

Accordingly, the city played a consequential, if ambivalent, place in Guerrero's analysis. It could be a force of moral degradation for (some) Indians, vagrants, and beggars. But it was also a place of moral and cultural uplift (*mestizaje* avant la lettre), where contact with modern culture and technology could transform atavistic Indians into industrial workers and consumers. This ambivalence would be shared by intellectuals and policymakers who would reflect for decades on the meaning of rural-urban migration, the socioeconomic profile of the country as a peasant or industrial society, and the place of the Indigenous peoples in the nation.[55] The answers to these questions would play out in the informal neighborhoods of the capital.

In conclusion, capitalist urbanization transformed and resignified spatial hierarchies that harkened back to the colonial era. By the turn of the twentieth century, the seminal separation between the Spanish and the Indigenous city had been replaced by a more expansive geography, with modern colonias built along a southwest-northeast axis and varying in market value and proximity to a transnational urban ideal. Social inequalities materialized in the sprawling city. While the language of race was never fully abandoned, Porfirian urban hierarchies were interpreted with the novel language of science (public health, criminology, psychiatry, sociology). Hence Alexander von Humboldt's "City of Palaces" became, in the words of Gonzalo de Murga, a "City of Contrasts."[56] The phrase was already something of a cliché in 1913, but its meaning was shifting: racial differences were subsumed under differences of class, hygiene, and access to modern urban amenities. De Murga did not write only as a dilettante sociologist meditating on the influence of cities over a traditional society (his article was entitled "Sociological Inklings"). He also spearheaded Mexico City's transformation, working as a land developer eager to maximize profits in a real-estate market divided between its bourgeois and its proletarian sides. Porfirian Mexico City was not simply interpreted with the preexisting language of the social sciences. The Porfirian city—modern, capitalist, segregated—was the lab in which this language emerged.[57]

Public Health and Informality

Sanitation was the master logic behind informality in Porfirian Mexico City. Like other nineteenth-century metropoles, the capital was an increasingly unsanitary place, plagued by such epidemics and diseases as "cholera, smallpox, scarlet fever, typhus, measles, whooping cough, and malaria."[58] Manuel Marroquín y Rivera, the engineer who designed the capital's new water system, calculated that contaminated water was responsible for three thousand deaths yearly.[59] Pasteurian bacteriology became the dominant paradigm in the 1880s without fully replacing the earlier miasma theory of disease. While engineers and physicians debated the etiology of water-borne diseases, they were cognizant of the relationship between public health, the supply of clean water, and the disposal of sewage.[60]

To put it in the simplest possible way, Porfirian authorities faced the interrelated challenges of bringing fresh water into the city while disposing of its wastewater. The "conquest of water" would consist of three interrelated hydraulic projects completed in the first decade of the century.[61] In 1900 the federal government completed the Grand Drainage Canal, a protracted project dating to the colonial period that evacuated the city's wastewater. A new sewage system was inaugurated in 1905, although additional work continued for years. Finally, the city updated its water system in 1912 by tapping fresh spring water from Lake Xochimilco and pumping it to holding tanks in Molino del Rey, in Chapultepec, then distributing it. The achievement of these waterworks seemed to announce a new epoch for Mexico and its capital. President Díaz boasted that the conclusion of the Drainage Canal rivaled in "importance Mexico's independence . . . redeeming the Republic from the servitude to the mud and the filth that poisoned the city."[62]

Porfirian authorities complemented hydraulic engineering projects with the drafting of city codes that regulated the provision of water and sewage.[63] This was only one example of an increasingly scientific state, set on harnessing the expansion of Mexico City. The Porfirian era spurred an explosion of decrees, codes, regulations, cadastral surveys, blueprints, censuses, and other technologies of statecraft.[64] Laws were not necessarily followed, but they always had consequences, though often unintended. They were a generative force that produced official and popular categories that shaped expectations about city life. Laws regulating municipal services, such as street pavements, sewage disposal, and potable water, prompted residents to expect these services. City codes and regulations by the stroke of a pen produced an array of activities, spaces, and populations outside of the law, the realm that would later be known as "informal."

Beginning in the 1870s, the city council drafted codes that stipulated sewage systems and public lighting, among other services. Wealthy colonias, subdivided by developers with capital and connections with city officials (at times developers and city officials were the same men), were normally provided with municipal services, paid for by the city council with the expectation that land taxes would make the investment profitable.[65] On the other hand, developers subdivided working-class neighborhoods without authorization from the city council, failing to provide services while promising purchasers that the municipal government would provide them.[66] Jesús Galindo y Villa, chronicler, city council member, and editor of the city's *Boletín Oficial*, lamented the existence of such working-class colonias, whose "owners failed to consult with the authorities about whether they can subdivide colonias, sell lots, and construct houses." He linked the disregard for municipal regulations with an increase in criminality and unhealthy living conditions:

> many so-called colonias were established throughout the city without the authorities' approval; at the same time, however, the houses built in these places were occupied, becoming foci of insalubrity or dens of thieves who, protected by the shadows of the night and the absence of public lighting, committed numerous crimes.[67]

Historians have sometimes viewed sanitary regulations as imposed by official authorities on the urban poor, who often resisted policies to modernize them.[68] But sanitary regulations were not merely imposed by authoritarian states. Neither were they simply disregarded. Instead, laws were negotiated—in the city bureaucracy, the courts, and the streets—between groups making competing claims. As the need for municipal services was promoted by sanitation officials, codified in legal documents, and disseminated in print media, city residents began to expect these services and organized to claim them. A legal and political battlefield emerged, pitting city officials, developers, and residents against each other. Authorities sought to regulate urban growth because of a concern for public health. Developers sought profits at different tiers of a segmented housing market.[69] Finally, city residents longed for—and increasingly demanded—sanitary homes and such public amenities as schools, markets, and green areas.

The metropolitan integration of the Valley of Mexico turned growth into a political, sanitary, and financial crisis. In 1903, in response to the "fever of constructions and subdivisions," the federal government stripped away the authority of the Federal District's city councils (including the council of Mexico City), creating instead a new metropolitan government, the Consejo Superior de Gobierno del Distrito Federal (Superior Government Council of the Federal District). This was a tricephalous authority, all three heads appointed by the president: the governor of the Federal District, the director of Public Works, and the president of the Consejo Superior de Salubridad (Superior Sanitation Council, CSS). The logic of these changes, as historian Ariel Rodríguez Kuri has argued, was to scientifically guide the growth on a metropolitan scale, undertaking public works projects for the entire Federal District.[70]

Created in 1841, the Consejo Superior de Salubridad steadily increased its power over the second half of the century, extending its jurisdiction over sanitary matters in the city.[71] The sanitary codes that it decreed, for instance, encompassed hitherto unregulated spaces, regulating the construction standards of homes, schools, and hospitals. As historian Claudia Agostoni noted, "because illness could be caused by almost anything, everything had to be considered."[72] The expansion of Mexico City during the Porfirian era prompted calls to limit urban growth and restrict the building of insalubrious housing. "Prohibitive measures are the most effective," a journalist wrote. "Sanitary regulations must include prohibitions to build insalubrious houses and must limit the expansion of the city toward unhealthy regions."[73] In response to these pressures, the city council denied municipal services to unauthorized neighborhoods.[74]

The city government passed a stricter code in 1903 to curb urban growth, the Reglas para la Admisión de Nuevas Colonias (Rules for the Admission of New Neighborhoods).[75] In order for colonias to be "admitted" into the municipal system, developers were required to demarcate areas for streets, green spaces, and public markets as well as lay out water and sewage infrastructure. The city council would reimburse these expenses by deducting developers' city taxes.[76] The 1903 code produced a division between admitted neighborhoods and nonadmitted neighborhoods, to which the city government was not required to provide municipal services.[77] Like future codes, the Reglas para la Admisión de Nuevas Colonias were influenced by contemporary sanitary codes and the sanitary movement more broadly.

The Consejo Superior de Salubridad was divided into subcommissions tasked with surveilling sanitary conditions across the city. These authorities directed their "medical gaze" at the city, which demarcated a new social geography.[78] Mexico's capital had always been an unequal city, but sanitary officials added a scientific veneer to long-standing prejudices, capturing in their reports a city divided by lines of sanitation and class. An inspector, for instance, contended that the first district was plagued by "numerous vecindades lacking urban services and all requirements that hygiene counseled." He described these vecindades as "filthy and abandoned houses without ventilation, overcrowded with a repugnant confusion of men and animals."[79] Sanitary inspectors portrayed barrios outside of the urban perimeter as spaces "at the threshold of our incipient culture of hygiene."[80] The language of sanitation and hygiene disseminated by city officials stigmatized poor residents, ascribed to them the unsanitary conditions of their homes, and blamed them for their living conditions. "There is unfortunately an enormous distance between public and individual action on matters of hygiene," according to an editorial in *El Imparcial*. "We will have a sanitary city but continue to have unhygienic individuals; water for cleaning but people who won't clean themselves."[81]

But authorities combined moral and cultural understandings of disease—inflected by racist views of indigeneity—with environmental views, which acknowledged that working-class residents were the victims of greedy landlords and hydraulic works that cemented and reinforced segregation.[82] The drainage system inaugurated in 1905 extended across wealthy and middle-class colonias but did not reach numerous working-class neighborhoods and barrios north of the city center.[83] "Aristocratic and elegant buildings" in the fourth district, an inspector noted, enjoyed excellent sanitary conditions. But the "barrios and suburbs" in the northern districts, whose residents were eager to follow sanitary regulations, suffered from a "lack of drainage and potable water."[84]

Houses not connected to the sewage system disposed of their waste through latrines and open-air sewage canals that outflowed to rivers and polluted underground water repositories. A sanitary official reported in 1895 that a latrine in a vecindad in the Plaza de los Ángeles was so large that an eight-year-old drowned in it: the "pond" measured three meters in length, one and a half meters in width, five in depth, and was entirely filled with fecal matter.[85] Two decades later, Alberto J. Pani described Mexico City as foul-smelling, vermin-ridden, and disease-prone: the "most unhealthy city of the whole world."[86]

Unequal access to sanitary housing prompted residents to organize improvement boards, tenant unions, and neighborhood associations and occasionally to riot. As historians have documented, the expansion of water and drainage systems had gone "from a novelty to a demand" by the first decades of the twentieth century.[87] Residents of the barrio of Zentecalco complained upon learning that the city government earmarked MX$11,000 to fight typhus while their streets, filled with "bumps" and "ditches," were a "breeding ground for the typhus microbes."[88] Across the city, residents organized associations to petition for water, but the city council rejected many petitions on various legal grounds. In 1912, for example, neighbors from Colonia La Tlaxpana requested that the city council incorporate their neighborhood into the municipality of Mexico City (they were located in Tacubaya) so that they could receive "public lighting, police, water, pavement, and schools." The city council denied their request. Residents of Colonia Vallejo made a similar petition, which the city council also denied, arguing that there was no contract for the neighborhood, which was, moreover, located in the municipality of Guadalupe Hidalgo, outside of the city limits.[89]

By breaching urbanization codes or being located beyond the city limits, working-class neighborhoods were outside of the law, justifying government denials of requests to provide municipal services. But the subdivision of unserviced and unauthorized neighborhoods remained a profitable business for developers and a necessity for families in need of housing. While the government lacked resources to service these neighborhoods, it also lacked the power (and often the will) to prevent their growth, which continued undeterred despite pleas from sanitation officials. In fact, the city council occasionally authorized new subdivisions with the caveat that it would not provide services.

This was the case of Colonia El Rastro, subdivided in 1897 in an area adjacent to the city slaughterhouse and Colonia La Bolsa. The municipal Public Works Commission pondered prohibiting the establishment of a neighborhood outside of the "urban perimeter," in a scarcely populated area where sewage disposal would be too costly. In the end, rather than forbidding the establishment of the neighborhood or extending the sewage system, the government granted special permission for the construction of the neighborhood, while deferring the provision of sewage services until the density of the area made it a necessity.[90] This was a striking decision that made explicit a practice that later governments would continue with less candor: granting tacit permission for the establishment of a neighborhood while refusing to provide it with municipal services.

Colonia Valle Gómez, Colonia Calzada de Vallejo, and Colonia Porfirio Díaz (established in the 1880s and located in the municipality of Guadalupe Hidalgo, north of the city) offer another example of the government's willingness to bend its own rules. Council member Luis de la Brena in 1912 requested that Public Works urbanize these neighborhoods, although they did not "comply with the legal requirements to have official existence." De la Brena grounded his request in pragmatism. He first noted that the neighborhoods were breaking the law and that the government needed to prevent the construction of new housing until residents were provided with municipal services. However, because the neighborhoods had a large population, he proposed that "if all the legal requirements could not be met, the *practical solution would be to negotiate with residents*, in order that at the very least some requirements were met" (emphasis added).[91]

De la Brena's request was sent to sanitary and Public Works authorities, who acknowledged the conundrum. Public Works asserted that de la Brena's points were valid, but the "illegal existence of these neighborhoods prevented Public Works from fulfilling its obligation to provide urban services." Legal responsibilities aside, "the existing disease required immediate solution," so they needed a "compromise" that would allow for official government sanction and cooperation with the distribution of municipal services.[92] Negotiating a compromise would not be easy, as city officials, residents, and developers made competing claims about the preeminence of the rule of law, sanitation, housing, and profit. This triangular battlefield, demarcated by the law but not reducible to it, would shape urban growth, politics, and citizenship throughout the twentieth century.

The social construction of a divided city had taken firm hold by the early 1900s. One city was modern, wealthy, sanitary, and officially sanctioned; the other traditional, Indigenous, unsanitary, and illegal—a division later subsumed under the formal/informal opposition. But this imaginary map hid a messier reality: countless neighborhoods found themselves in ambiguous legal situations, with uneven access to municipal services, and in an uncertain position within or beyond city limits. Attempts by city officials to map the city according to its legal status proved enormously difficult. A 1908 report offered a confusing picture, with plenty of unauthorized neighborhoods, neighborhoods that existed only on paper, neighborhoods that had changed names, and neighborhoods in limbo because their developers had failed to follow city codes.[93] Large swaths of the city found themselves in a legal labyrinth impossible to navigate, and the number of unauthorized neighborhoods continued to grow over the following decades.

The colonial, Porfirian, and postrevolutionary periods were characterized by continuities and ruptures, particularly regarding the question of urban informality. The term itself carries the weight of centuries of urban regulations, spatial inequalities, and social stigma, dating back to the seminal division between the Spanish grid and the Indigenous settlements surrounding it. While the project of separation between the Spanish and Indian republics was never fully enacted, Priscilla Connolly has argued that the orderly Spanish city did create a normative ideal, with which Indigenous barrios could be disapprovingly contrasted. "Colonial urbanism was thus based on a double standard in which the very precise legal dispositions concerning who should live where, and how, existed more in representation than in reality, while at the same time legitimizing the segregation of the disordered periphery from the formal elite center."[94] This was the beginning of modern urban informality.

Sanitary codes demarcated a basic opposition that would later be translated into the language of formality and informality. This opposition built on a familiar colonial matrix. But the Porfirian notion of an unsanitary city was not merely a continuation of an earlier colonial understanding of the relationship between the city center and its barrios and pueblos. The link between capitalist urbanization, public health, and the law that emerged during the Porfirian period created a rupture in the history of the city and heralded a period of instability. Growth and modernization dislocated the axes and limits of Mexico City—even as its belly button remained firmly in place. By the early twentieth century, the areas north and east of the colonial grid were already in the process of urbanization outside of the law. At the same time, the sanitary city triumphantly expanded southwest along Reforma Avenue, incorporating municipalities like Tacubaya in the process. Public health was the master logic dividing the sprawling Porfirian city, drawing a line between bourgeois and plebeian, modern and traditional, formal and informal.

The informal city, however, was amenable to formalization: residents were eager to receive municipal services, but Porfirian city codes dictated that unauthorized neighborhoods were not entitled to municipal infrastructure, a stipulation that stigmatized both neighborhoods and their residents as inherently unsanitary. The same codes that Porfirian city officials deployed to curb growth, however, could be appropriated by residents to claim the right to sanitary housing. These claims proliferated in number and gained legitimacy in the aftermath of the Mexican Revolution, when the "housing problem" gained visibility in the politicized postrevolutionary city.

2

Revolution in the Hinterland, Revolution in the City

Mexico City regent José Manuel Puig Casauranc presented a survey to his advisory council (Consejo Consultivo) in April 1930. The picture was dismaying. The capital had gained 600,000 residents since the end of the revolution, reaching 1 million.[1] But dozens of neighborhoods lacked "potable water and drainage, pavements and sidewalks, public lighting and police, markets, schools, temples, and transportation services." Puig Casauranc blamed "previous administrations [that] authorized the establishment of numerous subdivisions without municipal services" as well as developers who failed to comply with their obligation to provide these services.[2] While city codes stated that developers were responsible for this provision, there was no enforcement mechanism for these rules. This meant that the development of many neighborhoods was based on the whims of developers and the demands of residents. According to Puig Casauranc, informal neighborhoods resulted from the confluence of poor families, greedy developers, and a government unwilling to enforce the law. "Unfortunately, people must be allowed to settle wherever they can, and in any way they can," he concluded.[3]

These words suggest that the city government was powerless to rein in developers and satisfy the housing needs of working-class families. But they obscure the growing role the government played as a broker between the two groups. While Puig Casauranc did not come up with a realistic plan to address the demand for affordable housing, his government became increasingly involved in neighborhoods outside of the law. Informal neighborhoods developed in conjunction with new modes of political power that emerged after the Mexican Revolution. The distribution of land in rural areas (through the institutions of the agrarian reform) was key to the allegiance of peasants to the state. Land, housing, and municipal services in Mexico City were also a political tool, a lucrative business, and a newly defined right. Accordingly, these goods were constantly negotiated by city officials, developers, and families in need of housing organized as settlers (colonos).

The nexus between these groups is the topic of this chapter. Throughout this period, the political arena of informality was demarcated by a foundational conflict among city officials, developers, and settlers over who was responsible for financing municipal services. In the wake of the revolution, settlers created a flurry of organizations to demand housing and services. They were caught in a contradiction: deprived of access to potable water, sewage systems, and paved streets but empowered by the ideals of social justice codified in the revolutionary Constitution of 1917. City authorities faced their own paradox: the challenge of controlling the growth of the city while placating revolutionary claims to it. Peripheral neighborhoods were the locus where settlers and officials staked, on the one hand, their revolutionary claims to the city and, on the other, their visions of a modern, sanitary metropolis. But peripheral neighborhoods were also a churning real-estate market that provided ample profit-making opportunities for developers capable of brokering between prospective homeowners and city officials.

The triangular battle of settlers, developers, and city officials gave rise to local brokers who amassed political power and wealth in the process. Halfway between political leaders and land impresarios, brokers gained influence in the decades after the revolution, becoming key figures in the governance of the city.[4] Brokers structured a land market outside of the law (plagued by property conflicts, uncertain lot limits, and inadequate urban infrastructure) and organized settlers into associations connected with the local and federal governments. By the 1970s and 1980s, these figures would come to be associated in the popular imagination with an all-powerful PRI, a metonym that obscured the specific work that they performed in structuring land markets and political representation.

After offering a brief introduction to the effects of the revolution in the capital, the first part of the chapter describes the neighborhood settler associations (*asociaciones de colonos*) that became a key political actor in postrevolutionary Mexico City—equivalent to the better-known peasant and worker organizations. I focus on the neighborhood association of Colonia Obrera, a place that became a flashpoint for sanitary concerns after the revolution. In the second section, I discuss two government-sponsored housing projects established in the 1920s and 1930s. The first one distributed lots to individual purchasers organized in a housing cooperative. The second involved a government-financed housing project designed by the radical young architect Juan Legarreta. Despite their differences, both experiments led to the emergence of extralegal markets articulated by brokers connected with political power. The third section analyzes the creation of the Departamento del Distrito Federal (DDF) in 1929, especially its dealings with neighborhood associations, brokers, and urban developers (although, as will become clear, brokers and developers were often one and the same). Finally, I analyze the rise of urban expropriations as a housing policy inspired by Mexico's agrarian reform. Land in postrevolutionary Mexico City, I argue, was not only a commodity to be bought and sold. It was demanded by citizens as a right and distributed by governments and political leaders eager to accrue power and build a clientele.

Neighborhood Associations in the Postrevolutionary City

The Mexican Revolution, fueled by rural grievances, was essentially agrarian and liquidated large landholders as a class. But the revolution was not only agrarian. The once widespread notion of a conservative capital removed from the revolutionary turmoil of the 1910s has been debunked. As historian John Lear has shown, Porfirian Mexico City had a vibrant working-class culture that expressed itself in unions, mutualist societies, and cooperatives. In the aftermath of the revolution, workers and the popular classes became a "permanent feature in urban life," gaining influence over national politics by virtue of their location in the capital.[5] The revolution represented a rupture for the city, in a matter of months transforming long-held notions of what was possible and creating a fertile ground for political organizing around labor and housing.[6]

The 1910s witnessed an upsurge of political mobilization. Workers, employees, tenants, and women organized food riots and strikes while the capital was occupied by revolutionary armies vying for national dominance. The cycle of mobilization and protest reached a high-water mark in the period 1914–1916, as the Conventionists (led by Emiliano Zapata and Pancho Villa) and the Constitutionalist army (led by Venustiano Carranza and Álvaro Obregón) in succession occupied a capital city plagued by inflation, supply shortages, and famine. Popular groups combined labor demands such as wage increases and an eight-hour workday with consumption demands, including rent controls and the supply of food and water. The mobilization climaxed in the summer of 1916, when workers and employees organized a general strike that brought the city to a standstill (it began when electrical workers cut off power). While Constitutionalist forces led by soon-to-be-president Venustiano Carranza ended up declaring martial law and repressing the strike leaders, they also met several demands and imposed rent controls and limits on evictions.[7] Approved the following February, the radical Constitution of 1917—often referred to as the world's first social constitution—codified the right to housing, alongside a battery of labor rights, in its sprawling article 123.

Until the 1920s, the politics of housing primarily involved renters: at least 85 percent of workers lived in vecindades and other rental accommodations.[8] Communists, anarchists, and other radical groups organized rent strikes in several cities during the revolution and its aftermath. Tenants in the port of Veracruz in March 1922 organized a renters' strike that at its peak included half of the city's population—30,000 tenants.[9] Strikers were repressed by federal forces, but radical governor Adalberto Tejeda decreed a rent law in 1923. Tenants in Mexico City went on strike a few weeks later, refusing to pay rent until protection measures were enacted. Strikers numbered 50,000 in June—in a city of 615,000—when their movement began to lose strength.[10] While tenant leagues and unions remained the most vocal groups in the politics of housing, settlers rapidly gained influence. Thereafter, the politics of housing became inseparable from the questions of land and municipal services.

Settlers in Mexico City in the 1920s made revolutionary claims to housing amid a remarkable postwar resurgence driven by capitalist urbanization. While growth rates decreased during the 1910s, the real-estate market was back in full swing the following decade. A total of twenty-eight neighborhoods had been established between 1900 and 1910. The number decreased to fifteen over a decade of war (1910–1920) but increased to thirty-two in the 1920s.[11] A real-estate craze swept the postrevolutionary capital, with parvenu generals reinventing themselves as urban developers. "This is why we made the revolution," a character of Carlos Fuentes's *Where the Air Is Clear* reflected, "so we could subdivide Mexico City."[12] Following earlier patterns, the housing market was segregated along an east-west axis. Sanctioned neighborhoods—designed by architects and enjoying municipal services and public amenities—were subdivided by developers in the wealthy southwest, whereas neighborhoods without municipal services and in defiance of city codes continued to expand toward the northeast and the southeast. In the 1920s the first group included neighborhoods like Chapultepec Heights and Hipódromo Condesa. The second included neighborhoods with "disastrous and threatening" sanitary conditions like Ex-Hipódromo de Peralvillo, Buenos Aires, and Obrera.[13]

Colonia Obrera was established a few blocks south of the Zócalo by industrial workers, some of whom fought with the Constitutionalist army during the revolution.[14] Developers had attempted to subdivide El Cuartelito—the land where Colonia Obrera stands—since the 1890s, but their proposals had been rejected by authorities bent on containing growth. An 1899 municipal decree stated that El Cuartelito was not authorized.[15] An official notice posted in the streets warned that the municipality "has not authorized the establishment of a new neighborhood" and therefore "will not provide municipal services, which the owners . . . will have to provide." To comply with the "provisions of the Sanitary Code," residents would have to finance "drainage, potable water, and other conditions."[16] "El Cuartelito is not a neighborhood and it does not exist," official records stated in 1908.[17]

Over the following decade, the central location of the neighborhood made it a lightning rod for authorities. By the 1920s, Colonia Obrera was so densely populated that its sanitary conditions were deemed alarming. The city government described this as a "shameful and serious problem, because [earlier governments] tolerated the subdivision of lots in the worst conditions and without services."[18] The area was served only by eight artesian wells, sanitary officials recorded. "Water stagnated in large puddles that poisoned the air."[19] Sanitary officials blamed conditions on the "irregular" and "unauthorized" character of the neighborhood. In response to the demographic and sanitary crisis that Colonia Obrera exemplified, the federal government prohibited the construction of houses in neighborhoods without municipal services in July 1924. The government also committed to enforcing contracts between developers and purchasers, compelling the former to fulfill their obligation to provide municipal services.[20] Neither banning construction nor overseeing developers would be a viable strategy to harness urban growth. Instead, postrevolutionary authorities ended up negotiating the financing of urban services with purchasers of lots and allowing numerous exemptions from the law.

Residents of Colonia Obrera requested an exception from the construction ban, arguing that they had purchased their lots before the decree and toiled for years "on the material and cultural improvement of the neighborhood."[21] While acknowledging the need to prevent the spread of epidemics, they argued that their settlement was a "consummated act": "a large number of houses had been constructed, many others were half-built, and the population surpassed ten thousand souls."[22] Residents blamed poor conditions on developers who deceived them with propaganda, selling lots without services at an enormous profit. In a 1930 letter addressed to President Abelardo Rodríguez, they described Colonia Obrera as "a garbage dump, where lots without services were sold at a rate of 27 pesos per square meter." Because the government had failed to oversee contracts between sellers and purchasers, developers "were profiting from the increase in land values created by the expansion of the city."[23] Rather than abandoning their neighborhood, residents wanted help to fix it. "We have freed our children from the tyranny of the landlord, but our lives remain burdened with anxiety: deprived of schools, light, pavements . . . we lack everything, even the police, which is extremely deficient."[24] Although residents were able to remain in their houses (which were not destroyed as threatened), municipal services would only be completed in the 1930s, more than a decade after the initial settlement.

Residents organized a union, the Sindicato de la Colonia Obrera de Bolívar (Union of the Bolívar Workers' Neighborhood), to negotiate with the government and collect funds to finance municipal services.[25] Similar neighborhood associations had existed since the nineteenth century, when they were formed to pool resources to pay for common expenses.[26] But postrevolutionary organizations multiplied and acquired a more radical bent, becoming key players in city politics.[27] Neighborhood associations deployed sanitary ideals to claim a right to healthy urban living and sought government support against developers. Such was the strategy of the residents of Colonia Portales, a neighborhood south of Colonia Obrera subdivided in the 1910s. Homeowners in Portales in the 1930s denounced developers for "breaking the Sanitary Code in force when the neighborhood was established."[28]

Colonia Portales was publicized in the press as a neighborhood for "decent families, living in attractive, hygienic, artistic, and self-owned homes."[29] But these lofty ideals soon turned into a more prosaic reality. In petitions to authorities for two decades, residents described the "disastrous" conditions of the neighborhood, afflicted by "typhoid fever, malaria, and microbes born from the filthy ditches." Organized as a union, the Sindicato de Colonos y Vecinos de Portales (Union of Settlers and Residents of Portales), residents accused developers of selling them "potreros por colonia": barren lands instead of the fully serviced neighborhood in their contract.[30]

Neighborhood associations appropriated the rhetoric of the revolution, making claims based on the 1917 Constitution and secondary laws. The Constitution acknowledged the existence of social groups endowed with rights.[31] Peasants and workers became the beneficiaries of laws and policies intended to uplift them, protect them against capitalists, and win their allegiance to the postrevolutionary regime. Inspired by workers and peasants, settlers asserted their right to housing. The Federación de Organizaciones de Colonos del Distrito Federal (Federation of Settlers' Organizations of the Federal District)—an umbrella organization that united residents from dozens of neighborhoods—based its demands on the 1917 Constitution and the 1928 Civil Code, which mandated a right to housing, both as an obligation for employers and as a state mandate to foster family patrimony.[32] Neighborhood associations also joined agrarian and worker leagues and parties, forging alliances against capitalists and landholders with a shared collectivist language. Residents from Colonia Portales transplanted the language of the agrarian reform to the city when they alluded to article 27 of the Constitution and its commitment to fix the *problema de la tierra*—the problem of land, which had previously been understood as an agrarian issue.[33] As I argue later in this chapter, the agrarian reform provided urban settlers with rhetorical and political ammunition to advance their own fight for housing.

In order to secure legal standing and negotiate with authorities, neighborhood associations began to register with the federal government in the 1920s.[34] Neighborhood associations forged relationships with congressmen (*diputados*) and senators, engaging in a vibrant metropolitan political arena and participating in national politics. In petitions to local and national authorities, settlers requested financing for municipal services, support in conflicts with developers, and housing measures that included rent controls, construction of public housing, and land expropriations. Residents from Colonia Moderna in 1926 formed an improvement board to finance public works for their neighborhood, which they described as a "swamp" where two thousand souls lived without sewage disposal, "electric lighting, and surveyance of any type, hence exposed to all dangers."[35]

They also demanded that the government compel lot purchasers to contribute to common payments, as voluntary contributions were not easily secured. In September 1930, in a petition typical of the period, neighbors of Nonoalco and Atlampa requested government aid to build schools, pave streets, increase policing, build parks and community centers, widen thoroughfares, and improve municipal services. Their organization, Hombres Libres del Trabajo de Nonoalco y Atlampa (Free Workers of Nonoalco and Atlampa), was registered with the national Ministry of Government and supported by congressman Samuel Villarreal, whom the organization had helped elect.[36] Federal members of Congress became the spokespeople for urban residents, a role that was increasingly significant as the population of the city grew and the capital increased its share of national representatives.[37]

Local neighborhood associations formed larger federations that jockeyed for influence with the city government and the Partido Nacional Revolucionario (National Revolutionary Party, PNR), the party created to unite Mexico's revolutionary leaders following the assassination of President Álvaro Obregón in 1928. Residents from Colonia Obrera joined residents of other outlying working-class neighborhoods in the Federación de Organizaciones de Colonos del Distrito Federal, part of a constellation of housing cooperatives, unions, and federations. These organizations became increasingly entangled with the government and the subsequent incarnations of the PNR: the Partido de la Revolución Mexicana (Party of the Mexican Revolution, PRM, formed in 1938) and the Partido Revolucionario Institucional (PRI, formed in 1946).[38] The relationship between neighborhood associations and government and party officials was increasingly institutionalized, becoming what many have seen as a powerful system of intermediation and control. However, we should not understand city politics in these early postrevolutionary decades as leading inexorably to the creation of an all-powerful political party.

President Plutarco Elías Calles and the rest of the architects of the PNR founded the party in order to deal with intra-elite conflicts but not to manipulate the masses, as teleological interpretations of the PRI would later put it.[39] Neighborhood associations competed against one another for land with the support of local brokers who were also in competition with each other. Serving as an intermediary between settlers and the city government could be profitable, as will become clear, and various brokers (land impresarios, revolutionary generals, agrarian authorities, and local leaders) were eager to do so.

Public Lands, Private Brokers

Housing became a citizen claim in postrevolutionary Mexico City. But housing was also a means to build political support, fulfill revolutionary promises of social justice, and—not least—make a profit. As described in the previous section, neighborhood associations organized to fight for municipal services in the 1920s. Settlers at that time encountered authorities eager to make housing the foundation of a political bargain and a profitable business venture. This section examines the histories of Colonia Ex-Hipódromo Peralvillo and Colonia Michoacana (also known as La Vaquita) as examples of the confluence of political patronage, politicized real-estate markets, and revolutionary promises of social justice.[40] While both neighborhoods were sponsored by the state, they ended up being plagued by conflicts about property and the provision of municipal services. These conflicts arose as government officials and local brokers used their positions to advance private interests. The state could not monopolize control over land and people, so peripheral neighborhoods became a fertile soil for the emergence of local political leadership and profit-making.

Colonia Ex-Hipódromo Peralvillo and Colonia Michoacana were located northeast of Mexico City, in what was becoming the heart of the city's working-class culture. A brainchild of President Álvaro Obregón, Colonia Ex-Hipódromo Peralvillo began as a project to distribute the lands of the old jockey club among working-class families.[41] Starting with the presidency of Venustiano Carranza (1917–1920), revolutionary leaders used housing to build political alliances and win mass support.[42] In 1917, in the midst of the political and economic crisis caused by the war, Carranza distributed land in the barrios of San Simón and Atlampa to landless families, one of the first times such an action was taken.[43] Popular groups and workers continued to petition for land, rent controls, and credit. Postal workers successfully petitioned President Obregón in 1921 for loans to purchase lots and escape the "exploitation and extortion they faced as tenants."[44] As federal employees, workers proposed a scheme through which they would receive government bonds and have the payments deducted from their salaries. Colonia Federal was established through a similar scheme in 1924.[45] Workers in these neighborhoods continued to suffer from the lack of municipal services, however, hinting at the limits of land distribution without a commitment to provide infrastructure.[46] The founding of Ex-Hipódromo Peralvillo must be interpreted in this context.

The availability of federal lands in Peralvillo prompted architects, developers, business owners, and a handful of opportunists to make proposals to the government. Architect Guillermo Zárraga, an employee at the federal Secretaría de Comunicaciones y Obras Públicas (Ministry of Communications and Public Works, SCOP), who would later head the city's Office of Public Works, submitted a worker housing project that included floor plans and budgets. While the building featured a neocolonial facade, a common feature in the 1920s, Zárraga made the bold decision to combine individual and collective dwellings, with individual bedrooms and common spaces around a central courtyard.[47] While his project remained unbuilt, it might have influenced Colonia Michoacana and other functionalist projects built in the following decade and designed by radical architects like Juan Legarreta and Juan O'Gorman, students of Zárraga.[48]

A developer named Elfego Lugo also submitted a plan for a neighborhood reflecting in all its splendor the "social tendencies of the time."[49] Describing other developers as "exploiting octopuses," Lugo proposed a partnership between the federal government and a homeowners' cooperative: the government would provide land while cooperative members would make monthly payments of MX$40 over a five-year period to amass enough capital to begin construction. The cooperative would then negotiate the provision of municipal services with the city. Many other projects were floated, for Peralvillo and for other federal lands.[50] The majority were characterized by the revolutionary rhetoric of social justice and collectivist legal structures like cooperatives.

In December 1922, following a study by an "expert group of engineers," Congress approved the creation of Colonia Ex-Hipódromo Peralvillo.[51] A government engineer subdivided the land, while Jesús H. Abitia brokered the negotiation between the government and the purchasers.[52] Abitia was close to President Obregón, having produced propaganda films in support of his 1920 political campaign.[53] Abitia, supported by the government, led the distribution of lots.[54] He even served as honorary president of the neighborhood, which carries his name in a few documents. It was common in the 1920s and 1930s to name neighborhoods after their political patrons. Abitia's role as a broker was essential, bolstering the authority of the federal government and contributing to the crystallization of a real-estate market. This type of broker, halfway between a political leader and a land impresario, gained influence in these years and would remain a key figure in the history of the city.

The early years of Peralvillo and the lands surrounding it were marked by a property conflict between residents, who received their lots from the federal government, and Macario Navarro, a general who claimed to own the land.[55] Unlike Abitia, who enjoyed the patronage of Obregón, Navarro derived his authority from more varied sources. Newspaper reports described him as a "wealthy landowner" who offered Congress a 300-hectare lot to be distributed among students.[56] He had been accused in the 1910s of invading lands belonging to Colonia Nuevo Rastro and Colonia Peralvillo.[57] Navarro filed a lawsuit in 1924 to claim ownership of Ex-Hipódromo Peralvillo. He deployed police forces to oust the residents.[58] Archival sources do not reveal how Navarro managed this, but the line between police forces and hired gunmen in postrevolutionary urban Mexico was blurry. The use of violence to extort those less powerful was widespread.[59]

Instances of land invasions and violent removal of residents were common in the 1920s and 1930s, hinting at the importance of politicking and extralegal violence as well as the limits of judicial power. The logic of land invasions and land grabs, as described by historian Matthew Vitz, was using landless families to bolster the claims of alleged landowners, wedding the claims of both.[60] In the context of uncertain property rights, the possession of land by families was a useful way to solidify claims. The line between protecting residents and exploiting them was tenuous, and brokers like Navarro were both reviled and beloved.

Like property rights, the allocation of municipal services was also fraught. Abitia led the distribution of lots in 1922 and 1923, but municipal services were the responsibility of the Junta de Mejoras Materiales (Board of Material Improvements), a board elected by residents that was entrusted with the collection of funds for the provision of water, sewage systems, electricity, and pavements.[61] The board was headed by Ramiro E. Martínez. To amass funds, it charged monthly fees and organized boxing matches, dances, and similar events.[62] Martínez was soon accused of stealing funds from the cooperative and overcharging its residents. A rival organization, the Sindicato de los Colonos del Ex–Hipódromo de Peralvillo (Union of the Settlers of Ex-Hipódromo

Peralvillo), led by José Arcipresto, was thus organized. Arcipresto accused Martínez of setting an excessive price for sewage works (MX$4 per square meter) and argued that he could secure a lower price (MX$2.60).[63] According to Guillermo Zárraga, who authored a report on the conflict, Martínez stole from the cooperative to fund a political campaign. Zárraga blamed Martínez but exonerated Abitia, describing him as an honest man but a terrible administrator. In his report, penned in June 1927, Zárraga argued that Abitia was the only person capable of resolving the conflicts in the neighborhood, an assessment that confirms Abitia's ongoing influence.[64]

Abitia continued to control the neighborhood as president of its Sociedad Cooperativa Plutarco Elías Calles (Plutarco Elías Calles Cooperative Society) for almost a decade. In 1935, however, he faced accusations similar to those made against Martínez. According to a group of residents organized in the Liga Pro-Defensa de los Colonos del Ex–Hipódromo Peralvillo (League for the Defense of the Settlers of Ex-Hipódromo Peralvillo), Abitia acted as a "lord and master" who "seeded anarchy" in the cooperative and profited from his role as president. He secured "excessive salaries" for himself and his associates that betrayed the "cooperative ideal." He stole from the neighborhood treasury and took loans that he did not pay back. Abitia also engaged in a more eccentric fraud—he had, after all, been a film producer. He sold the cooperative a film projector and initiated the construction of a movie theater (later suspended by authorities).[65]

These abuses elicited protests that escalated into violence and even the death of one cooperative member. Conflicts between cooperative leaders and accusations of corruption and embezzlement were common and continued to take place in Ex-Hipódromo Peralvillo as in other neighborhoods. Archival traces of them abounded for decades, despite continuous government efforts to put an end to the chaos by streamlining the link between the government and residents.[66] The federal government conducted an investigation in 1935, which concluded that Abitia's cooperative "had not fulfilled its social function . . . since it only benefited a small group of leaders who exploited residents."[67] The government stripped the cooperative of its power, assuming control of the urbanization of the neighborhood and the distribution of property titles.[68] Rather than resolving conflict in the neighborhood, however, the government intervention empowered one organization over another, a common occurrence. Virtually every working-class neighborhood in Mexico City experienced a similar conflict between two or more rival organizations seeking official sanction and eager to amass capital and political power.

By 1930, less than a decade after its founding, an official report described Colonia Ex-Hipódromo Peralvillo as "lacking all public services, as its developers did not do anything but sell lots, without concerning themselves with hygiene and public health."[69] Remarkably, the report failed to consider that the neighborhood was initially a state project. Neither did it analyze the process through which such a project was taken over by brokers and land impresarios. In any case, the confluence of political power, business opportunity, and citizenship claims in Ex-Hipódromo Peralvillo was all too common and casts light on later experiences.

In the early 1930s—a decade after the creation of Colonia Ex-Hipódromo Peralvillo—the city government initiated a more assertive experiment that went beyond the distribution of land and the organization of cooperatives. In 1933 it announced with much fanfare the construction of three housing projects for workers and employees: Colonia Balbuena, Colonia San Jacinto, and Colonia La Vaquita, located a few blocks away from Ex-Hipódromo Peralvillo, on land claimed by Macario Navarro.[70] The projects were designed by a cohort of architects inspired by functionalism and the tenets of the Congrès Internationaux d'Architecture Moderne (International Congresses of Modern Architecture, CIAM). The group of "radical architects," as they came to be known, included Enrique Yáñez, Augusto Pérez Palacios, Carlos Tarditi, and Juan Legarreta, the winner of a 1932 contest for the design of a minimal home for workers. Legarreta led the design of the three housing projects, borrowing and adapting ideas from his classmates.

In the end, 700 houses were built between 1933 and 1936 and sold at a subsidized price to government employees.[71] While the dwellings housed a minuscule number of families in terms of the needs of the city, they were highly symbolic projects, amalgamating a revolutionary rhetoric with radical ideas about architecture and urban planning. At the inauguration ceremony of the San Jacinto project, city regent Aarón Sáenz explained that the houses fit into the rational city that his administration was engineering. Located on the outskirts of the city, San Jacinto would lead the way for harmonic urban development by becoming a "model urbanization zone."[72] Subsidized by the city government, the houses would emancipate workers from "the pigsties where they lived, [vecindades] that resembled jail cells and death chambers . . . where tenants' bodies and souls were infamously exploited by owners."[73]

Historians of architecture have studied Legarreta's minimal homes as radical experiments and precursors of a more muscular housing policy that galvanized in the 1940s. But these projects also show how easily state projects could spawn land markets outside of the law. In her detailed study of La Vaquita, historian Claudia C. Zamorano Villarreal provided evidence of the transformation from a formal public housing project into an informal real-estate market. La Vaquita was inaugurated by President Lázaro Cárdenas in

December 1936. According to oral histories, the name was changed to Colonia Estado de Michoacán (and then Michoacana) following the suggestion of Cárdenas, because many residents, like the president himself, hailed from that state. However, at the time of the inauguration only 228 houses had been completed, less than 50 percent of the number contemplated in the original project, owing to the early death of Legarreta and budgetary constraints. Most of the houses built did not follow the original design but represented a simplified and cheaper version, known as type-Z houses.[74]

Eventually, two neighborhoods, Ampliación Michoacán and Ampliación 20 de Noviembre, would be established in the unbuilt sections of Colonia Michoacana at the behest of local brokers. While the precise origins of these neighborhoods are unclear, the existence of empty blocks—earmarked for sports facilities in Legarreta's original project—in an area of the city where numerous organizations were jockeying for land created pressure to subdivide the area. This pressure was felt in many other neighborhoods, where land invaders and developers eyed empty swaths of land (where public facilities like schools, markets, or community centers were planned) as prospective neighborhoods.[75] To make matters worse, La Vaquita was surrounded by neighborhoods—Socialista, Patria Nueva, Lázaro Cárdenas, and Macario Navarro—with cooperatives fighting among themselves and with the city government. In 1934, for example, "residents who had received their lots from General Macario Navarro" were violently dispossessed of their houses by "a group of thirty armed men led by the developer Alejandro Romero."[76] Land was a valuable asset, and both political leaders and real-estate developers were bent on controlling it, often by using violence.

At that point, Jerónimo López, a resident of Colonia Michoacana, spearheaded the creation of Colonia Ampliación Michoacán. López hailed from the State of Veracruz, something of a revolutionary laboratory for housing politics. Upon arriving in the capital, he became the leader of the short-lived Partido Socialista de las Colonias Proletarias (Socialist Party of Proletarian Neighborhoods), where he advocated for an urban alternative to Mexico's agrarian reform. "In the same way *agrarismo* was the solution for the peasant, *urbanismo*[,] . . . the distribution of houses to the urban poor, is a solution for the housing problem, a relief for the working class, and one problem less for the planning of cities."[77] López, however, was enmeshed in conflicts with local brokers and, according to press reports, at times resorted to violence against rival groups of settlers.[78] The city government in 1941 sold the land designated as Ampliación Michoacán to the Bloque de Colonos Revolucionarios del Distrito Federal (Revolutionary Settlers' Bloc of the Federal District), the larger federation with which López's Partido Socialista de las Colonias

Proletarias was affiliated. Most purchasers were already in possession of the lots, so the sale simply formalized their ownership.[79]

Colonia Michoacana's evolution from a proud state housing project to a neighborhood settled by brokers like López is mirrored by the experience of Ex-Hipódromo Peralvillo and Colonia Gabriel Ramos Millán (analyzed in chapter 5). These were all government-sponsored neighborhoods, which made good on revolutionary housing promises. But these neighborhoods were also resources that local brokers (more or less independent from the state) could take over to make a profit or build a political clientele. Colonia Ex-Hipódromo Peralvillo and Colonia Michoacana destabilized the division between official state-led housing projects and informal ones spearheaded by private actors, with varying degrees of support or acquiescence from the government. Scholars have long been aware of how informal neighborhoods could be regularized over time, following the provision of property titles and municipal services. But many neighborhoods went through the opposite process. Established as state projects, they ended up bearing many markers of informality: property conflicts, incomplete municipal services, and self-construction.

Urban Expansion and Political Control under the Departamento del Distrito Federal

The housing project of La Vaquita was led by the city government, the Departamento del Distrito Federal (Department of the Federal District, DDF). The DDF had been created in 1929, in a climate of euphoria about the resurgence of Mexico City and a growing anxiety over the provision of municipal services. The decision followed a political and technocratic logic. Politically, the DDF eliminated the autonomy of local municipalities, putting the Federal District under the grip of a regent appointed by the president (a state of affairs that lasted until 1997).[80] Along with this rationale to centralize power, President Obregón borrowed technical arguments from architects, engineers, and urban planners who lamented the city council's incapacity to guide the metropolitan expansion of the city. In the opinion of architect Luis Prieto y Souza, the sacrifice of a democratic body was a small price to pay for "securing the unity of Mexico City and the proper distribution of urban services."[81] The metropolitan integration of the Valley of Mexico could be led more efficiently by a single expert body, rather than by an assortment of inchoate city councils. Broader (regional) and deeper government powers were needed to deal with an increasing population and a metropolitan scale.

Since the "problems of urbanization encompass the entire Valley of Mexico," argued Public Works director Vicente G. Almada, a single office ought to be in charge of public works throughout the entire Federal District.[82]

The Valley of Mexico was an extraordinarily diverse mosaic of small towns, Indigenous pueblos, ranches, and fields. Metropolitan integration was a tall order. The DDF published a lavish two-volume *Atlas general del Distrito Federal* (1930), an instrument of state legibility and territorial control. Through its description and inventory of the Federal District, the *Atlas* attempted to match a government body with a defined territory. Unsurprisingly, the volume reveals a statecraft project as well as its limits. Its maps, for example, were based on outdated cadastral surveys and did not include recent neighborhoods that had not been sanctioned by the city government. The maps of several *delegaciones* (boroughs) offer the incongruous image of a few blocks and roads surrounded by blank spaces, as if territory that was not fully urbanized was not worthy of inclusion. The *Atlas* also described delegaciones such as Iztacalco and Iztapalapa as agrarian, which was undoubtedly the case, while failing to acknowledge the existence of recently settled neighborhoods. (Iztacalco is a borough in southeast Mexico City; Ixtacalco is a small town in this borough.)[83] By offering descriptions of colonial Mexico City that failed to acknowledge its Indigenous suburbs, the *Atlas* erased the unplanned city outside of the law, relentlessly expanding outward.

The growth of the city, the incomplete reach of its municipal services, and the informal character of its peripheral neighborhoods became a multifaceted challenge for the new governing body. In April 1930, fifteen months after taking over the DDF, Puig Casauranc found himself explaining this conundrum to the Consejo Consultivo. He listed dozens of neighborhoods bereft of municipal services and public amenities. The area amounted to thirty-six square kilometers, and the budget required to address these insufficiencies added up to 100 million pesos, an extraordinary sum well beyond the city budget.[84] Puig Casauranc accused developers of exploiting working-class residents and failing to comply with the law. He vaguely referenced his efforts to resolve conflicts between settlers and fraudulent developers. While his attempt to have developers pay for the missing municipal services failed, the situation created an opening for his government to deal with the problems of urban growth, the financing of municipal services, and political representation in an integrated manner.

Incapable of reining in developers, the DDF became an intermediary between the settlers and the developers. This required controlling the neighborhood associations and federations of settlers that flourished during the 1920s, over which the city government had little control.[85] To streamline

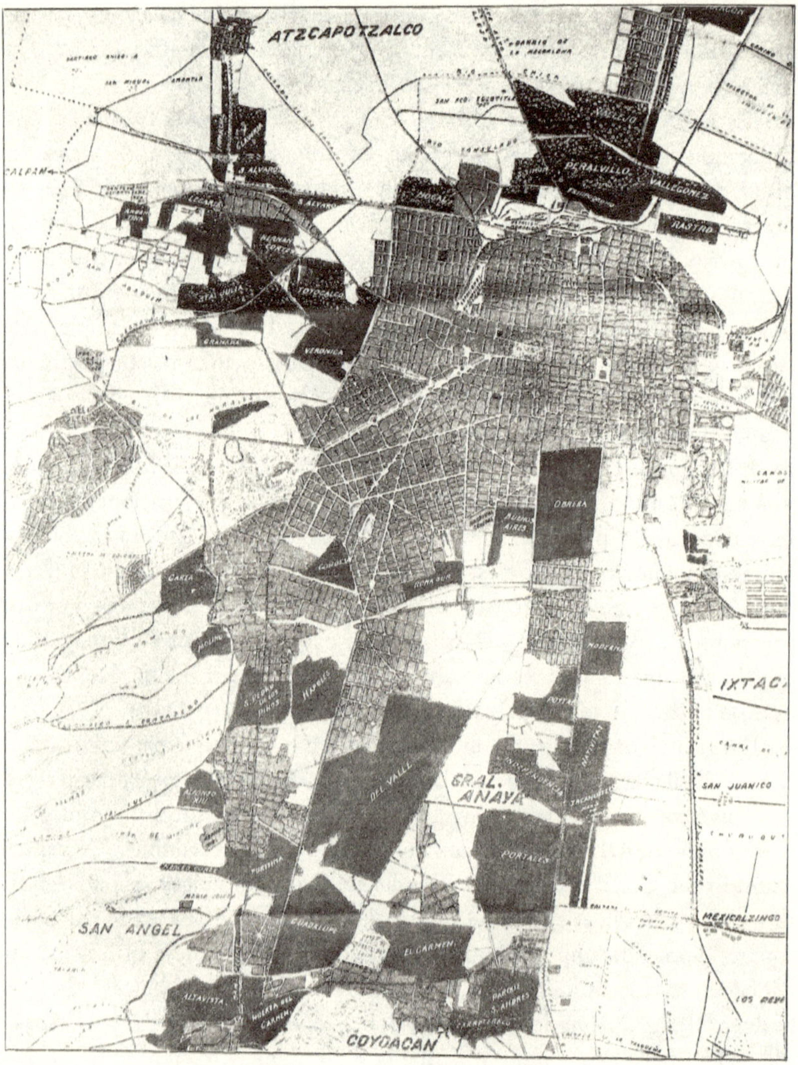

Figure 2.1. "Map of Mexico City and the Metropolitan Region." *Nuestra Ciudad*, May 1930. Hemeroteca Nacional Digital de México. Regent José Manuel Puig Casauranc presented this map to the Consejo Consultivo in April 1930. The map was published, along with a report listing neighborhoods without urban services, in the DDF's official journal and other publications.

its relationship with these organizations, the DDF created the Oficina de Cooperación (Cooperation Office) in 1931. Under the authority of Public Works, the Oficina de Cooperación was tasked with setting the amount residents were required to pay for infrastructure works, mainly the provision of municipal services that previously had been the responsibility of developers.[86] According to the 1933 Ley de Cooperación, residents could contribute cash, land, or labor to install municipal services.[87] To provide water, drainage, and pavements, Public Works collaborated with local improvement boards by providing funds, technical assistance, and oversight.[88] The Oficina de Cooperación was hailed by the press as a progressive measure to aid residents. However, its existence tacitly acknowledged the government's failure to compel developers to pay for municipal services, even when stipulated in their contracts.[89] But the office and the law were pragmatic responses that allowed for the installment of municipal services on an ad hoc basis. By fusing the political organization of residents with the financing of municipal services, cooperation provided a rubric for urban expansion and political control.

The DDF increasingly embraced a progressive rhetoric of cooperation. Its aim, regent Cosme Hinojosa declared in 1935, was "to provide water, drainage, and pavements to poor neighborhoods. . . . This is not only justified by our revolutionary commitment to end privileges and inequalities. . . . it is also based on the practical consideration that these inequalities and privileges [have] momentous consequences for the community."[90] The Oficina de Cooperación showcased the importance that working-class neighborhoods acquired for the government, both as a constituency that ought to be served and as a political asset, a duality that characterized the relationship between the government and settlers for years to come.

Originally in charge of coordinating the financing of municipal services, the Oficina de Cooperación morphed into an office tasked with "organizing and promoting worker neighborhoods."[91] The office gained political prominence as it negotiated with developers and settlers. Eventually, the Oficina de Cooperación began to sanction the leaders of neighborhood associations, becoming the broker between settlers and the city authorities. Evidence of this role is visible in Colonia Emilio Carranza, a neighborhood close to Ex-Hipódromo Peralvillo established by Alejandro Romero, the archetype of the corrupt and abusive developer.[92] According to residents, Romero imposed "predatory contracts" and deployed extralegal forces to deprive them of their lots if payments were not made. Yet the neighborhood "had not received urban services as ordered by the law."[93] The head of the Oficina de Cooperación, engineer Manuel Rodríguez Gutiérrez, investigated the matter and mediated between the two parties, though archival records do not provide a record of the outcome of his travails. Rodríguez Gutiérrez surveyed other working-class neighborhoods, leading investigations into the legal and political conflicts plaguing them and reporting to the president.[94]

Like Macario Navarro, Jesús Abitia, and other brokers, the head of the Oficina de Cooperación was sometimes seen as a benefactor for settlers, but he was also accused of exploiting them. This was the case of Rafael de Villa, who succeeded Rodríguez Gutiérrez and was accused of dispossessing settlers of their lots and belongings. Villa was removed from his post in 1938 by the city regent, according to party officials and neighborhood leaders, because he was "working against the unity of the colonos of the Federal District."[95] While the precise causes for his removal are not clear, his position as head of the Oficina de Cooperación was a constant predicament, as virtually all working-class neighborhoods were divided between rival organizations, and the Oficina de Cooperación was essentially tasked with choosing sides. As an employee of the DDF, de Villa also found himself in an impossible position between the city government and neighborhood leaders, increasingly—but by no means straightforwardly—agglutinated around the PRM. The conflict between party leaders and city authorities would never be fully resolved. While party leaders would continue to support urban residents' demands for land and municipal services, the DDF had limited resources and was stretched thin in its efforts to control the relentless expansion of the city.

In the DDF's view, the "anomalous situation" of "poor people's neighborhoods" was caused by fraudulent sellers who did not have "real possession of [the lots they sold]."[96] To fix this political and legal problem, the government intervened in working-class neighborhoods in several ways.[97] First, as we have seen, the government became a broker between lot purchasers and landowners, collecting lot payments and urbanization fees from the former and making payments to the latter. The government also purchased lots that it subsequently sold to city residents. Finally, the government expropriated lots in order to sell them to lot purchasers. This was the case in the neighborhoods in La Vaquita, where Macario Navarro and other leaders had been jockeying for lots and residents: Macario Navarro, Patria Nueva, Socialista, and Lázaro Cárdenas, all expropriated in the 1930s.[98] All of these neighborhoods were led by cooperatives that had abused residents and failed to fulfill their "social function," far from an unusual occurrence.[99] In response, the government expropriated the lots, canceled the permits of the cooperatives, and instructed lot purchasers to stop making payments to them.[100]

Before expanding on the significance of urban expropriations as a housing policy, it is worth summarizing the role that the Oficina de Cooperación acquired in the 1930s, not least because the office would remain active for decades, under different names (first as the Oficina de Colonias, then as the Procuraduría de Colonias). The Oficina de Cooperación was created to finance municipal services in working-class neighborhoods, many of which were plagued by legal conflicts involving developers, neighborhood associations, and settlers. But the office quickly acquired a more political role, becoming a government organ tasked with sanctioning neighborhood associations and their leaders as well as more actively promoting worker neighborhoods. As a consequence, the fiscal and legal crisis created by the growth of peripheral working-class neighborhoods outside of the law became the basis for a political arrangement, wedding the city government and working-class residents.

Urban Expropriations during Cardenismo

Urban expropriations represented the most forceful housing policy deployed by the DDF as well as its most effective tool to settle property conflicts. Since the turn of the twentieth century, the primacy of collective welfare (as defined by the state) over individual property rights had been advanced by legal thinkers around the world, enabling governments to expropriate land for the sake of "public utility."[101] These statist principles had been embraced by Porfirian ideologues influenced by French positivism. But these ideas gained momentum and became radicalized in the aftermath of the Mexican Revolution. The power of the state to expropriate land and resources in the subsoil, enshrined in article 27 of the 1917 Constitution, became a cornerstone of the revolutionary state project. Article 27 provided the legal basis for the 1938 expropriation of the oil industry and for the agrarian reform, which ebbed and flowed but reached a climax during the presidency of Cárdenas, the most radical period of Mexican postrevolutionary history. The agrarian reform transformed property relationships in the countryside and liquidated the assets of the landholding class. But it also indelibly marked struggles over land in urban Mexico, a fact that still has not been properly acknowledged by the historiography.[102]

In Mexico City and in other regions, urban expropriations were intertwined with the agrarian reform, warranting a short overview of this process. The agrarian reform started early in Mexico City, gaining momentum in the 1920s. Following the revolutionary decree of January 6, 1915—the legal foundation for the agrarian reform—dozens of pueblos around the city petitioned for land grants and restitutions.[103] Most of the land distributed was located in the peripheral delegaciones, in areas that had been targeted by developers as prime sites for residential subdivisions.[104] In fact, the specter of agrarian reform accelerated the urbanization of these areas: landowners subdivided and sold their lands as a strategy to prevent expropriation, because agrarian laws typically targeted large landholdings.[105] Whether or not land grants were awarded depended, among other conditions, on the rural or urban status of the communities requesting land and the rural or urban status of the land in question.

But defining this status was no simple task, especially in places experiencing rapid urbanization. When the neighbors of Colonia Independencia petitioned for land from the Narvarte estate, the estate lawyers argued that the residents were not agricultural workers, that Colonia Independencia was an urban settlement, and that their land was within city limits, hence outside of the jurisdiction of agrarian authorities. The petitioners denied the urban character of Colonia Independencia and asserted their status as peasants: "It is false that this neighborhood is urbanized: there are no streets, drainage, electricity, water, police . . . or any indication that a settlement will be established here." Residents described themselves as "poor people making a living from agriculture," adding that "if they had other occupations, it was due to the lack of agrarian lands."[106] Similarly, residents from the pueblo of Magdalena Mixihuca were denied a land grant because the local agrarian commission ruled that they were not a rural community but an urban barrio.[107] Residents responded that they were once a pueblo: if they were "reduced to misery" and "dispossessed," it was due to the loss of their lands during Porfirian times.[108] Both neighborhoods would eventually receive land grants. As these legal arguments reveal, however, the lines between the urban and the agrarian realms were far from clear.

Neither was there a strict line between peasant and worker organizing. As we have seen, urban settlers deployed the rhetoric of the agrarian reform to petition for land. At the same time, as the city encroached onto formerly agricultural land, many agrarian leaders transformed themselves into urban brokers who derived power from selling land and politicking on behalf of landless "urban" families or families newly understood as urban.[109] Before Cárdenas restructured the PNR into clearly defined sectors in 1938—including peasant and worker sectors—workers, peasants, and settlers crafted alliances in the capital and other cities.

In this context of the ambiguity of the "urban" and "agrarian" realms, state and federal governments with a radical bent established working-class urban neighborhoods, resorting to an expansive interpretation of "public utility"—the sine qua non for lawful expropriations—inspired by the agrarian reform and revolutionary ideals more broadly.[110] The radical government of the State of

Veracruz, led by governor Adalberto Tejeda (the man responsible for the 1923 state rent law), for example, ordered expropriations to build social housing in cities and established *colonias agrícolas* (agricultural neighborhoods, nonetheless settled by industrial workers) on the outskirts of cities like Xalapa.[111]

Urban expropriations had an obvious political logic, given the popular pressure from landless families headed by savvy brokers. But the pressure struck a chord because it had a foundation in Mexico's revolutionary jurisprudence. Because article 27 declared that all land originally belonged to the nation, it established a legal framework where property rights to soil and subsoil could be interpreted as "derivative, precarious, and in coexistence with different modalities of property."[112] Expropriation was also justified by the 1928 Civil Code, which declared that "the government acquisition of lots in order to sell them for the constitution of family patrimony or in order to build houses for rent for low-income families, through the payment of a modicum rent," was "of public utility."[113] Whereas the 1917 Constitution had been drafted with an agrarian country in mind, the Civil Code was a direct response to the global crisis of liberalism, which manifested itself in urban problems like labor and the housing question.[114] Finally, as the following chapter shows, urban expropriations (especially in Mexico City) were driven by the desire to rationalize the settlement of working-class neighborhoods according to functionalist planning principles, which were gaining ground. In other words, urban expropriations could combine the national property of land codified in the Constitution, the collectivist ethos of the Cárdenas era, and the principles of a functional city espoused by urban planners in the 1930s.

Expropriations for worker neighborhoods triggered *amparo* lawsuits brought by landowners (amparos are legal actions designed to protect constitutional guarantees), unleashing conflicts that sometimes turned violent. In 1934 the Supreme Court ruled in favor of landowners in Veracruz whose lands had been expropriated and ordered the "destruction" of neighborhoods in Xalapa, Córdoba, and Amatlán.[115] In response to this ruling, a group of senators led by General Cándido Aguilar proposed a constitutional reform to increase the government's authority to expropriate land in cities. The senators argued that because the Cárdenas government placed "the rights of the popular masses over the rights of the individual," the law ought to reflect that hierarchy.[116] The proposal was not approved, but in 1935 the Supreme Court ruled that urban expropriations were lawful by arguing that, like their agrarian counterparts, they "indirectly fulfilled the needs of the collectivity." The court compared the "division of agrarian latifundia for the benefit of the peasant classes with the subdivision and urbanization of lots to build sanitary worker housing."[117]

The Supreme Court's ruling exemplifies Mexico's "social revolutionary jurisprudence"—to use legal scholar Rodrigo Meneses Reyes's term—a legal movement to deploy the Constitution to transform society according to revolutionary ideals.[118] That same year, the minister of the economy, Francisco Mújica, drafted the Expropriation Law of 1936, which opened the door for the redistribution of urban land modeled on the agrarian reform. Expropriations, Mújica asserted, could be based not only on "public utility" but also on "reasons of social interest," such as the subdivision and distribution of agrarian landholdings or the construction of worker neighborhoods.[119] Industrial, commercial, and financial groups lambasted the Expropriation Law of 1936. It also evoked fears among homeowners, who saw it, in the words of one daily newspaper, "as a threat to private property."[120] Resident associations, however, welcomed the law as a godsend. The Liga Nacional de Sociedades Cooperativas (National League of Cooperatives) congratulated Cárdenas, and hundreds of resident associations doubled down on their petitions for land.[121]

Expropriations were not an uncontested policy enacted by a powerful and progressive government. Furthermore, they were seldom used to create worker neighborhoods from scratch. More often, they were a means to regularize possession by residents without a title or in the midst of conflicts with developers who had failed to distribute urban services.[122] In other words, expropriations were a political solution to a legal conflict. Once the government owned the expropriated land, the thinking went, it could sell it to residents, guaranteeing their rightful possession and winning their political loyalty. A policy *and* a political tool adapted from Mexico's agrarian reform, urban land expropriations politicized the real-estate market and strengthened the authority of the state and political brokers allocating land. This project, which acquired a remarkable degree of institutionalization in the 1940s, is the topic of chapter 4.

During the twentieth century, Mexico's federal government distributed millions of acres of land to peasant communities. The institution of the reform endowing the agrarian corporation (ejido) with land under a sui generis property regime was a political and legal response to the inequality of nineteenth-century agrarian society,[123] as interpreted by revolutionary intellectuals.[124] The consequences of this transfer of land are hard to overstate. More than half of Mexico's territory was distributed among ejidos and for the most part remains so today.

Urban land did not carry the same weight as a foundational myth for the postrevolutionary regime. But it was far from inconsequential. In the wake of the revolution, housing and land became a crucible for citizenship but also a means to build political support, fulfill revolutionary promises, and make a profit. For the working classes, access to land and housing was mediated by city officials, brokers, developers, and political leaders who sought to insert themselves into the production and distribution of housing. The relationship between working-class families and these actors became particularly salient in the informal peripheries of the city. These neighborhoods—lacking municipal services, in defiance of city codes, and plagued by property conflicts—represented a political arena where the financing for municipal services, the access to lots, and even state expropriations were negotiated, often by bending the law.

Beginning in the 1920s, the city government viewed the unruly expansion of the city as a daunting technical and financial problem. However, this expansion also presented an opportunity to make urban housing the cornerstone of a political bargain. The DDF's approach to urban growth and political control in the 1930s would remain in place for decades. But the city government never harnessed the full support of the hundreds of neighborhood associations that continued to demand housing, land, and municipal services in the aftermath of the revolution. While party officials and the political branches of the city government attempted to satisfy these demands (and curry favor), others, more technocratic in nature, sought to regulate the expansion of the city in the name of expert governance. The political and technocratic classes continued to be at odds as they sought to manage the expansion of the city, as the following chapters describe.

3

Planning and Informality

It is an enduring belief—commonsensical to the point of banality—that Mexico City is an unplanned city. The city's urban crisis, geographer Peter Ward asserted in 1990, did not occur "because planners had got it wrong" but "because planners didn't exist as such."[1] During the 1930s and 1940s, denunciations of the anarchy of Mexico City centered on two matters: the weakness of planners and the absence of a master plan.[2] "There is neither a master plan nor urban planners," the Sociedad de Arquitectos Mexicanos (Society of Mexican Architects) declared in 1945: "Instead there is politics, practical solutions, and engineering."[3] These ideas still resonate. Neither architects nor planners in the middle third of the twentieth century used the term "informal," but they championed the vision of a planned city as a foil against the disorder, poverty, and irrationality that would later animate the term. It is a truism to understand Mexico City through oppositions such as planned and unplanned, regulated and disorderly, formal and informal. Scholars in the last decades have challenged these dichotomies, but they continue to shape how we view cities.[4]

This chapter addresses the paradox of an unplanned city with an efflorescence of planning offices. Planning ideas spread like wildfire in 1920s Mexico, a decade of national reconstruction and the expansion of state institutions. Mexico's first planners collapsed the line between a narrow definition of urban planning, mainly concerned with architectural matters, and a much broader one that encompassed technical mastery over the entire national territory and its population. In 1930 the Ministry of Communications and Public Works organized a National Planning Congress in an effort to bring together disparate individuals and agencies working on these goals into a common project, "organizing the national unity . . . planning a united, homogenous, kind, beautiful, and smiling Mexico for all Mexicans."[5] That same year, President

Pascual Ortiz Rubio signed a National Planning Law drafted by architect Carlos Contreras, the leader of Mexico's planning movement.[6] The planning ethos gathered steam during the presidency of Lázaro Cárdenas, a high-water mark for state intervention at the service of a radical political project. Speaking at the Sixteenth International Congress on Housing and Planning (ICHP) in Mexico City in 1938, future secretary of education Luis Sánchez Pontón confidently declared that "the Mexican Revolution, which started as something sentimental [*algo sentimental*] and then turned political, ended up becoming a technical undertaking: that is to say, a program of actions based upon science."[7]

This optimism was short-lived. By the late 1930s, thirteen different offices were tasked with planning Mexico City, creating a labyrinth of bureaucracy rather than a paragon of technical efficiency.[8] Planners failed in terms of their own goals. The city spiraled out of control, generating increasingly pessimistic prognoses of urban decline. Reminiscing about his tenure as chief of the Master Plan Office in the 1950s, architect Reinaldo Pérez Rayón acknowledged the futility of his work, accepting that "reality would have overtaken any plan."[9] But the failure of planners was far from inconsequential. Like the sanitation codes described earlier, planning laws carved out a political arena where city officials, brokers, developers, and settlers pursued conflicting visions and interests: controlling urban growth and crafting an orderly city, establishing political alliances with settlers, making a profit in a hot real-estate market, and accessing homeownership. Although the influence of planners was contested, the "fundamental juridical superstructure" upon which urban development was based was established during this period.[10] Planning laws demarcated formal and informal modes of city-making, placing many residents and their neighborhoods outside of the law. This did not in any way mean that these residents were excluded from the city. It simply meant that they had to organize to reclaim their place in it, sometimes by deploying the language of planning and sometimes by resorting to other modes of politics.

In this chapter I describe the visions of planners and assess their impact on the ground. I move from the general to the particular as the chapter progresses, starting with a bird's-eye view of the city as planners saw it and zooming in to more granular analyses of local conflicts over street openings, neighborhood subdivisions, and the distribution of municipal services. I start by describing the growth of urban planning as a field of expertise in the 1920s. In the next section, I focus on planners' failed efforts to assemble a master plan in the 1930s, centering on their plans for delimiting an urban perimeter and pursuing industrial zoning. In the third section, I analyze the planning process—more specifically, the subdivision of a neighborhood grid—in neighborhoods violating planning regulations and plagued by property conflicts. Finally, I illustrate this planning process with a case study of Colonia Gertrudis Sánchez, a neighborhood subdivided by private developers in violation of planning regulations that was eventually upgraded by the Department of Public Works. Throughout the chapter, I analyze planning as it moved from the realm of expert debates to everyday conflicts. In other words, I treat planning as a bureaucratic practice enmeshed with conflicts on the ground rather than as an architectural practice engaged with abstract ideas.[11]

The Dissemination of Urban Planning

The discipline of urban planning emerged in response to the perceived ills of the nineteenth-century city epitomized by metropoles like Berlin, London, and Chicago but familiar to Mexican city officials since the Porfirian era: overcrowding, anarchic growth, and unsanitary conditions. As an alternative, planners conjured utopian visions—the Garden City, the City Beautiful, the functionalist city—that were disseminated across the world at the turn of the twentieth century.[12] These visions would come to life, planners hoped, through the use of master plans, zoning regulations, and other tools that sought to guide the expansion of cities. They were premised on a new relationship between government and urban space, the technical and authoritarian relationship that James Scott called "seeing like a state."[13] Porfirian officials, for example, surveyed Mexico City according to its sanitary conditions, drafting sanitary codes to curb the construction of unhygienic dwellings. The same preoccupations compelled Alberto J. Pani to propose zoning regulations, which he transplanted from Germany, as a solution for Mexico City's high mortality rate.[14] Following the revolution, urban planning replaced sanitation as *the* field of expertise that justified government intervention in public space.[15] Many continuities existed between these disciplines, but planning offered a more ambitious approach to the urban question, combining the knowledge of architecture, engineering, public health, and geography, among other disciplines.

Carlos Contreras was the figurehead of Mexico's planning movement. As the son of the sculptor Jesús F. Contreras, his background bears testament to the continuity between Porfirian and postrevolutionary elites, evident across architectural and planning circles. Contreras studied architecture at Columbia University in the early 1920s and was influenced by the Burnham Plan of Chicago (1909) and especially the Regional Plan of New York and Its Environs (1928), which became a model for several initiatives that he launched in the 1930s.[16] As Francis Violich (a US planner who spun professional networks across Latin America in the 1930s) noted, Contreras was "trained in the United States." He "knows our methods, and is in constant touch with us through the American Society of Planning Officials."[17]

Contreras launched his planning crusade in March 1925, when he published a call in the daily newspaper *El Universal* to plan cities, regions, and the country as a whole.[18] The same year he established the Asociación Nacional para la Planificación de la República Mexicana (National Association for the Planning of the Mexican Republic, ANPRM), dedicated to finding solutions to the "national and regional problems of city planning as well as housing."[19] The association's journal, *Planificación*, disseminated the planning ethos as well as showcasing the work of Mexican and international planners. Over the next two decades, Contreras wrote opinion pieces, drafted federal and local planning laws, developed planning projects for several cities, and organized the First Planning Congress in 1930 and the Sixteenth International Congress on Housing and Planning (ICHP) in 1938. Through these actions, Contreras strove to establish for planners and himself what sociologist Andrew Abbott calls "professional jurisdiction" over the urban question, an authority premised upon expert knowledge.[20]

The most concrete materialization of this vision of modern planning was Mexico City's master plan or *plano regulador*, as Contreras translated the term. Contreras justified the need for the plano regulador with a Comtean aphorism: "Savoir pour prevoir afin de pourvoir" (To know in order to predict in order to control).[21] This project was a research program to study the city and its surrounding region, a call to assemble maps, blueprints, censuses, and other statistics.[22] To amass this information, Contreras spearheaded the creation of a Regional Planning Committee for Mexico City. The committee was divided into three working groups. The first studied the topography and climate of the Valley of Mexico: the distribution of its population; its roads, waterways, and sewage system; and its industrial, residential, commercial, and recreational zones. The second focused on Mexico City's role as a center of government, commerce, education, and industry as well as the role of its legal regime in regard to production. The last group, which studied the living conditions of the population, was divided into several subcommissions that at times merged with other working groups: housing, health, schools, and recreation, among others.[23]

Members of the committee included architects, doctors, engineers, lawyers, and the versatile Gerardo Murillo (painter, writer, folklorist, and vulcanologist, better known as Dr. Atl). Miguel Ángel de Quevedo, the country's most important environmentalist and a member of the Porfirian intellectual elite, headed the subcommittee for public parks. Architects Carlos Ituarte and Manuel Ituarte, Vicente Mendiola, José Villagrán García, and José de la Lama were distributed across various subcommittees, such as housing and schools. Edward H. Bassett, the "father of American zoning," and French architect Jacques H. Lambert were designated as external consultants. Lambert visited Mexico as a technical advisor in 1932, preparing a report on the country's planning laws and a project of renewal for the Zócalo.[24] Bassett's participation, while mostly nominal, was not casual, as the Mexican Committee was modeled after its noteworthy American counterpart, the Committee for the Regional Plan of New York and Its Environs, on which Bassett played a decisive role.[25] Contreras also invited historians Manuel Toussaint, Federico Gómez de Orozco, Justino Fernández, and Edmundo O'Gorman to join his planning crusade. Urban growth could only be guided once historians identified the "basic elements of the urban nucleus": old maps of the city, Toussaint wrote, presented the planner (its physician) "with a history of its diseases."[26]

The elements of this survey were not new, but their amalgamation in a single project amounted to a radical paradigm shift. As Françoise Choay reminds us, the "idea of the *big city* as a unified entity [as opposed to 'a collection of juxtaposed parts'] was still foreign" in the first half of the nineteenth century. Upon his arrival at the Hotel de Ville in 1853, the prefect of the Seine, Baron Georges Haussmann, had a "detailed and accurate plan of the whole city, the first of its kind," hung in his office.[27] The plan gave the illusion of a discrete object upon which policies could be enacted, a bird's-eye map that distorted reality through procedures of scale and projection,[28] allowing planners to think big, from afar and from above figuratively and now literally: aerial photographs were integrated into the city survey.[29] Master plans altered the measure of space and time. Instead of catching up with the growth of the city, they purported to predict and guide growth. Instead of dealing with architectural solutions for discrete problems—the opening of a street, the design of a public square—master plans offered a regional approach to the city that encompassed the entire Valley of Mexico.[30]

Representing the city as a legible and discrete object was appealing not only to planners but also to the wider public. The Sixteenth International Congress on Housing and Planning in 1938 organized by Contreras included an exhibit at the Palacio de Bellas Artes. This Art Nouveau museum and concert hall, inaugurated in 1934, was located only a few blocks away from the city center. The public flocked to the exhibit, which included scale models, blueprints, photographs, geological surveys, and myriad other artifacts: a blueprint of Paris, pictures of daily life in Jerusalem, worker housing projects in Bogotá, and a blueprint of Johannesburg's subterranean electric network.[31] A "marvelous scale model of Mexico City," however, was the most popular attraction. Visitors stared admiringly at the model (ten by seven meters) built by more than thirty people with the help of aerial photographs.[32] A cadastral map of the city also attracted close attention. The map showed in various colors "areas destined for different kinds of housing." Journalists remarked on the difference between the "legal perimeter" of the city and its built environment, which was significantly larger and allocated for urban development.[33]

Both the scale model and the cadastral map offered reassuring representations of Mexico City as a legible object, with clear limits, in which policy interventions could be made. Indeed, the entire exhibit—which also featured projects for public housing, schools, and hospitals—bore testament to the power of planning to capture the imagination of the public. Contemporary newspapers shared this enthusiasm, referring to "planning," "zoning," and a "master plan" as the solutions to urban disorder. This was not a coincidence: the exhibit took place as planners were working on Mexico City's long-awaited master plan, which, in the optimistic words of *El Universal*, "would establish urban zones in order to end the architectural anarchy of the city."[34]

A decade later, most observers agreed that the master plan had failed, not to speak of its translation into a public works program. Of course, the project faced external political, bureaucratic, and financial challenges. But other challenges were intrinsic and went to the heart of the discipline of planning itself. What categories did planners use to survey the city? How could they translate their diagnoses into a master plan?

The Master Plan

Contreras began working on a master plan in the 1930s at the Department of Public Works of the DDF. The city's planning bureaucracy was incohesive and plagued by internal conflicts. In theory, planning was overseen by a Planning Commission, with authority over the Department of Public Works, the Master Plan Office, and other planning committees.[35] But the proliferation of planning offices bewildered city officials.[36] Engineer Salvador Arroyo, head of the Master Plan Office in the 1940s, noted that planning laws "ought to specify the functions of each of the city's planning organs in order to avoid their interference or the undue absorption of attributions of some organs by others."[37] But this was not the case: no one knew exactly what the purpose of each office was. The problem was not a scarcity of planners but the confusion that reigned among them.

Contreras headed the short-lived Comisión de Programa, which conducted city studies until its dissolution in 1932.[38] The following year he published *El plano regulador del Distrito Federal*, in which he synthesized the work he had developed since 1925. Contreras's *Plano regulador* divided Mexico City into ten zones categorized by function: residential, commercial, industrial, agricultural, educational, military, forest reserves, archeological and architectural zones, a civic center, and "zones of unlimited use." Defining these categories was simple enough, but matching them with the actual city was a different matter: large swaths of Mexico City had not been surveyed, and the city lacked the spatial homogeneity that the plan projected onto it. High-income residential zones were easy enough to define. But locating industrial zones was more arduous; large industries were still scarce and small shops like bakeries and tailors were "disseminated all throughout the city."[39] Translating the city into abstract planning categories was a delicate task that produced a partly fictional document. Because transforming the city to fit the master plan was impossible, Contreras found a middle ground: his master plan was at once a descriptive and a prescriptive document, an ambiguity from which later plans would also suffer.

While historians have noted the significance of Contreras's 1933 master plan, it was in fact a modest undertaking.[40] It read like a work in progress, concluding with a call for more studies to produce a more comprehensive plan. Contreras himself heeded this call as head of the Master Plan Commission, created in 1935.[41] The work of the Master Plan Commission is partial and scattered across archives, reflecting the administrative chaos already described, but the remaining evidence allows us to reconstruct its debates over two key issues: urban growth and industrial zoning.

While postrevolutionary planners were preoccupied with urban growth, nineteenth-century Mexican elites had been obsessed with territorial loss and population decline as irrefutable manifestations of national decay. The human loss inflicted by the Mexican Revolution, which prompted the exodus of hundreds of thousands to the United States, infused new life into these demographic anxieties. Engineer Alberto J. Pani, anthropologist Manuel Gamio, and demographer Gilberto Loyo were only a few members of a postrevolutionary elite concerned with underpopulation and racial decay. "Narrow and dusty streets, often without running water and sewers, threaten the resistance of a race, even if it is a bronze one," Enrique C. Aguirre argued in 1930 as he proposed an ambitious public parks program directed at the city's youth.[42] Inspired by fascist Italy's pronatalist ideas, Loyo—Mexico's premier demographer and a collaborator on *Planificación*—drafted the General Population Laws of 1936 and 1947, which included plans to promote early marriages and large families and prohibit contraceptives.[43]

Loyo was convinced of the urgency of increasing Mexico's population, but the capital represented an opposite challenge. By the turn of the century, the overcrowding in central tenements and the expansion of the city through unplanned neighborhoods were widely recognized as a public health emergency. The sense of crisis worsened after the revolution, reaching a fever pitch in the months leading to the census of 1940. Loyo, who also organized the census, drew attention to the "urban elephantiasis" threatening Mexico City as peasants abandoned the countryside, lured by promises of urban "comfort and frivolity" disseminated among the masses by Hollywood movies.[44]

The fear of overpopulation triggered by demographic statistics convinced planners of the need to reduce the population. In 1937 Contreras calculated a future population of 2 million inhabitants by the year 1985, a number he already found alarming (the actual figure would be closer to 15 million if we consider the metropolitan area).[45] In 1940 Master Plan Commission members Federico O'Reilly and Juan Antonio Lainé made a series of growth projections for the Federal District. According to their calculations, Mexico City's rate of growth would decrease and the Federal District would have between 4 and 5 million inhabitants by 1990, in a country of 30 million.[46] These were reassuring numbers, but other projections offered nightmarish scenarios. According to engineer Geo Camp, the city would have a population of 20 million in 2030—in a country of only 40 million! Rural-urban migration would reduce the population of the countryside, driving the city to implosion. Camp's numbers were dismissed, but planners, economists, and demographers remained alarmed by overpopulation. A haunting image began to take shape in the 1940s: a gigantic capital city standing atop a rickety national body. In the following decade, architect and urban critic Mauricio Gómez Mayorga predicted that the city would consume the entire country, which would then face starvation. In hundreds of articles published in newspapers and architectural journals, Gómez Mayorga would emerge as the most relentless opponent of urban growth, a position inseparable from his views on the problem of urban informality and his elite dread of the urban poor.[47]

The 1940 census did not settle the matter. Population figures were contradictory, hinting at a disturbing pairing that would become clear a decade later: an overcrowded inner-city "slum" coupled with scattered but rapidly growing informal neighborhoods in the peripheral delegaciones. While wealthy neighborhoods such as Chapultepec Heights enjoyed low population density, working-class neighborhoods like Peralvillo and La Merced suffered from intense overcrowding.[48] Central districts (*cuarteles*) III, IV, VI, and VII offered staggering figures, with more than 20,000 residents per square kilometer. A 1935 housing survey identified 100,000 overcrowded and insalubrious houses

Table 3.1. Population and population densities in Mexico City and the Federal District in 1940

	Area sq. km	*Population*	*Density (residents per sq. km)*		*Area sq. km*	*Population: Mexico City and Federal District*	*Density (residents per sq. km)*
Mexico City	**134**	**1,464,556**	**10,930**	**Federal District**	**1,483**	**1,773,627**	**1,196**
Cuartel I	18.1	199,980	11,049	Azcapotzalco	32.7	62,998	1,927
Cuartel II	11.9	133,711	11,236	Coyoacán	58.7	35,218	600
Cuartel III	5.8	154,985	26,722	Cuajimalpa	68.7	6,005	87
Cuartel IV	3.7	103,493	27,971	G. Madero	78.7	41,258	528
Cuartel V	5.5	97,158	17,665	Iztacalco	21	11,233	535
Cuartel VI	4.1	108,618	26,492	Iztapalapa	115	25,374	221
Cuartel VII	7.1	145,699	20,520	Magdalena C.	66	13,147	199
Cuartel VIII	9.2	118,495	12,880	Milpa Alta	266.2	14,789	56
Cuartel IX	23.4	146,230	6,249	Álvaro Obregón	86.2	32,318	375
Cuartel X	10.3	64,068	6,220	Tláhuac	80.2	13,841	173
Cuartel XI	20.8	105,783	5,086	Tlalpan	300.7	19,253	64
Cuartel XII	12.5	74,758	5,980	Xochimilco	127.2	33,310	262

Source: México: Dirección General de Estadística, *6° censo general de población: 1940.*

where half a million people lived. The survey authors proposed replacing these houses with hygienic units in order to protect their residents from "tuberculosis, rickets, typhus, and all the vileness, depravity, and disease that are incubated in [these] pigsties."[49]

Despite these visions of overcrowded slums, Mexico City was a flat and low-density city. Or at least much of it was. Assessing the 1940 census, urban planner Hannes Meyer—previously director of the Bauhaus school, at the time in exile in Mexico—concluded that Mexico City had one of lowest population densities in the world: its 1,464,556 residents were spread across 134 square kilometers, amounting to an average of 109 residents per hectare.[50] While planners zoomed in on the overcrowded central slums as the urban problem par excellence, they also remarked on Mexico City's extension and low density. The city's peripheral delegaciones—technically part of the Federal District but not of the city proper—had extremely low population densities in the 1930s. During the Porfirian era, delegaciones were sparsely populated, mostly rural, and widely imagined as bucolic spaces distinct from the city.[51] While land continued to be dedicated to agrarian uses, most delegaciones were in the midst of demographic growth that the 1950 census would render obvious. Iztacalco, Iztapalapa, and Azcapotzalco tripled their populations between 1940 and 1950. Gustavo A. Madero quintupled its population over the same decade.[52] These delegaciones, located east and north of the city center, were the hot spots of informal urbanization, settled by working-class residents and built in defiance of planning codes.

Inner-city "slums" and peripheral settlements were pathologized with opposing diagnoses: while slums were viewed as cesspits of disease, immorality, and crime, peripheral settlements were seen as cultural deserts that bred social anomie.[53] While inner-city neighborhoods may have lacked adequate sanitation, peripheral settlements represented a more pressing challenge when it came to expanding municipal services. Because Mexico City had expanded in a disorderly manner, vacant areas lay between the central city and some of these neighborhoods, rendering the distribution of municipal services expensive and technically daunting. With such considerations in mind, planners pushed for a policy of urban concentration that avoided horizontal growth beyond the city limits.[54] While planners embraced regional visions of urban development, they were also concerned—especially in the short run—with containing the growth of the city.

Defining an urban perimeter (*unidad urbana*) became an obsession. Concerns about the city limits were architectural, financial, political, and cultural. Should Mexico be an extended city or should it grow in density and height? Should peripheral delegaciones serve as a green belt or industrial centers? How far could water, electricity, and roads be extended? Where exactly did Mexico City end? The Banco Nacional Hipotecario y de Obras Públicas (National Mortgage and Public Works Bank, BNHOP), a credit institution that financed public works including housing, advocated for collective housing as an antigrowth policy. Collective housing limited horizontal growth by creating a denser city; it also enabled the creation of public spaces and increased the ratio between taxpayers and the provision of city services. Single-family housing had the opposite effect, augmenting the urban area and placing a higher burden on municipal finances. It also increased traffic to and from the city center, complicating planning and zoning regulations.[55] Architect Manuel Ortiz Monasterio made similar arguments at a session of the Master Plan Commission devoted to the definition of an urban perimeter. Ortiz Monasterio favored concentration over dispersion, which he recommended promoting with bans on urban development.[56] Most planners favored concentration because an overextended city required wider nets of public works and was thus more costly.

In November 1940, after months of work, the Master Plan Commission set an urban perimeter.[57] Mexico City was defined as "the part of the basin of the Valley of Mexico that is already served or that can be served by the water and sewage system of the city." This definition was consequential. Zoning regulations would only be applied within the urban unit, while settlements outside of it would be considered independent from Mexico City.[58] As a result, the Department of Public Works would not have the same obligations toward these peripheral areas as it did toward Mexico City proper. While the definition was established in terms of urban infrastructure, the physical limits of the city were delimited by rivers and topographic features. The northern edge followed the Río de los Remedios, while the volcanic zone of the Pedregal marked the southern limit. An imaginary altitude line following the Río Hondo represented the western edge. The city's eastern limit, finally, was marked by the Grand Drainage Canal.[59] Whereas the western border made a turn in order to include the wealthy neighborhood of Lomas de Chapultepec, using the Grand Drainage Canal as the eastern border of the city left several working-class neighborhoods outside of the city proper. The eastern limits placed working-class neighborhoods east of the Grand Drainage Canal outside of the law, reproducing a logic evident since the Porfirian period: the erasure of neighborhoods on the urban periphery.

The urban unit was outdated from its inception. Exceptions to it were granted as early as September 1941, and a new city code in December 1941 rendered the urban unit redundant.[60] However, the delimitation of the unidad urbana continued a long history of city officials rendering peripheral working-class settlements invisible.

Planners not only wanted to define the city limits. They also aspired to divide the city according to land use, the practice known as zoning. Planners ascribed a strategic importance to industrial zoning, for they believed that Mexico City was on the cusp of a transformation from a "bureaucratic" to an "industrial" city.[61] In the wake of the global crisis of 1929, planners were part of a broader technocratic elite that embraced industrialization as part of a larger mission of modernization, development, and economic nationalism.[62] "To industrialize," wrote minister of the economy Antonio Ruiz Galindo in the 1940s, "does not mean only building factories and transforming raw materials into finished products; it also means opening up new markets, carrying the benefits of production to the farthest corners of the country, and educating the people in the consumption of those articles that will raise the living standard."[63] These ideas crystallized in an economic program known as import-substitution-industrialization (ISI), which fostered industrialization through state investments in infrastructure, tax exemptions, tariffs to protect the national industry, and the state's role as a mediator between capital and labor. Planners thus became participants in a larger economic transformation driven by the capital city.

Import-substitution-industrialization policies increased production in Mexico City, which became the country's industrial engine and, more ominously, the center of a "macrocephalic" urban system.[64] During the 1940s, the number of factories in the capital rose from 4,920 to 12,704; their share of the national industrial output spiked from 8.7 percent to 20 percent.[65] Planners understood industrialization as a net good that was nonetheless plagued by perils. In the words of David Cymet Lerer and Guillermo Ortiz Flores, architects employed by the Office of the Master Plan, the "pairing of railroads and industry" was a "thorn in the urban organism that hindered healthy urban growth."[66] The establishment of factories and industrial plants in the northern delegaciones of the city—Azcapotzalco and Gustavo A. Madero—was accompanied by the creation of working-class neighborhoods adjacent to the factories that employed their residents.[67] Working-class neighborhoods like Tlatilco, Atlampa, and Peralvillo suffered from "noises and dangerous and pestilent emanations."[68] "Infrahuman slums," Cymet Lerer and Ortiz Flores asserted, are the "natural corollary of industry."[69]

The Master Plan Committee strove to find a balance between "encouraging industrial development" and mitigating the "disturbances" it created.[70] Planners were bombarded by a flurry of conflicting petitions in the 1930s. Industrialists requested permits to establish factories throughout the city, while residents petitioned to remove factories from their neighborhoods.[71] Engineer Geo Camp, committee member and industrial consultant, argued that planners should not determine the location of industries but instead grant "industrialists the freedom to choose the most convenient sites."[72] This was the modus operandi during the 1930s, as planners granted permissions for industrial zoning in an ad hoc manner, a policy that probably contributed to the decentralization of industrial production.[73] But in 1938 and 1939 the Master Plan Committee decided to concentrate industrial production in a few demarcated areas. The master plan, Contreras wrote, should "reduce as much as possible industrial nuisance" and "prevent the installation of factories in residential areas."[74] Engineer Fernando Ríos Venegas drew a comparison between the failure to "regulate residential neighborhoods" at the turn of the century and the opportunity for planners to harness industrial growth in the 1930s. Planners, he insisted, should "discipline the establishment of factories" and forbid locating them outside of industrial zones.[75]

In November 1940 planners proposed creating twelve industrial zones.[76] Zone One, a large area north of the city where several working-class neighborhoods were located, was declared a general industrial zone, fit for all industries except those emitting pestilent odors and noxious liquid waste. Other areas were zoned according to their specific topography. This was the case of the sand deposits in Tacubaya and Mixcoac, identified as industrial Zone Nine. Zones Two and Eight, located alongside the Grand Drainage Canal, were designated for animal-processing industries and those emitting noxious liquids and gases. As with the demarcation of the urban unit, planners ignored the fact that several working-class neighborhoods were located alongside the Grand Drainage Canal. Like the urban perimeter, the industrial zoning project was born outdated. A few months after its proclamation, the DDF granted exemptions to industrialists who were already in the process of establishing factories outside of demarcated zones when the code was passed.[77] A handful of industrial decrees were passed in the following decade, leading architect Carlos Lazo to identify twenty industrial zones in 1949.[78] Industrial zoning suffered from the same ambiguity between description and prescription: it followed preexisting patterns of industrial development, which it nonetheless sought to codify.

Both the urban unit and industrial zoning were part of a 1941 planning law.[79] Based on the studies conducted by the Master Plan Office and approved by the Planning Commission, this secondary law was envisioned as a first step toward the completion of the master plan. But the legal and practical significance of the urban unit and industrial zoning was unclear. Previous legislation had already established that neighborhoods outside of the urban perimeter were not entitled to receive municipal services. While industrial zoning was not fully enacted, it did influence policy decisions on a case-by-case basis. Zoning regulations signaled which areas of the city were demarcated for industrial production, prompting investors to purchase land and construct industrial plants.[80] And the Department of Public Works rejected projects to build neighborhoods close to these industrial areas.[81] These rejections were sometimes disregarded by developers, but residents of unsanctioned neighborhoods in industrial zones were placed outside of the law. Whether followed or not, the guidelines for industrial zoning reoriented production and sent a clear signal that some areas of the city were unfit for residential purposes.

While the urban perimeter and industrial zoning were part of a yet-to-be-completed master plan, the document remained shrouded in legal uncertainties. In 1946 Carlos Contreras, Enrique Guerrero, José Luis Cuevas, and other architects and planners argued that Mexico City's Planning Law needed to provide resources to finalize this "fundamental Document."[82] In the following decade, journalist Adrián García Cortés remarked on the absurdity that Mexico City's 1953 Planning Law defined planning as the "organization and coordination, by means of a [nonexistent] master plan, of the functions of city life." As he sarcastically wrote, planning was "the organization of urban life according to something that does not exist."[83] Planning was defined in relationship to the master plan: the former was a means to achieve the latter.[84] But the master plan only gained legal teeth once it was backed by a presidential decree, an executive order, or an expropriation decree to complete projects of public utility. Rather than guarantee that projects were undertaken, however, these orders and decrees configured a political arena where planners, city officials, and settlers confronted each other over the question of who financed municipal services, who oversaw the subdivision of new neighborhoods, and who controlled the allocation of lots in these neighborhoods.

Planning Informal Neighborhoods

But how and why did settlers resist planning initiatives? Residents from working-class neighborhoods contested projects to open streets and establish public facilities that impinged on their neighborhoods, especially when these projects disrupted the allocation of lots. Colonias proletarias, as these neighborhoods began to be called in the 1930s, were sanctioned by the municipal Oficina de Colonias (Office of Settlements), which replaced the Oficina de Cooperación in 1941. As I describe in the following chapter, colonias proletarias were part of a sui generis governance regime and enjoyed significant political leverage by virtue of their connection with city officials and party representatives. Working-class neighborhoods were often subdivided by private developers who violated planning codes. But sooner or later planners intervened to distribute municipal services and adjust their grid, an intervention that historians have not analyzed. Mexico City's urban grid must be understood at the interface of two logics: the top-down logic of planners bent on creating a rational street grid and the logic of local actors—brokers, developers, and settlers—attempting to amass political power, make a profit, and carve a space for themselves in the city.

Articulating a general street system was a top priority for planners. Several neighborhoods built after the revolution were disarticulated from the city center and from each other, lacking thoroughfares. Traffic in the city center was quickly becoming a public emergency, eliciting concerns about the death of the historic center.[85] The DDF widened San Juan de Letrán Avenue in the

1920s and opened 20 de Noviembre Avenue, a south-north axis leading to the Zócalo.[86] In the following decade, planners started working on the extension of Reforma Avenue and Tacubaya Street, which would create a diagonal and an east-west axis, respectively. In addition to this system of vertical, horizontal, and diagonal avenues, planners contemplated the construction of peripheral boulevards that would structure space in a radial manner.[87]

Planners were horrified by what they viewed as a patchwork of disjointed neighborhoods in need of integration. Mauricio Gómez Mayorga could not hide his frustration: "Each subdivision pretends to be an independent city with its little streets and avenues [and] its diagonals leading nowhere. These patches are unconnected, don't even have north-south avenues communicating them."[88] Many neighborhoods lacked schools, markets, and green areas. Planners were also concerned that houses in working-class neighborhoods were built by residents, in defiance of construction codes, with subpar materials, and incrementally. Residents first built a single-room shack and over the course of years added additional rooms and upgraded construction materials. This mode of construction, called self-construction (autonconstrucción), would become widely regarded as a "solution" to housing needs in Mexico City and other Latin American cities by the late 1950s.[89] But autoconstrucción was still considered a problem in the 1940s. Planners and architects saw it as costly, irrational, and an obvious manifestation of the deterioration of housing standards.[90]

Planners were bent on fixing colonias proletarias, a task that involved upgrading individual houses as well as opening much-needed public spaces. Perhaps most ambitiously, colonias proletarias had to be integrated into the metropolis by opening avenues across the city, superimposing a general street system on the existing mosaic of neighborhoods. This integration forced planners to deal with political, technical, and jurisdictional questions. Did planners have the power to open streets or was their role limited to providing recommendations (which then could be put in place through executive orders)? Could they use eminent domain to open streets and avenues? What projects justified removing residents from their neighborhoods? Should planners focus on citywide projects or local ones?

Many of these questions were related to matters of scale. Planners saw the city as a cohesive whole, but they most often intervened at the level of specific neighborhoods. The Master Plan Office completed a project for a general street system in 1947, which it turned over for discussion at the Growth Commission. Members of this commission considered the project incomplete, consisting of "general lines but deficient in the details."[91] The Master Plan Office identified the city's main thoroughfares, but the project did not include the "detailed" technical information that indicated how widening and extending them would impact neighborhoods.[92] Planners often debated what type of project to submit to the Planning Commission for approval. Should the commission approve a general project or a more detailed one? When detailed studies existed, planners were reluctant to divulge them, lest they spark opposition. Commission member Fernando Ríos Venegas opposed a detailed plan, arguing that a small-scale blueprint—a "planning skeleton" composed of the city's main thoroughfares—should be submitted instead. Once this project was approved, it could be implemented by Public Works, thereby completing the master plan.[93] The image of the planning skeleton is helpful: urban planners considered their mission from a general perspective, setting guidelines that ensured a harmonious urban development.

The neighborhoods growing in between the main thoroughfares of this "planning skeleton" were described by Gómez Mayorga as a "cancerous tissue," a "wide and confusing ring of disorder."[94] Many were old barrios that had been absorbed by the city in the twentieth century, like Romita, the subject of a planning study in the 1940s.[95] Others, like nearby Colonia Buenos Aires, had been built during the 1910s and were characterized by irregular streets and incomplete urban services. The DDF expropriated large sections of Colonia Buenos Aires in 1941 to install municipal services and build a hospital. Residents protested the expropriations and fought, with little success, for the hospital to be relocated to the outskirts of the city.[96] Other colonias proletarias built in the 1930s also suffered "planning problems," which the Department of Public Works sought to ameliorate with "special brigades of engineers and topographers."[97] Planners were eager to better integrate these neighborhoods into the street system. For all their differences, these neighborhoods can anachronistically be defined as informal, viewed by planners as problems in need of intervention.

The fight to control urban growth by imposing urban perimeters and passing more stringent city codes was a losing battle. Neighborhood associations persistently and often successfully petitioned the government for land and municipal services, even when their neighborhoods were built against the law or located outside of the urban perimeter. In response, planners complained of the political muscle mustered by settlers. Speaking at a session of the Growth Commission, architect Luis Ángeles noted:

> We have encountered a number of recently subdivided neighborhoods whose residents are building [their homes] wherever they wish and are asking the licenciado [regent Fernando Casas Alemán] for water and drainage without considering the difficulties of undertaking such works. We are asked to

> complete fast planning of these places. Maybe we will get more personnel to address this situation in the Federal District, which is preferable to the ongoing chaos.[98]

Capultitlán, one of many colonias proletarias north of the city, exemplifies how planners undertook this "fast planning." In December 1946 city authorities requested a "planning study" for Capultitlán.[99] The project devised by the Department of Public Works adjusted the neighborhood grid but threatened to dispossess a group of residents, who rejected the proposal. Like all colonias proletarias, Capultitlán was represented by a neighborhood association whose leaders were sanctioned by the Oficina de Colonias. As in most colonias proletarias, another association was also active, even though it was not sanctioned by the Oficina de Colonias. The Department of Public Works "planning project"—a blueprint demarcating a system of lots and streets—pitted the two associations against each other: while the official association approved the blueprint, the unofficial one, which included the residents at risk of dispossession, unsurprisingly rejected it. Both groups presented their cases to the Growth Commission in the summer of 1947. This was an unusual occurrence: sessions were usually attended by experts who argued over urban matters vehemently but in technical terms. On this occasion, however, the commission offered a venue to those "threatened by the planning of Capultitlán."[100] Often insulated from local battles over street openings and the provision of municipal services, planners had the chance to participate in a neighborhood conflict firsthand.

At the heart of the matter were the two blueprints that the neighborhood groups used to advance their claims. The official neighborhood association accepted the blueprints produced by the Department of Public Works. Its members carried credentials provided by the Oficina de Colonias and were supported by an unnamed representative who also attended the planning session. Members of the opposing group—referred to as *los inconformes* (the dissatisfied)—brought their own blueprints to the commission session, which they claimed had been drafted by city planners in accordance with the master plan. It was common for blueprints to circulate among planning offices, and planners often disagreed over their preeminence, date, and authorship. It is significant that both groups acknowledged the legitimacy of official blueprints, which they used to support their claims. It is also worth noting that both groups were *already* residing in Capultitlán. The blueprints under discussion would not lay the grounds for settlement but rather would confirm rightful possession for some residents, leaving others in more uncertain terrain, outside of the blueprint.

Blueprints were critical for receiving alignment licenses, property titles, and municipal services. "Residents of colonias proletarias," explained a member of the Growth Commission, put "intense pressure on Public Works to get blueprints of their neighborhoods signed."[101] This pressure, exerted by residents in conjunction with political figures like representatives and the regent, was acutely felt by planners. On another occasion, planners discussed the need to relocate a group of residents from Colonia Tlatilco due to the proximity of their lots to the railroad tracks. Engineer Salvador Arroyo cautioned against the proposal. Residents had begun negotiations with the city government, so removing them would create a "political problem." Arroyo recommended that the colonia "remain untouched."[102]

The sequence of events in Colonia Capultitlán—where planners attempted to modify an already-existing settlement—is reminiscent of processes analyzed by scholars of *urbanismo popular*. Emilio Duhau and Ángela Giglia explained that streets and basic urban infrastructure in Mexico City's popular neighborhoods were built once space had been distributed among settlers. "Therefore, the creation of public space is the outcome of the initial settlement, and not the other way round, as in modern urbanism."[103] "Modern urbanism" refers to the city-building sequence that Mexican planners had long attempted to put in place: the drafting of a subdivision by private developers, its approval by planning authorities, the installation of municipal services, and, finally, the construction of individual houses and the settlement of the neighborhoods. In Capultitlán and similar neighborhoods, streets were opened and urban services distributed when land had already been subdivided, settled, and built on by residents. Peter Ward described a similar sequence in Sector Popular, established in 1947:

> At the outset the land was poorly drained, buildings were flimsy, provisional structures and there was a high degree of insecurity as to whether or not the settlement would be eradicated. However, in 1952 the government expropriated the land and sold it back to the squatters providing them with the incentive to make substantial improvements both to the settlement as well as permanent investment in their homes. Drainage . . . was installed by levying quotas from each neighborhood. In addition the improvement association (*junta de mejoras*) set aside areas designated for future school and playground development.[104]

Ward referenced the expropriation of the neighborhood and the relationship between the government and its neighborhood association, as described in chapter 2. But as my analysis of Capultitlán should make clear, the expropriation of the land and the improvement of the settlement were politically fraught processes, rife with risks for residents who had purchased their lots but had only tenuous legal claims to them. As Salvador Arroyo summed it up, "people build their houses wherever and however they wish and then conflicts ensue. *If it is hard to plan a colonia, it is even harder to adjust that planning*" (my emphasis).[105] Planners were not planning proactively, Arroyo lamented, but instead retroactively attempting to remedy a deficient system of streets, lots, and blocks, catching up with the construction of new neighborhoods. "Neighborhood blueprints must follow the master plan," Public Works officials insisted time and again.[106]

It is impossible to provide a general sequence of how informal neighborhoods came to be. Surveying and subdividing land, opening streets and installing water and pavements, distributing and occupying lots, building houses, licensing property titles: all of these actions followed a unique sequence in each neighborhood, depending on factors such as land ownership, location, and the political connections of the residents. Similarly, neighborhoods differed in how they were planned, who planned them, and to what degree the Department of Public Works intervened in their planning. To illustrate these modalities of planning, I turn to the history of a single neighborhood: Gertrudis Sánchez.

Colonia Proletaria Gertrudis Sánchez

Gertrudis Sánchez was established in 1939, just west of the Grand Drainage Canal, the border that the 1941 urban perimeter demarcated as the city limits. The area grew astonishingly in the 1930s, becoming an industrial hub and home to numerous working-class neighborhoods. The early years of Gertrudis Sánchez were rocked by property conflicts that pitted residents against each other, the DDF, and the alleged owner of the land, General Macario Navarro. As described in the previous chapter, Navarro was the contested owner of large swaths of land, which he subdivided and sold as lots in multiyear installments to working-class families. His friends described him as an "honest man, an old revolutionary, and a true patriot,"[107] while his foes accused him of belonging to the fascist Golden Shirts organization. I cannot ascertain which claim is true, or whether Navarro was the legitimate owner of the land, but his political power depended on his ability to distribute land among homeless families, safeguard their possession, and charge them for their lots and the installation of municipal services.

While the land in Gertrudis Sánchez belonged to a private individual who was selling lots to purchasers, the neighborhood was also a colonia proletaria

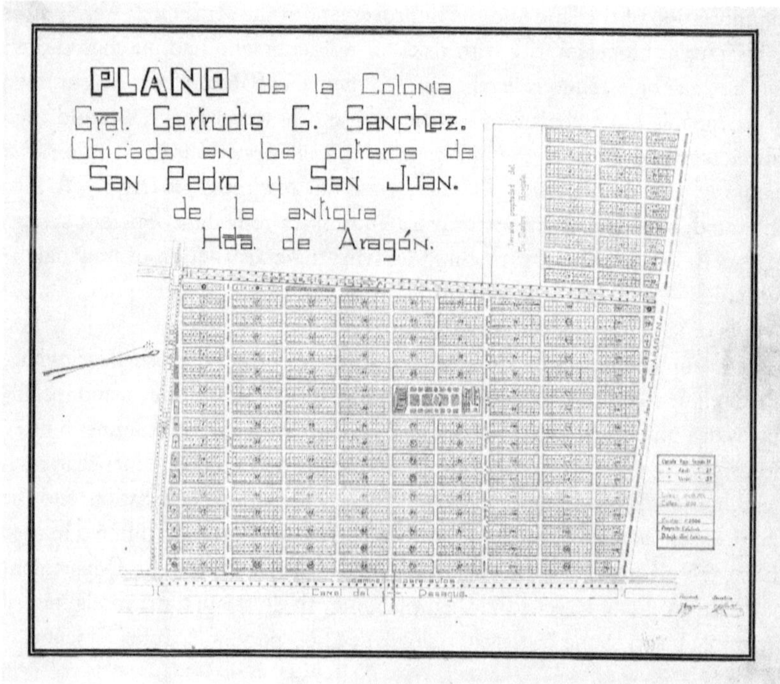

Figure 3.1. "Plano de la Colonia Gertrudis G. Sánchez: 1943." AHCDMX, Planos y Proyectos, box 121, file 14. Ponce's original subdivision features his signature alongside Guzmán's, hinting at a period predating the conflict between the two men. The signatures of the president and the treasurer of the neighborhood legitimized what was in essence a real-estate plan: a blueprint defining a system of blocks and lots to be sold.

under the authority of the Oficina de Colonias. Like its predecessor, the Oficina de Cooperación, the Oficina de Colonias acted as an intermediary that charged the residents fees, paid them to the owner, and sanctioned the neighborhood authorities: Juan Guzmán (president) and Teodoro Ponce (secretary and treasurer). Shortly after the establishment of the neighborhood, a rift developed between the two men. In 1940 Guzmán accused Ponce and the Oficina de Colonias of selling Navarro's lots and keeping the payments.[108] He also accused Ponce of charging illegal fees and threatening residents with dispossession of their lots. For example, Ponce collected MX$7,000 for a bridge that apparently only cost MX$600. In a letter to President Manuel Ávila Camacho, Guzmán described Gertrudis Sánchez as a "public market" where municipal employees profiteered off residents.[109] Ponce was not only in charge of handling the finances of the neighborhood but also subdivided it and allocated its lots, a role that provided plenty of opportunities to make a profit. Although the particulars of the conflict are hard to trace, a logic does emerge. Both Navarro and Ponce (the latter in conjunction with the Oficina de Colonias) claimed to own the land in question and were building political power and making a profit by selling lots.

Planners were still out of the picture, but not for long. In 1942 Public Works tasked special brigades of topographers with addressing the "multiple planning problems" in several neighborhoods north of the city, including Gertrudis Sánchez.[110] Ponce's original layout was a complete disaster, "hecho con las patas" (botched up), as planning officials graphically put it. The modifications by Public Works—expressed in an official blueprint dated June 1943—followed Ponce's original layout but expropriated a number of blocks and designated them for public use.[111] Such expropriation proposals were fairly common. Following planning codes and ideas about the necessity of public amenities, planners often sought to reclaim land from developers for public use.

The attempt to create these spaces in Colonia Gertrudis Sánchez represented a mixed blessing. Schools, markets, and green areas were sorely needed, and residents doggedly fought for them. However, these spaces were won at the expense of settlers living outside of the official blueprint, who were left facing eviction. In the summer of 1944 a group of such settlers protested against their removal from the neighborhood because of public works to be undertaken on their lots (sources do not specify the nature of these projects). Residents asserted their standing as proletarians, therefore protected by the Oficina de Colonias.[112] In a letter to President Manuel Ávila Camacho, they demanded fair compensation for their loss, including the improvements they had made to their homes and the surrounding area.[113]

Public Works authorities were unmoved. In the ensuing battle between planners and settlers, Department of Public Works director Guillermo Aguilar Álvarez contended that his office had studied the planning and zoning of Gertrudis Sánchez, concluding that the land residents claimed was zoned for public services. Adding insult to injury, Aguilar Álvarez stated that residents had built their homes without the necessary permits; while acknowledging their "status as proletarians," he insisted that residents had to follow city codes.[114] Residents pleaded ignorance, explaining that the engineer who sold them their lot had recommended they build their homes as soon as possible. They were particularly appalled that Public Works offered compensation after work had been terminated and not before abandoning their homes. "It is a shame that despite the victory of the Revolution" the weak continued to be oppressed, particularly considering that it was a "public functionary who testified to their condition as such."[115] What happened to these claimants is not certain, but in the end Public Works did gain a number of blocks dedicated to public spaces. A 1957 survey assessed that 1,603 dwellings in the neighborhoods required upgrading, while 1,347 shacks (*barracas*) should be eradicated. But the survey described the civic center of the neighborhood as well located, composed of two elementary schools, a public market, and a church.[116] This area remains dedicated to public spaces.

I cannot say that Colonia Gertrudis Sánchez was a "representative" neighborhood. I am not sure one can make such a claim about any neighborhood, once we look at conditions on the ground. However, this place does illustrate the politics of planning in informal neighborhoods. As the following chapters show, the DDF was divided between technicians in the Department of Public Works and political officials clustered around the Oficina de Colonias. Planners acted with the authority provided by their professional credentials, and political officials were in the business of garnering support and making a profit through corrupt politicking. While planners were bent on integrating neighborhoods into the urban grid and fixing their planning problems, political officials sought to harness the demands made by settlers.

Planners embraced the dichotomy between formal and informal neighborhoods, which they understood as defined by construction codes, official blueprints, and zoning ordinances—all of which, in theory, were based on a master plan. But the actual practice of urbanization disrupted this dichotomy. Neighborhoods like Capultitlán and Gertrudis Sánchez were not planned in accordance with the law, but they were deeply entangled with planning laws, city officials, and political brokers. They were not "official" neighborhoods, but they were very much recognized by city planners and administrators. Most historians believe that planning efforts were futile and that planners were defeated by the forces of the real-estate market, populist politics, and urban growth. In this chapter I have offered a different interpretation: official blueprints—which followed planning guidelines set by the master plan—were at the heart of local city politics. While they were not always followed, they always articulated political conflicts, validating some claims to land and delegitimizing others.

Debates over industrialization and urban growth might seem theoretical, but the studies undertaken by planners were translated into zoning codes, expropriation decrees, and street opening projects, all of which had an impact on local neighborhoods. Department of Public Works officials intervened in Capultitlán and Gertrudis Sánchez because planners were eager to connect the neighborhoods with the rest of the city and because they were located in an industrial area of strategic importance. Informal neighborhoods were shaped by urban planners who sought to impose a city grid over a patchwork of neighborhoods as much as by brokers who allocated lots and land developers who profited from a politicized real-estate market. These neighborhoods violated city codes, lacked municipal services, and were subdivided by men like Teodoro Ponce—brokers eager to capitalize on their position of leadership. Once planners intervened in these neighborhoods, the logics of planning, profit, and politics clashed. While the opening of public spaces represented a common good, it threatened to dispossess individual families and reduced profits for developers.

Planners were not all-powerful, but neither were they powerless. Their influence is most evident in the existence of public spaces in neighborhoods where the pressure to sell land was almost unbearable. Even today the presence of schools, markets, and green spaces in these neighborhoods bears witness to the power of Public Works—the power to remove residents or the power to prevent them from settling in public areas. Working-class neighborhoods like Gertrudis Sanchez were not part of the "lettered city," to use Ángel Rama's term.[117] Clearly, they were designed not in accordance with a vision of the ideal city but with the goal of maximizing profit. But neither were they unplanned or lawless—as Gómez Mayorga put it—because Public Works officials eventually intervened.[118]

While scholars increasingly advocate for abandoning the formal-informal dichotomy, it is not always easy to demonstrate exactly how formal urbanization and informal urbanization are entangled. Gertrudis Sánchez and similar neighborhoods illustrate how the technocratic logic of planning clashed with informal real-estate markets and claims to housing made by working-class residents, all playing out together in one neighborhood. The master plan did not "end the architectural anarchy of the city," as journalists augured in the late 1930s.[119] But neither was it inconsequential. The master plan—and the urban codes, zoning regulations, and official blueprints that stemmed from it—configured a political arena where city officials, land impresarios, political brokers, and city residents fought for their own interests and urban visions, which were then projected into the city grid.

4

A Proletarian Metropolis

Mexico City's informal neighborhoods displayed extraordinary variety in their legal status and relationship with the city government. Beginning in 1941, however, colonias proletarias—as these places came to be known—became the centerpiece of a political project to build a proletarian metropolis.[1] While many colonias proletarias were established in the 1920s and 1930s (among them Ex-Hipódromo Peralvillo and Ampliación Michoacán, referenced in chapter 2), it was not until the second half of the 1930s that the term was popularized. The number of colonias proletarias skyrocketed during the 1940s, when they became institutionalized as an aspect of housing and planning policy. By the 1950s, there were close to three hundred. Half of them were established between 1941 and 1952, mostly in the peripheral delegaciones, beyond the urban perimeter that planners had decreed in 1940. This was the Golden Age of colonias proletarias.[2]

This chapter analyzes the government policy toward colonias proletarias during the 1940s. While there is no doubt about the territorial and political relevance of colonias proletarias, their significance as a matter of policy is less clear. Writing in the 1970s, political scientist Wayne Cornelius claimed that the Mexican government had never completed a "comprehensive survey" of colonias proletarias, implying an ad hoc approach.[3] Others acknowledged government intervention in colonias proletarias but argued that it was "never announced . . . as [an] official planning policy."[4] Most contemporary references to colonias proletarias highlighted their violation of city codes and falsely asserted that they were settled by squatters, claims that suggested they were a direct challenge to the government. Colonias proletarias, according to a 1955 article, were "built by squatters who invaded a piece of land and constructed a shack."[5] This chapter argues against these interpretations,

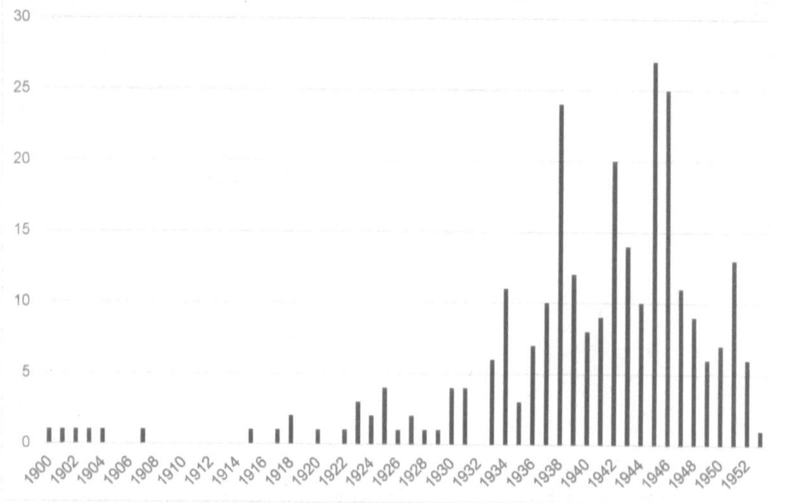

Figure 4.1. Number of colonias proletarias in Mexico City in 1953 by date of establishment
Source: Based on data from David Cymet Lerer and Guillermo Ortiz Flores, *El problema de las colonias proletarias, Ciudad de México.*

demonstrating instead that colonias proletarias were in fact governed by the DDF through specific policy interventions.

The chapter is divided into three parts. First, I describe colonias proletarias as an example of urban corporatism, in which settlers formed political organizations influenced by national and transnational models of collectivism. These neighborhood associations interfaced with the city government, becoming the key channel of political participation for settlers. In the second section, I focus on the city government, examining how different municipal offices handled colonias proletarias. As the previous chapter has shown, the Department of Public Works was responsible for planning and distributing services to colonias proletarias, while the Oficina de Colonias was tasked with awarding property titles, distributing lots, sanctioning local leaders, and handling neighborhood conflicts. In the last section, I view colonias proletarias in the context of the Mexican political system, specifically the ways in which government and party officials sought to integrate settlers into vertical and monopolistic government structures. I focus on one important organization—the Coalición de Colonos (Settlers' Coalition)—that often battled with city and party officials, even though it also collaborated with both. By underscoring divisions within the city government and among settler organizations, I show how politics in colonias proletarias were too complex to be subsumed under the analytic shorthand of the PRI, the intermediary between the urban masses and the state.

My understanding of colonias proletarias as neighborhoods outside of the law *and* governed by the state might strike some readers as contradictory. Informal neighborhoods, as I proposed earlier, are not the anti-state but the state's bastard child. Likewise, colonias proletarias resemble an illegitimate urban form in pursuit of acceptance—a central part of the city that could also be something of an embarrassment, at least for architects and middle-class observers. Mired in ambiguities, colonias proletarias represented political arenas where government projects of social uplift and corporatist political control, original modes of urban planning, and revolutionary claims for housing coexisted.

The multiple meanings of the term further reinforce this point. At least three—administrative, architectural, and political—are worth mentioning. First and foremost, colonias proletarias were an administrative category within the DDF, sanctioned by an ad hoc office (the Oficina de Colonias) and governed through a series of written and nonwritten practices. Second, regardless of their administrative status, colonias proletarias were actual places defined by architects in terms of their infrastructural privations. They were located on the urban periphery, largely made up of self-built houses, and lacked adequate water, drainage, pavements, and other services.[6] Finally, colonias proletarias were a vibrant political arena: both the "context and substance of urban citizenship" claimed by hundreds of thousands of settlers and a ripe ground where brokers and politicians politicked and built power by assembling a clientele.[7] Colonias proletarias embodied the contradictions of the government's imperative to maintain order in the midst of momentous urban transformation, the visions of a modern city advanced by planners, and the claim to housing made by working-class families.

Revolutionary and Transnational Origins

Colonias proletarias became a viable urban policy during the global ascent of corporatist politics and social citizenship, embodied in Mexico by a "social revolutionary jurisprudence."[8] Like its international counterparts, Mexican corporatism was a response to the crisis of liberalism punctuated by World War I, the Russian Revolution, and the Great Depression. In Mexico corporatism provided a rubric to give representation to social groups mobilized during the revolution.[9] The organizing of such groups as units of governance was in line with a legal paradigm that legal scholar Duncan Kennedy calls "The Social," a "conceptual vocabulary" that permeated legal thought in the first decades of the twentieth century and reached a high-water mark in the interwar years.[10] Although the politics of this legal doctrine could adopt left-wing or right-wing forms, its chief enemy was classic liberalism, labeled as overly deductive and individualistic. Instead, it considered all members of society to be interdependent and society as an irrefutable social fact—as evidenced by social sciences such as history, economics, and sociology. Proponents of "The Social" held social welfare, rather than inalienable individual rights, to be the law's normative ideal. In the words of one Mexican jurist, the law was a tool for social transformation, an "instrument at the service—and only at the service—of the needs and aspirations of mankind."[11] Or, as a representative put it in his defense of colonias proletarias, they filled a "positive social need that the State ought to safeguard through adequate laws."[12] The Mexican Constitution of 1917 and the 1928 Civil Code exemplify the paradigm of "The Social." The preamble of the Civil Code referenced the dramatic transformation brought by "economic development, the empowerment of unions, the growth of cities, the ascent of a democratic spirit, new scientific discoveries, and the rise of cooperation."[13]

Corporatist politics and the paradigm of "The Social" deeply influenced postrevolutionary Mexico City. During the debates that led to the creation of the DDF in 1928, Vicente Lombardo Toledano, the leader of Mexico's labor movement and a figure close to planning circles,[14] advocated for a "democratic-corporatist" government in which social groups, rather than individuals, were represented.[15] These principles were put in practice at the Consejo Consultivo, an "original experiment" in "functional democracy," as regent José Manuel Puig Casauranc called it.[16] Although the Consejo Consultivo had a limited advisory role, as a venue where government matters were discussed among representatives of labor, capital, and professional organizations, it contributed to the galvanization of corporate interests among workers, employees, industrialists, and others. "The composition and character of Mexico City's Consejo Consultivo," urban scholar Diane Davis has argued, "prefigured" the corporatist political system put in place by the PRM and refined by the PRI.[17]

Corporatism also provided a lingua franca for policymakers and politicians defending an array of interests. "Primitive communities are no longer responsible for municipal development," the leader of the Sindicato Único de Trabajadores del Distrito Federal (Federal District Government Workers' Union) explained in 1947 in a municipal reform proposal. Unions like his own, which he described as a "clan" representing more than 15,000 members, were a "communal force more powerfully linked to the life of the great metropolis."[18] As described in chapter 2, myriad neighborhood associations petitioned for municipal services, rent controls, and urban expropriations in the 1920s and 1930s. These petitions deployed the rhetoric of "The Social" as expressed in the Constitution of 1917: the belief in the interdependency of society and the primacy of the collective over the individual.

While colonias proletarias avant la lettre had been established at the behest of the federal government since the 1920s, this housing form acquired a more distinct legal profile after 1940. The passage of the Reglamento de Asociaciones Pro-Mejoramiento de Colonias (Code for Neighborhood Improvement Associations, called Reglamento de Colonias throughout this chapter) in March 1941 serves as a historical marker. It sought to control and uplift families living in colonias proletarias.[19] An exemplary corporatist law, it captured the ironies of Mexico's twentieth-century *dictablanda* (soft dictatorship): progressive yet authoritarian, protective yet controlling the working class, fiercely nationalistic yet part of global ideological currents.[20] While planning laws tended to regulate the built environment, the Reglamento de Colonias focused on the political life of colonias proletarias. The code grouped residents in government-sanctioned associations created for the purpose of "defending their rights, improving urbanization and urban services, and establishing new neighborhoods" (article 1). These official associations would replace earlier ones, whose "fake leaders . . . used their positions to exploit the masses."[21] The DDF had attempted to rein in these organizations for over a decade, but its efforts had proved futile. To prevent abuses by leaders, neighborhood associations were prohibited from requesting fees, which could only be paid to the Oficina de Colonias. To further strengthen government oversight, the code decreed that only one association could exist in each neighborhood and made nonsanctioned associations illegal (articles 8 and 9). This restriction was intended to prevent conflicts between rival associations (which had existed for years) by creating a single intermediary between residents and the DDF.[22]

The Reglamento de Colonias attempted to shield residents from speculation and market forces by dictating that lots purchased from the government (commonly following expropriation) had to be used to constitute "family patrimony," a mode of property that declared lots inalienable and restricted the amount of land families could own.[23] Mexico's postrevolutionary experiment in urban corporatism was firmly based on nuclear families owning single homes, which was the overwhelming preference of settlers. Agrarian laws also restricted the sale, rent, and use of ejido lands as collateral for loans. Both regulations countered nineteenth-century property law in the belief that an unfettered market could only harm the popular classes. In the words of the city government, "family patrimony" would "secure a home for low-income families, limiting the [market] use of real estate to protect those under the care of the head of the household."[24]

Many neighborhood associations welcomed the Reglamento de Colonias, praising it as a shield from "exploitation by capitalists and dispossession of their lots."[25] But it was rejected by some. The president of Colonia Emiliano Zapata filed a lawsuit against the proclamation of the code, arguing that it restricted homeowner rights. Legal scholars have also pointed out that the prohibition against forming improvement associations unsanctioned by the government was unconstitutional.[26] In any case, the "family patrimony" restrictions included in the code did not prevent residents from selling, renting, and accumulating multiple lots, which remained a common practice.[27] Neither were the restrictions on establishing multiple associations in each neighborhood followed. Neighborhood associations continued to multiply, as evidenced in previous chapters and in the following sections. However, the code intensified the competition among local leaders to become the official intermediary between residents and the government. Infighting between rival associations could sometimes turn violent, especially when landless families invaded settled neighborhoods. To prevail, neighborhood leaders assembled large numbers of residents who could pressure representatives or stage a large protest. Resident groups always claimed to have the law on their side in these confrontations.

In conclusion, the regime of colonias proletarias was not only an improvised response to the housing needs and demands of settlers. While the DDF adopted a reactive and piecemeal policy toward them in the 1930s, a more cohesive policy was discernible by the following decade. As the Reglamento de Colonias illustrates, the DDF envisioned colonias proletarias as the territorial building blocks of a working-class city—an urban equivalent of the agrarian ejidos. The code stipulated that residents of colonias proletarias would be shielded from market forces through the "family patrimony" mode of property and protected from abusive leaders by government-sanctioned neighborhood associations. These regulations were inspired by a series of legal doctrines (which I have called "The Social," following Duncan Kennedy): a belief in the interdependency of members of society and the existence of social groups as well as the conviction that the purpose of the law was to safeguard the welfare of these groups.

The Governance of Colonias Proletarias

Colonias proletarias were governed by an alternative legal framework and were not subject to the same agencies and regulations that presided over "regular" neighborhoods. While colonias proletarias were sanctioned by the Oficina de Colonias, regular neighborhoods were approved by the Department of Public Works and subject to the rules established in the 1941 Reglamento de Fraccionamientos (Subdivisions Code).[28] Passed in December 1941, this planning code restricted land use and building types and stipulated that urban developers were responsible for financing municipal services. A dual regime of public works and urban planning thus emerged in the 1940s: both regular neighborhoods established under the 1941 Reglamento de Fraccionamientos and colonias proletarias, where the obligation to provide municipal services was "transferred [from developers] to the authorities."[29]

While the Reglamento de Colonias managed the political organization of residents, the DDF put colonias proletarias at the heart of its vision for urban planning. In a 1943 decree, regent Javier Rojo Gómez declared that the "establishment and improvement of houses for the urban poor" was "of public utlity."[30] The decree also established planning guidelines for colonias proletarias. For example, following zoning principles, it ordered that they be located in specified areas, outside of industrial zones and far from middle-class neighborhoods.[31] The decree stipulated that once residents built houses, the government would provide municipal services and tax exemptions. As one contemporary newspaper put it, once a colonia proletaria was established, "the Department of Public Works will decide on the planning and distribution of urban services, which will be completed in cooperation with residents."[32]

These laws reveal the extent to which the policies toward colonias proletarias had a systematic character and were not simply enacted in response to ad hoc political crises. They also show that the dual planning regime of the 1940s did not emerge spontaneously but was a deliberate policy. An article in *El Universal* in 1951 noted that, on the one hand, "regular neighborhoods [*fraccionamientos*] had to comply with a large number of requirements to be sanctioned by authorities: titles registered with the authorities, cadastral surveys, a planning project, a deposit covering urbanization costs." On the other, developers in colonias proletarias were not obliged to "undertake urbanization [and] public works."[33]

However, this account, like the 1943 decree itself, offers an illusion of clarity in describing what was in reality a confusing regime of governance shared between the Oficina de Colonias and the Department of Public Works. Planning officials, bent on modernizing the city, and political officials, eager to maintain political stability, constantly locked horns.[34] While authorities were in theory obligated to provide municipal services, residents were responsible for the cost. How much was paid, under what conditions, and for what services was up for negotiation.[35] Neighborhood leaders constantly petitioned city authorities for help to complete public works and protested against injustices committed by the Oficina de Colonias and the Department of Public Works. While colonias proletarias paid city taxes, these payments were lower than those made by regular neighborhoods and were negotiated with the Oficina de Colonias.[36] Residents of colonias proletarias did not have rights, only concessions granted in a piecemeal fashion. While these concessions were codified in law, they were granted only after residents mobilized and politicked, with the mediation of brokers and the blessing of government officials. While this system was discretionary and often abusive, colonias proletarias represented a promise of integration into the city through homeownership for settlers.

In comparison with vecindades in the city center, homeownership rates in colonias proletarias were extremely high. According to a 1952 study, 70 percent of colonia proletaria residents were homeowners; the rest were renters.[37] In contrast, tenancy rates in the main affordable housing alternatives were 99.3 percent for *tugurios* (slums) and 86.9 percent for *jacales* (shacks).[38] In 1956 demographer Raúl Benítez Zenteno calculated that 76.8 percent of residents in colonias proletarias were homeowners.[39] The promise of homeownership, coupled with a decline in the construction of rental accommodations in the 1940s, led thousands of families to purchase a lot in colonias proletarias. The city was transformed by a centrifugal pattern of growth during this decade, increasing its extension while its population density decreased in the peripheral areas.[40]

This pattern is exemplified by the well-known history of Jesús Sánchez, the family patriarch depicted in anthropologist Oscar Lewis's *Children of Sánchez*. Sánchez was renting a room in a vecindad in Colonia Morelos when Lewis met him in the 1950s. But he had purchased a lot in Fernando Casas Alemán, a colonia proletaria in delegación Gustavo A. Madero in the northeast of the city (next to Colonia Gertrudis Sánchez), and a second lot in Iztapalapa, in the southeast.[41] Sánchez purchased his first lot after winning a raffle and over the years built a house, which gave him enormous pride. Lewis described Sánchez's house as a "kind of fortress, the four walls of which presented an unbroken stretch of cement except for the door in the narrow front end of the building."[42] Crucially, he captured it as a work in progress, pregnant with promise, a perspective that would become widespread in the late 1950s. But whether colonias proletarias would improve or deteriorate over time was still an open question a decade earlier.[43]

Handling colonias proletarias was not a simple task, for they were both a matter of public concern, pathologized by virtue of their deficient infrastructure, and a matter of governance, which required negotiating with local leaders. Accordingly, officials compiled data on colonias proletarias as both physical neighborhoods and political communities—critical information for distributing municipal services, fixing street systems, allocating lots, and awarding property titles.[44] But the city government was no Leviathan exerting its power in the name of technical efficiency and political control. Data were incomplete and fragmentary, a natural outcome of the government's inability to survey its territory. The municipal cadastral plan remained incomplete throughout the 1940s, an obstacle with ramifications beyond the fiscal arena because it was used not only to tax property but also to define boundaries between lots.[45] In the delegación of Coyoacán, to give but one example, the Oficina de Colonias ignored the number of lots in six (out of twelve) colonias proletarias. Most neighborhoods in this delegación had not been surveyed and lacked an official blueprint. Approximately 20 percent of colonias proletarias lacked official blueprints (approved by Public Works) in the 1950s.[46] Possession claims in these neighborhoods were mired in uncertainty.

As evidenced by the histories of Capultitlán and Gertrudis Sánchez, the existence of an official blueprint was a key step toward the distribution of municipal services, but it also posed threats to residents.[47] Most colonias proletarias were subdivided by private developers and settled before city officials approved their layout and distributed services. The approval of an official blueprint, followed by the distribution of municipal services, fixed the neighborhood grid. However, the decisions about who had rights to lots were made not by the Department of Public Works but by the Oficina de Colonias. Jealously controlled by the Oficina de Colonias, these censuses were a key tool of political control, for they allowed officials to distribute lots and eventually property titles. City officials long aspired to assemble a single list of colonias proletarias and their residents, but the mission was never completed.[48]

Partial data and bureaucratic miscommunication were key components in the governance of colonias proletarias, contentiously shared by the Department of Public Works and the Oficina de Colonias. Technical officials working at the Department of Public Works saw it as their mission to integrate colonias proletarias into the urban grid and provide them with municipal services. But they were also determined to limit the city's expansion. "Public Works must be consulted before neighborhoods are established on federal lands," government planners habitually complained, as "providing services to these places can become an impossible load for this office."[49] The Oficina de Colonias informed Public Works when a neighborhood became sanctioned as a colonia proletaria, notifying the department whether or not its personnel had subdivided the land and requesting the completion of official blueprints.[50] But miscommunication between both offices was common, and information was unevenly shared. According to a 1957 investigation, 244 of the 280 colonias proletarias were sanctioned by the Oficina de Colonias, while 36 lacked official recognition, "which deprived them of the most urgent urban services."[51]

The Oficina de Colonias acted as the intermediary between government authorities and settlers.[52] In addition to sanctioning the leaders of neighborhood associations, it approved public works, collected fees, and awarded property titles.[53] Crucially, property conflicts bolstered its authority because they extended its margins to politick and broker between competing settler groups. In any given year, the office dealt with numerous conflicts across the city: thousands of settlers were represented by rival brokers and urban federations petitioning for land, property titles, and municipal services. In 1945, for example, the Oficina de Colonias issued new contracts to residents from Colonia Moderna who had been affected by the expropriation and survey of the neighborhood. The office also fused two neighborhoods—Américas Unidas and Niños Héroes—whose resident associations had been embroiled in a long-standing conflict.[54] The heads of the Oficina de Colonias were consistently accused of profiting from the corrupt practices that it was intended to remedy in the first place: embezzlement, charging arbitrary fees, and distributing lots among their political clientele. Officials in the Oficina de Colonias could amass considerable support while gaining numerous enemies. They were sometimes beloved but more often reviled.[55]

The Oficina de Colonias received petitions from families and brokers with whom it forged patron-client relationships and business enterprises.[56] When residents of Colonia Juventino Rosas requested that the city government "legalize the lots that they had purchased," the head of the Oficina de Colonias, Rafael Suárez Ocaña, responded that the neighborhood was not recognized as a colonia proletaria but that his office would work toward that end.[57] Scholars have documented the long bureaucratic procedures conducted by residents in order to receive legal recognition from the Oficina de Colonias. The requirements included forming an executive committee, drafting an official blueprint, carrying out a resident census, and creating a neighborhood association.[58] Neighborhood leaders who forged relationships with the Oficina de Colonias became brokers whose power increased in relation to their capacity to obtain services for the neighborhood. By the early 1970s, the office was swarming with petitioners requesting land titles and government aid. Scholars writing during this period identified these actors as "urban caciques" who exerted control over colonias proletarias through the distribution of lots. Their power, however, depended on support from the Oficina de Colonias and later the PRI, which could easily abandon them if they became discredited and ceased to fulfill their mission as brokers and guardians of social peace.[59] The president of Colonia Ramos Millán, for example, was removed from his position by the Oficina de Colonias once his abuses were exposed by the press.[60]

The relationship between the Department of Public Works and the Oficina de Colonias resembled the fraught but complementary division of the Mexican state between a technocratic and a political class, with offices charged with overlapping responsibilities and members defined by distinct professional backgrounds and goals. The Department of Public Works primarily consisted of engineers who embraced an ideal urban vision and viewed themselves as detached from local politics. The Oficina de Colonias, by contrast, maneuvered between city technocrats, political party leaders, and organized settlers.[61] This maneuvering often required bending the law, favoring one resident group over the other, and negotiating with a wide array of political leaders, from federal representatives to leaders of neighborhood associations. This politicking chipped away at the ideal city envisioned by technocrats, but it was necessary to maintain a measure of order.

Politics in Colonias Proletarias

The DDF and the PRM viewed colonias proletarias as political units that would support the government through collective mobilization in exchange for the funneling of resources to neighborhoods. The relationship between settlers, the party, and the city government continued the emphasis on mass politics of the Cárdenas presidency, which had intensified—and come under new pressure—in the national and international context of the 1940s.

The disappointing election results of President Manuel Ávila Camacho (1940–1946) in Mexico City prompted the party to strengthen local structures. World War II pushed Ávila Camacho toward a policy of "national unity" in syntony with the corporatist rhetoric that had given rise to colonias proletarias.[62] War and inflation led the government to coordinate production, prices, and salaries with capitalists and workers. War also prompted a series of experiments in urban governance. In July 1942 Ávila Camacho decreed the "freezing" of rent in Mexico City, which tenant leagues had long demanded.[63] Expropriations to form colonias proletarias became more viable in the context of war, and one neighborhood—Colonia Escuadrón 201—was established for Mexico's celebrated World War II veterans. Popular urban groups were emboldened, also demanding further rent controls, the drafting of a law to promote popular housing, and the establishment of a bank to finance home improvements and build worker housing.[64]

In January 1944 the partnership of the PRM, the city government, and colonias proletarias was celebrated at the Palacio de Bellas Artes, where the presidents of 150 colonias officially accepted their positions.[65] The secretary of the PRM pledged his support to settlers so that they could "resolve their specific problems." "The unity of the colonos," proclaimed Lauro Ortega, president of the Federación de Ligas del Sector Popular del Distrito Federal (Federation of Popular Sector Leagues of the Federal District), was "a necessary condition for the solution of their problems."[66] This was at best wishful thinking, as Ortega's trajectory reveals. A few years earlier, Ortega and the PRM had been accused by representative José Muñoz Cota, leader of the Federación Mexicana de Colonos Proletarios, of dispossessing settlers and seeding discord in working-class neighborhoods.[67]

The Federación Mexicana de Colonos Proletarios was one of four citywide federations that grouped dozens of neighborhood associations in the late 1930s.[68] Conflicts abounded, alongside land invasions. Sometimes these conflicts seemed to mirror national and international cleavages. Many associations were accused of being controlled by foreigners, right-wing groups like the *sinarquistas* and the Golden Shirts, Communists, and other political factions. Conversely, associations claimed to be part of political cliques or named their neighborhoods after presidents, regents, and other local figures. Foreign landowners did exist, and Communist organizers were active in some colonias proletarias, but conflicts within neighborhoods were structured not by ideology but rather by legal claims to possession that were difficult to reconcile. The unity of settlers could not be achieved because settler groups were competing against one another for expropriated land, often a zero-sum game. In the end, the PRM and the PRI, the final avatar of Mexico's revolutionary party, were incapable of grouping residents of colonias proletarias under a single authority. Urban settlers would never become a pillar of Mexican corporatism to the same extent as peasants and workers.

To bring to life this political world, I focus on the Coalición de Colonos (Settlers' Coalition), an organization joined by a handful of neighborhood associations that were not sanctioned by the Oficina de Colonias. Established in 1945 and led by Salvador Flores, the Coalición de Colonos became the most important foe of the Oficina de Colonias over the remainder of the decade. There is evidence that the coalition was affiliated with the Confederación Nacional de Organizaciones Populares (National Confederation of Popular Organizations, CNOP, the hodgepodge popular sector of the PRI), but it should not be seen as subservient to either the CNOP or the PRI. The Coalición de Colonos pursued a two-pronged strategy. First, it organized rallies and mass events with the goal of building a following that could influence

Figure 4.2. "Congreso de Unificación de las colonias proletarias del D.F." Celebrated around 1950 in Colonia Bondojito, this event sought to bring residents from colonias proletarias in districts 1, 2, and 3 into a single federation. It was led by Carlos Zapata Vela, head of the Oficina de Colonias. Archivo General de la Nación, Fondo Hermanos Mayo, 1a Parte, Cronológico, HMA/CR1/04690.

local and national authorities. At the same time, the coalition organized land invasions in neighborhoods controlled by government and party officials, such as places expropriated by the government, where lots had been distributed to the residents by the Oficina de Colonias. This modus operandi reveals the limits of the control that both the PRI and the Oficina de Colonias enjoyed over urban politics. While scholars have tended to reduce the government and the party to a homogenous entity, the reality of politics on the ground serves as a caution against ascribing too much power to the PRI and the city administrative apparatus.

In September 1945 the Coalición de Colonos organized its first housing congress, "The Housing Problem in Mexico," at Mexico City's Teatro del Pueblo.[69] In an ambitious petition sent to President Ávila Camacho, the organization made several demands: (1) a plan for the development and construction of popular housing; (2) the expropriation of 15 million square meters in Iztapalapa and other delegaciones; (3) approval of the establishment of Colonia Modelo by the city government, putting it under the control of the coalition; (4) 200 million pesos for the construction of popular housing; (5) granting the expropriated terrain of Lomas de Becerra to the coalition to distribute among the "popular" classes; (6) the establishment of a bank for development and popular construction; (7) the coalition's participation in these proposals.[70] The coalition also demanded that the leaders of the Oficina de Colonias be replaced. "Ever since gangster José Garibay Centeno became head of [the office]," the coalition complained, "settlers have suffered from dispossessions, assaults, assassinations, and all sorts of exploitation and abuses."[71]

Some of these requests, like the plan to build popular housing, were of a general nature. But others were more targeted, aiming at government intervention in specific land conflicts. The coalition had its sights set on a large area southeast of the city (including parts of the delegaciones of General Anaya, Iztapalapa, and Iztacalco) and was negotiating with the government for the distribution of municipal services in several colonias proletarias, including Ampliación Niños Héroes, Progreso del Sur, El Triunfo, and San Andrés Tetepilco.[72] The coalition also demanded that lots expropriated by the government be distributed among its members, claiming that leaders who had colluded with the Oficina de Colonias had taken over these lands illegally.[73]

The coalition was not only in conflict with the Oficina de Colonias. It also rejected an ambitious project by architect Mario Pani to build twenty-one housing units on government-owned lands in the area. (Only one unit, Unidad Modelo 9, was built on a 57-hectare lot in Iztapalapa.)[74] Pani viewed the southeast quadrant of the city as "mostly virgin," "untouched," and covered by "ejidos and green areas" and therefore amenable to the construction of large housing projects.[75] But the coalition rejected this description of the area as an empty space, as it rejected "Soviet-style" housing solutions designed by "desk theoreticians."[76] It demanded instead to be charged with the establishment of colonias proletarias and the distribution of lots among its members. Like the lands of La Vaquita a decade earlier, General Anaya, Iztapalapa, and Iztacalco were a battleground where numerous organizations were jockeying over land on the brink of expropriation.

Colonia Ampliación Niños Héroes—also known as Américas Unidas—illustrates how these battles played out. Today the neighborhood, situated between Colonia Narvarte and Colonia Portales, is well connected to the city by avenues and subway lines. But in the 1940s it was on the fringes of the city, close to ranches and agrarian fields and used as a landfill when Américas Unidas was settled in 1942.[77] As in most colonias proletarias, residents were divided between two associations: an official association, sanctioned by the Oficina de Colonias, and a rival group of so-called squatters who were defended by the coalition and PRI representatives. This was a different conflict from the one already laid out between the Oficina de Colonias and Public Works. In this case, it was a struggle between the city government and the PRI, whose national representatives often defended settlers from the city government. This dispute between national PRI representatives and the city government would reach a breaking point in the 1960s, as later chapters describe.

This specific fight began with the sale of the land in Américas Unidas, owned by Concepción de Hoth. The sale was brokered by the Oficina de Colonias, which drafted a neighborhood blueprint and set a price for the lots.[78] This arrangement was accepted by the official neighborhood association, led by Adalberto Pliego.[79] But another group of settlers, headed by Salvador Flores, the leader of the coalition, rejected the deal. Flores claimed that his followers had lived in the area before it was sold by de Hoth, improving it through their hard toil. He accused de Hoth of altering the original neighborhood plan, raising the price of lots, and failing to provide municipal services.[80] Flores claimed that de Hoth had "stirred up" Pliego and the (official) residents of the neighborhood against the families that he defended, who had been living in the area "for five or six years."[81] He contended that these families had property titles but were nonetheless facing eviction through legal ruses and police violence.[82]

Pliego denied the denunciations, accusing Flores of politicking with the goal of building a political following, "searching for uneducated settlers, making them false promises, and rejecting the [neighborhood's] blueprints and divisions."[83] Pliego described Flores as an immoral leader "sowing discord" and creating a "state of permanent agitation."[84] He accepted the deal with de Hoth and feared that the expropriation Flores requested would be detrimental to his followers. Other settlers accused Flores of "threatening to kill them and dispossess them of their lots."[85]

In 1945 the government expropriated swaths of land in the neighborhood in an attempt to end the property conflicts plaguing the area. But the expropriation resolved a legal problem only to create a political one. Flores complained that the land was "handed over to gangsters and exploiters of residents who negotiated these land distributions and made business deals outside of the law."[86] Another leader of the coalition, Roque Plata Belmont, accused José Garibay Centeno (head of the Oficina de Colonias), Leonilo Salgado, and José Ambrosi of organizing "crazy invasions" and illegally selling lots. Flores would later claim that there were 3,000 empty lots in the city that could be distributed among his followers. He requested that the government compile a census of settlers, which could prevent neighborhood leaders from accumulating lots or distributing them to "paper settlers" (*colonos de paja*).[87] These property conflicts lasted for years. In 1952 a government plan to open a street in the neighborhood prompted the Department of Public Works to investigate property claims and determine which residents were in actuality "invaders."[88] But the intervention of surveyors and the drafting of an official blueprint did not accomplish this. In September 1953 Flores requested a second expropriation in the neighborhood in one of his last battles (he died in December of that year).[89]

In June 1949 the coalition organized its Third Housing Congress at the Teatro del Pueblo. Lasting three days, the congress was attended by more than 800 people, including the leaders of both the coalition and fifty neighborhood associations, regent Fernando Casas Alemán, and at least two police intelligence agents who penned a confidential report. The coalition continued to demand expropriations and discussed a number of grievances against landowners and the Oficina de Colonias. The congress featured the following presentations: (1) the problem of popular housing; (2) the creation of new popular neighborhoods; (3) credits for the construction of popular housing; (4) problems of juridical order, possession, and property in Mexico City; (5) state intervention in colonization and housing, considered problems of public order; (6) authentic and clandestine popular neighborhoods; (7) planning and zoning problems in the Federal District; (8) private property and public utilities in relationship to the housing problem; (9) expropriation law; (10) public services, schools, parks, markets, and urbanization in popular neighborhoods; and (11) decrees and laws related to the problem of land and housing in the Federal District. In addition, the coalition demanded that authorities prepare a census of vacant lands and lots that could be declared to be of public utility and expropriated. It also requested that Mexico's 1936 Expropriation Law be strengthened and that landowners be forced to set fair prices for lots, paid over ten years in installments.[90] Together, these demands amounted to a major revision and strengthening of the city's corporatist legal edifice. The coalition wanted more expropriations, more public housing, and a more muscular welfare state. But it also demanded a privileged role as the intermediary between this state and settlers.

Regent Fernando Casas Alemán attended the last day of the congress and claimed to stand in solidarity with the coalition in support of acquiring lots and building homes while respecting the legal order.[91] Ironically, the Oficina de Colonias—under Casas Alemán's own authority—had accused Flores of inciting countless illegal invasions. But Casas Alemán also warned that the actions of a few "senseless agitators" threatened to erode the support for his government, alluding to a recent "massacre" in Colonia Escuadrón 201. The neighborhood had been established in 1944, following a presidential expropriation. The land was distributed among workers belonging to different unions, including World War II veterans from Esquadrón 201.[92] The owner of the land, a Spaniard named Vidal Alonso, objected to the expropriation, eventually winning an *amparo* from the Supreme Court.[93] Alonso explained that during the presidency of Ávila Camacho "landowners lost their property at the hands of audacious leaders who led land invasions." The conflict between Alonso and settlers spilled over into the press, which informed readers of the thousands who were demanding the "expulsion of the *gachupín* Vidal Alonso" for charging fees that settlers could not pay.[94] In response, Alonso published an open letter accusing political leaders of harassing him and "engaging in the immoral business of attracting landless families and selling them lots under the pretense of organizing colonias proletarias."[95]

The ruling in Alonso's favor did not settle the property conflict; it merely demarcated a battleground where a number of political groups quarreled for years. The court ruling prompted the police to intervene, launching a prolonged war of attrition against the residents.[96] Sources from secret intelligence agents record a wide array of actors defending settlers: neighborhood association leaders, PRI representatives, Communist organizers, and university students.[97] Skirmishes between these groups and police forces plagued the neighborhood between 1947 and 1949. As one researcher put it, in that period their youth "was forged in years of street-fighting." The last confrontation took place on June 8, 1949—less than a week before the inauguration of the Third Housing Congress. The conflict was finally resolved by President Miguel Alemán Valdés, who prompted Vidal Alonso to "cede his rights" to the land to the city, which in turn distributed the land among groups in the area.[98] A legal conflict was initially resolved through violence then through politicking and finally, it appears, through back-channel negotiations.

This is one example of countless conflicts where the coalition and similar organizations played a role. In addition to leading dozens of land invasions,[99] Flores and the coalition protested against citywide projects. When the Planning Commission discussed the extension of Reforma Avenue in 1950, for example, the coalition protested that the project would entail the destruction of thousands of vecindades.[100] Over years of organizing, the coalition constantly denounced "the government's protection of those who exploit settlers and enable big businesses."[101] But the same accusations were leveled against Flores and the coalition, who were often described as invaders who manipulated naïve residents. The difference between legitimate and illegitimate leaders, "authentic and clandestine" neighborhoods,[102] and "residents in possession of their lots who embodied citizenship" and "squatters manipulated by opportunist leaders" is blurry, as always, but political actors were bent on defining these lines, which were ultimately political.[103]

Figure 4.3. Residents of Colonia Ampliación Simón Bolívar protesting against fraudulent leaders. Archivo General de la Nación, Fondo Hermanos Mayo, 1a Parte, Cronológico, HMA/CR1/04690.

Archival sources describe Flores as an antagonist of the Oficina de Colonias and a land invader. Indeed, he spent an occasional stint in jail.[104] But his organization was made up of thousands of members: he was well connected within the Oficina de Colonias as well as with the city regent, representatives, and other political actors. When Flores died in December 1953, thousands of settlers attended the funeral, allegedly paid for by President Adolfo Ruiz Cortines. The newspapers said he died a poor man, something of a folk hero.[105] They made no reference to the deep enmity that he had encountered in the city government through years of opposition and invasions.

The nature of the relationship between the coalition and the PRI is hard to ascertain.[106] PRI representatives sometimes joined the coalition, and Flores tried to use his following to become a PRM official in 1944.[107] PRI representatives took part in political rallies organized by the coalition, pledging to support settlers' demands for municipal services.[108] But the question is ultimately anachronistic because it presumes the existence of what later scholars would call the "PRI-government apparatus," a powerful and unitary machine of political control.[109] Some scholars have stressed the accomplishment of the Mexican state in meeting the demands of the urban poor, while others have focused on its authoritarian character and its successful control of the "urban masses" for the sake of capitalist development.[110] But the "PRI-government apparatus" was nowhere to be found in the 1940s, if it ever existed. The city government was divided between the technical officials of the Department of Public Works and the political officials of the Oficina de Colonias. At the same time, there was fierce competition among political brokers to represent settlers and amass a following, which would provide opportunities both to win elected office and to make a profit. PRI representatives sometimes supported the Coalición de Colonos, but these alliances ought to be explored on a case-by-case basis.[111] It is enticing to view Flores and brokers like him as setting the stage for the final consolidation of the "PRI regime." But such an interpretation turns the PRI into a teleological monolith, rendering it the inexorable endpoint of urban politics in Mexico City. By taking for granted the idea of the PRI, it prevents us from "seeing political practice as it is": local leaders competing against one another, presenting claims on behalf of urban residents, and making a profit through the control of a politicized real-estate land market.[112]

Like the distinction between formal and informal neighborhoods, the line between official colonias proletarias with lawful residents and squatter settlements inhabited by invaders was blurry and arbitrary, but it demarcated a political arena in which city officials and residents could negotiate claims to the city. This political arena involved multiple groups and organizations: government officials (both technicians and politicians), party representatives, political brokers, land developers, landholders, and families in need of housing. Colonias proletarias held distinct meanings for each of these groups. They were corporatist political units, neighborhoods in need of upgrade, sites for grassroots organizing, political bounties, and profitable real-estate investments. Amid this ambiguity they rose to prominence, confounding contemporaries and historians alike.

In the 1940s this system of governance was embedded in the language of corporatist politics, ideals of social citizenship, and revolutionary promises of social justice. In this favorable context, urban residents were emboldened to request expropriations, push for the drafting of planning and housing laws, and organize federations like the Coalición de Colonos. As the next chapter demonstrates, the political conditions for making claims to housing were transformed in the 1950s, a decade when dreams of modernization gained ground over the revolutionary promises of social justice, which slowly eroded.

5

From Proletarian to Marginal Neighborhoods

Colonia Gabriel Ramos Millán was one of the last neighborhoods established in the heyday of colonias proletarias. The first settlers arrived at the Tlacotal y Bramadero Ranch where the neighborhood was to be built in December 1950. The event was captured by the Mayo Brothers, the exiled Spanish photojournalists who settled in Mexico in 1939. One photograph depicts families arriving with their scant possessions: bed frames and mattresses, suitcases, boxes, and domestic animals as well as wood planks, metal plates, and other materials for building a house. Tents and makeshift homes are visible in another image, along with families waiting in line by a water truck, buckets in hand. Iztacalco, where Tlacotal y Bramadero was located, was (and still is) the smallest delegación in the city and one of the least populated, with 11,000 residents in 1940. A peripheral delegación, outside of the city perimeter delimited by planners in 1941, it consisted largely of agrarian estates, ranches, and canals. Early photographs of Colonia Ramos Millán have an eerie quality: it resembles a refugee camp, void of roads, light posts, sidewalks, and other signs of urbanization. No traces of Mexico City are visible.

The Mayo Brothers captured what chronicler Carlos Monsiváis called the "ceaseless growth of the marginal" in an overflowing city.[1] But the photographs obscure more than they reveal. Despite the depiction of quiet nobility among the neighborhood's first settlers, rather than looking like a refugee camp, Ramos Millán was something of a showcase. The Mayo photographs, commissioned to promote government actions on the housing front, are evidence of this centrality. Laudatory newspaper articles accompanied the photographs. "The shantytown is gone," read one, "and its residents have a new home."[2] Ramos Millán was a model colonia proletaria, the object of much attention from architects, working families, political brokers, city officials, and even a presidential hopeful. The neighborhood was the personal

Figure 5.1. "Traslado de colonos que habitaban en el Río San Joaquín a los terrenos de las cercanías de Ixtapalapa." This photograph, which was previously unpublished, depicts the arrival of the first settlers of Colonia Gabriel Ramos Millán. It probably did not evoke much optimism about the future of the place. Archivo General de la Nación, Fondo Hermanos Mayo, 1a Parte, Cronológico, HMA/CR1/04785.1.

project of regent Fernando Casas Alemán (1946–1952), who was considering a run for the presidency with the support of settlers. Preeminent modernist architect Mario Pani even designed a housing complex for new residents. City officials and political brokers were active in Ramos Millán, working to allocate lots among thousands of petitioners.

The men and women who arrived in Tlacotal y Bramadero in the winter of 1950–1951 were intimately aware of the webs of patronage in which they were entangled. Each family carried a voucher signed by Carlos Zapata Vela, head of the Oficina de Colonias, that secured a lot in the neighborhood.[3] The army set up tents and built improvised shacks for these first families. The city government deployed water trucks. Colonia Ramos Millán quickly became one of Mexico City's largest neighborhoods, with a population of 30,000 in 1955.[4] During its first decade of existence, it went from a temporary settlement to a working-class neighborhood provided with schools, a clinic, and other public facilities. A tantalizing welfare state seemed to be crystallizing, supported by a growing economy and a developmentalist state that invested in urban infrastructure and subsidized cities and their populations.

Over the course of only a decade, however, Colonia Ramos Millán went from a showcase colonia proletaria to a "marginal" settlement, at least if we are to trust the title of a 1963 thesis that surveyed the neighborhood a decade after its foundation.[5] Following contemporary research on the topic of rural-urban migration, the author focused on the residents of the neighborhood, whom she considered unprepared for city life. These assumptions, unmistakably a product of their time, were soon to be discredited. But their deployment in Ramos Millán elicits critical questions. Why did colonias proletarias (or at least the discourse around them) deteriorate so rapidly? Was this deterioration real or imaginary? What is the relationship between the deterioration of colonias proletarias, their stigmatization, and the political legitimacy that they enjoyed during the 1940s?

The changing fate of colonias proletarias had many causes, including major local and transnational developments. Ernesto P. Uruchurtu replaced Fernando Casas Alemán as regent in Mexico City in 1952, putting in place an antigrowth policy that restricted the creation of new colonias proletarias. But the stigmatization suffered by colonias proletarias was also part of a broader regional transformation whereby working-class neighborhoods in Mexico and Latin America in general came to be understood as part of a hemispheric urban crisis made palpable by rural-urban migration, "explosive" growth, and the proliferation of squatter settlements. Colonias proletarias, which had been seen as a fairly successful housing policy, came to be interpreted as a local iteration of the Latin American problem of informality, rendered visible in widespread images of marginality: rural migrants, unpaved streets, and makeshift dwellings.

The first section of this chapter reconstructs the history of Colonia Ramos Millán from the 1930s to the early 1950s, when multiple groups made claims to the land where the neighborhood was built. The countless projects, laws, and decrees that fixed this place in space set the stage for years of conflicts between landholders, peasants, industrialists, planners, city officials, political brokers, and settlers that convey the political interests and ideological visions undergirding urbanization in mid-century Mexico. The second section considers the actions of the Coalición de Colonos to gain a foothold for its clients in Colonia Ramos Millán. As in other colonias proletarias, property and planning conflicts constituted a fertile ground where political brokers thrived, allocating lots and negotiating the provision of municipal services. The third section zooms out to examine the city government under Uruchurtu, considering policies that sought to limit urban growth for environmental reasons. Finally, I analyze how scholars reinterpreted—and misunderstood—colonias proletarias as squatter settlements symptomatic of a failed modernization, an approach exemplified by labeling Colonia Ramos Millán a "marginal" settlement.

Agrarian Reform, Industrial Development, and Public Housing in Iztacalco

While it is squarely within the hustle of Mexico City today, in the early twentieth century Iztacalco was on the fringe of the city, southeast of the city center. The 1930 *Atlas general del Distrito Federal* described it as an area of "little historical importance," a dismissive view that glossed over a long history stretching back to the fourteenth century.[6] "Very little is left of the grandeur and importance [of Iztacalco] in the time of the Mexica kings and emperors," wrote a 1930s chronicler. "Most of its residents are Indians who cultivate small agrarian lots and chinampas [floating fields]."[7] The majority of Iztacalco's four thousand inhabitants resided in the towns of Ixtacalco and Santa Anita, located on the western fringe of the delegación (closer to Mexico City). The ranches, paddocks, and estates that constituted its remaining area were left unnamed and unmapped by the *Atlas*. In fact, the whole eastern half of Iztacalco was omitted from it, confirming how little the city government valued the place.

Iztacalco was an amphibian and essentially agrarian area, crisscrossed by canals and rivers and dominated by chinampas where cereals, alfalfa, and flowers were grown. During the colonial period and the nineteenth century, these products were transported by boat to Mexico City through the Canal de la Viga, which ran all the way from Chalco to La Merced, the central market of the city. But this aquatic universe was changing fast. Rivers, canals, and lakes suffered a long process of desiccation. By 1900, tramway lines connected Ixtacalco and Santa Anita to Mexico City. The Sanitation Council closed the Canal de la Viga in 1915. Bordering Santa Anita, to the east, lay the Rancho de la Viga, which would later become Colonia Independencia and already bore signs of urbanization in the shape of a grid only partially shown in the 1930 *Atlas general*. Under the radar, developers subdividing Iztacalco were transforming this agrarian zone into a hotspot of urbanization.

Nostalgic voices today lament the disappearance of the chinampas, canals, and rivers that characterized the southeast of the Federal District, but the transformation of this environment into a dry urban one was seen at the time as the ineluctable face of progress. "Cultural advancement and the needs of mankind," wrote a medical student investigating parasitic diseases in Santa Anita during the 1940s, "have transformed the pueblo and its residents." In

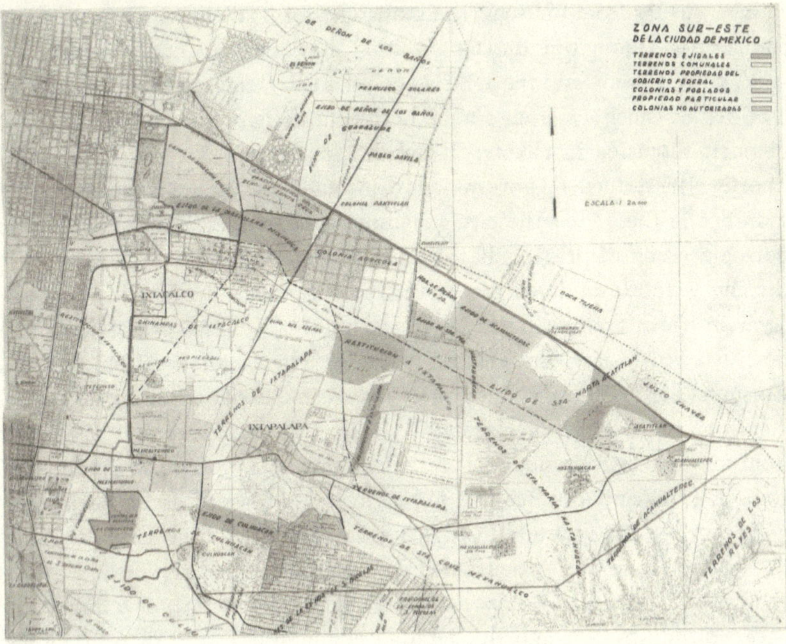

Figure 5.2. "Zona sur-este de la Ciudad de México." AHCDMX, Obras Públicas, box 658, file 1. This map captures a moment in the process of urbanization in Iztacalco in the 1950s. Colonia Gabriel Ramos Millán is surrounded by federal lands, private lands, agrarian lands (ejido and communal properties), and unauthorized neighborhoods. City authorities and planners like Mario Pani viewed this area as a favorable site for the construction of public housing.

a matter-of-fact manner she concluded: "Santa Anita has transformed into a colonia, chinampas have disappeared, and the old canals have become roads."[8]

Luz Calderón inherited the Tlacotal y Bramaderos estate from her husband, Ángel García Lascuráin, in 1934, just as the agrarian reform gained steam under the Cárdenas presidency. Calderón's property was targeted by several agrarian communities requesting land grants: Ixtacalco, San Juanico Mextipa, Mexicaltzingo, and Colonia Independencia. A judge decreed an expropriation in 1935, ruling that her estate be divided among the four neighboring communities.[9] It is unclear what happened during the interim, but in 1941 Calderón filed a lawsuit against the expropriation, winning a favorable ruling the following year. However, the agrarian communities counterattacked and requested a land restitution, approved by the local Agrarian Commission and the city regent in 1945.[10] This bundle of legal claims, counterclaims, and rulings was far from unusual. The availability of land grants triggered fierce competition among peasant communities, large landholders, and settlers.

While Calderón and the agrarian communities engaged in this protracted legal battle, other actors entertained different designs. The industrialists and planners discussed in chapter 3 saw the area as ripe for industrialization. Shortly after the federal government distributed land grants to peasant communities in the 1930s, the city government established industrial zones to pursue a vision of progress based on industrial development. Many lots in the city were expropriated twice over the course of a decade, first to create agrarian ejidos then as industrial zones, housing projects, or public amenities such as Mexico's Universidad Nacional.[11] In September 1942 architect Enrique Guerrero designed a project for an "industrial subdivision [*fraccionamiento*] in the ranch of Tlacotal."[12] Close to the city center but far enough from more exclusive residential areas, Iztacalco held promise as an industrial zone. A presidential decree in 1944 earmarked "Tlacotal and other contiguous ranches" for future industrial development.[13] Months later, an industrial corporation—the Sociedad de Fraccionamientos Industriales (Society of Industrial Subdivisions)—purchased the ranch, prompting a new legal battle between industrialists and the agrarian communities until then in conflict with Luz Calderón. Industrialists argued that Public Works had approved their project and noted that the 1944 presidential decree represented a "frank invitation to industrialize the area."[14] A new presidential decree, published in January 1946, settled the matter by overruling the claims of the agrarian communities.

But Tlacotal y Bramadero would not become an industrial powerhouse. Despite its status as a communal landholding or an industrial zone, a silent migration was underway, driven by thousands of families settling in the area after purchasing lots from developers and ejido authorities who sold their agrarian lands outside of the law. Most of these transactions were illegal, which explains why official documents sometimes fail to register these subdivisions. But thousands of self-built houses are visible in aerial photographs of Iztacalco taken in 1945, one-story structures along unpaved streets. This process of capitalist urbanization, coupled with government efforts to harness and politically exploit it, transformed the area. In the end, the politics of housing would decisively stamp Iztacalco, turning it into the working-class neighborhood that it remains today.

In an interview with *El Universal* in May 1949, regent Fernando Casas Alemán announced the acquisition of a 1.5 million square meter tract from the Compañía de Fraccionamientos Industriales de México.[15] Casas Alemán's plan for Ramos Millán was more assertive than many of the government expropriations during the 1940s. Rather than resolving a conflict between owners and residents, the usual modus operandi of expropriations, he sought to create a colonia proletaria from scratch: purchasing the land, subdividing it, distributing municipal services, and building a housing project. In September 1949 architects Mario Pani and José Luis Cuevas presented the Planning Commission with a housing project for the lot, the unexecuted "Unidad de Vivienda Tlacotal y Bramadero."[16] In addition to designing the project, Pani was the technical planning advisor for Iztacalco. His engagement with the project was dual, as an architect and as the planner responsible for the city section where it stood. From his modernist bird's-eye view of the city, the Unidad de Vivienda Tlacotal y Bramadero was one of twenty-one housing complexes (*unidades vecinales*) located in Iztacalco and its surroundings.[17] Pani built some of these units, but his grand design was never completed (see chapter 6).

The Casas Alemán interview reveals a political gambit, for the regent was courting the support of settlers as a potential presidential candidate.[18] Appointed by the president, regents were weak figures, bereft of a political base and democratic legitimacy.[19] Casas Alemán worked hard to win the favor of working-class families. He toured colonias proletarias, promising municipal services, much to the dismay of Public Works officials reluctant to place such burdens on the treasury. As we have seen, in June 1949 he attended the Third General Congress of the Coalición de Colonos, where he was welcomed by an enthusiastic crowd hailing him as the future president. Casas Alemán offered attendants his support "as a friend, a public official, and a humble servant of the humble people."[20] For a regent eager to build a political base, Ramos Millán represented a source of patronage to be distributed among thousands of settlers.

Countless families petitioned the government for a lot in Colonia Ramos Millán. Many lived in homes and neighborhoods threatened by modernization projects close to the city center, like the urban renewal of Atlampa, contiguous to the railroad station at Nonoalco. Most petitioning families lived on the margins of the San Joaquín River, which snaked northwest of Mexico City and crossed a military zone, a handful of industrial plants, and colonias proletarias such as Pensil and México Nuevo. Hundreds of families had settled on federal lands by the river, which was about to be piped. The government had considered moving these families to Iztacalco since the early weeks of 1948.[21] In December 1950, after more than two years of negotiations, the Oficina de Colonias began relocating families to Colonia Ramos Millán at the other end of the city. "The shantytown [*ciudad perdida*] that for more than seven years had been a nightmare for metropolitan authorities [the settlement

Figure 5.3. "Recorrido del jefe de la Oficina de Colonias del D.F., C. Zapata Vela." Carlos Zapata Vela, the head of the Oficina de Colonias, surveys the dismantling of the so-called lost city along the San Joaquín River. Archivo General de la Nación, Fondo Hermanos Mayo, 1a Parte, Cronológico, HMA/CR1/04785.1.

by the river margins] has disappeared," a newspaper article reported. The relocation was led by the head of the Oficina de Colonias, Carlos Zapata Vela, with the help of the army and representatives.[22] Soldiers tore down the shacks by the riverbanks, government trucks transported people to Iztacalco, and employees from the Oficina de Colonias distributed lots.

The intervention of the government was tangible, hailed by reporters who described the relocation as an "extraordinary improvement for the residents of the shantytown." After living by the margins of a river (more accurately described as a "sewage canal"), residents would move to 120-square-meter lots to be paid for in installments.[23] While the Oficina de Colonias relocated families, the federal government distributed food and vaccines. The government also brokered an agreement with the agrarian communities that still had claims to the area.[24] Buses began operating in Colonia Ramos Millán in the summer of 1951. A few weeks later, thousands of residents received their property titles during the grand inauguration of a market and a bridge that connected the two sections of the neighborhood, Tlacotal and Bramadero.[25] Judging by the press, the place was a resounding success.

Broker Politics

Following the relocation of the first settlers, government control over Colonia Ramos Millán eroded, undermined by myriad political groups and brokers active in the neighborhood. Those early settlers arrived with vouchers signed by Carlos Zapata Vela, securing a lot in the neighborhood. Upon taking possession of their lot, they received an official contract; once lot payments were completed, a land title would be provided. For every settler in possession of a voucher, however, there were thousands of others vying for a lot, putting immense pressure on the Oficina de Colonias. Petitioners came from all over. Many were public employees, including cleaning workers, teachers, and employees from the Ministry of Agriculture.[26] Many others came from neighborhoods such as Buenos Aires, Atlampa, Escuadrón 201, Peralvillo, Nonoalco, and Guerrero, where residents had lost their homes to floods or other disasters.[27] And a few came from outside the city, mostly from the nearby states of Mexico, Michoacán, Guanajuato, and Hidalgo.[28] These were low-income settlers acquainted with the broker politics of colonias proletarias and connected to the city's patronage networks. In the chaos of overwhelming demand, efficiently streamlining requests for housing would prove impossible.

In 1951, as the neighborhood grew rapidly, Conrado Mercado became the first president of Ramos Millán.[29] The neighborhood was owned by the DDF, so the Oficina de Colonias—on paper at least—had the power to distribute lots as it saw fit. As the intermediary between government and residents, Mercado was key to this distribution. Over the following years, he earned an infamous reputation, accused of perpetrating abuses that commonly afflicted residents of colonias proletarias: dispossessing residents of their lots; selling the same lot more than once; and charging fees for obscure administrative expenses. In a typical case, a woman named Vicenta González denounced Mercado for selling her a lot belonging to someone else. González paid MX$400 for her lot but did not receive a receipt for her purchase. After forty-five days living in the neighborhood, during which she built a house, a man named Aurelio García Sierra identified himself as the owner of the lot. González demanded that her payment be reimbursed or a new lot be provided.[30]

Likewise, a man named Erasto Castillo claimed to have purchased two lots from Mercado for a down payment of MX$1,200. Like González, Castillo did not have a receipt; like her, "while working on his lots on a Sunday," he was confronted by a man claiming to be the "legitimate owner" of the land. Castillo reported Mercado to Rafael Suárez Ocaña, Carlos Zapata Vela's replacement as director of the Oficina de Colonias. Mercado and his cronies, Castillo claimed, "run this place at will, harass its residents, and use their profits to keep out of trouble and justice at arm's length."[31] A teacher named Lauro Gorocica Concha purchased a lot from the city government at the Oficina de Colonias, where an employee requested a MX$25 fee to complete the transaction and provide the land title. Gorocica Concha still had not received his title months later, hearing continuous excuses and insults at the Oficina de Colonias and being told that there was nothing to be done because the land title was lost somewhere in the cadastral office.[32]

These stories reveal a thriving real-estate market shrouded in uncertainty about property ownership and the legitimacy of municipal and other authorities. As explained before, under the pretense of shielding residents from market forces, the Reglamento de Colonias prohibited speculation and restricted the sale of lots to middle-class and upper-class residents. All evidence points to the futility of these measures. Colonias proletarias clearly provided residents and authorities with countless profit-making opportunities. Despite legal prohibitions, residents partitioned, sold, and rented lots, business ventures that often spiraled into conflicts over the right to own and occupy land. These informal land markets have been documented by historians, and their existence is confirmed in Colonia Ramos Millán.[33] According to a 1960s survey, over half of residents were owners, while the others rented.[34]

This legal uncertainty created the conditions for Conrado Mercado to exert his power. As there was no official blueprint of the neighborhood and most residents lacked property titles, Mercado and Rafael Suárez Ocaña had the power to assign lots, manipulate their boundaries, and negotiate the provision of municipal services. Blueprints and resident censuses were tools of political control that the Oficina de Colonias jealously guarded, as evidenced by the constant petitions for information from government offices filed by landless families and nongovernment political brokers. Conflicts between the Oficina de Colonias and settlers abounded. Although accusations of abuses and frauds were common, publicly acknowledging them could put pressure on the authorities. In the summer of 1954 *La Prensa* published a story portraying Mercado as a swindler. It ran another story later that year about an Italian engineer named Ambrosi who bought a large amount of land and was illegally renting houses and rooms to tenants. The following spring, *El Popular* reported that city officials were charging illegal fees for the installation of water pipes.[35] In response to these scandals, Suárez Ocaña removed Mercado from the presidency of Ramos Millán in 1954. But Mercado continued to operate in the neighborhood, running for its presidency again the following year.[36]

Organizations like Salvador Flores's Coalición de Colonos thrived amid the chaos. The Coalición de Colonos had been involved in Ramos Millán since at least 1948, when Flores wrote to the president requesting lots in the neighborhood. His petitions over the following years were met with lackluster and vague responses from the Oficina de Colonias, which claimed that no lots were available or that it was in the process of revising contracts and the neighborhood plan.[37] In 1952 Roque Plata Belmont, an ally of Flores and a member of the Coalición de Colonos, negotiated the transfer of 200 families from the barrio of Atlampa to Colonia Ramos Millán. Atlampa, a notorious slum, was located north of the city center, close to the railroad tracks where Spanish filmmaker Luis Buñuel shot *Los olvidados*—a point that Plata Belmont did not fail to mention.[38] Conditions were dire. The families' houses suffered from continuous floods and were on the brink of collapse. The Red Cross described them as "pigsties" where miserable people dwelled in the utmost promiscuity.[39] Suárez Ocaña visited Atlampa in December 1953, confirming the conditions and recommending the relocation of the families to Colonia Ramos Millán.[40] Nonetheless, the move stalled. In the summer of 1954 the Oficina de Colonias told Plata Belmont that no lots were available. Plata Belmont accused Suárez Ocaña of betraying the Atlampa families who had been promised lots in Ramos Millán. He claimed that an engineer from the Oficina de Colonias had already subdivided 241 lots earmarked for the relocation.[41]

It is unclear whether these families ever received the promised lots. But while Plata Belmont negotiated these matters with the Oficina de Colonias, Salvador Flores organized a land invasion in the neighborhood's public park. According to Mercado, the invaders were led by the "so-called doctor" Salvador Flores, together with Jesús Chávez and Estanislao Padilla. Mercado referred to them as "outsiders" who sought to undermine his authority, "set the residents against him," and create a rift in the neighborhood.[42] Flores's "invasion" was part of a pattern visible across years of organizing. In the case of Colonia Ramos Millán, it fit into a longer history of claims over the land where the park stood. A year before the invasion, in the summer of 1952, residents had protested against the subdivision of the park, the "sole spot in the neighborhood where one could breathe fresh air."[43] But the area was under pressure from landless families, developers, and authorities. In fact, Mercado himself was accused of subdividing and selling lots in the park, "enriching himself at the expense of the sacrifice of the children of the neighborhood."[44] Mercado denied the accusations, stating that everyone knew of his efforts to "safeguard the park while [his] enemies subdivided it in order to honor commitments made with several groups."[45]

Both Mercado and Flores were accused of sponsoring illegal subdivisions and invasions. But it is futile and probably impossible to know who was an "invader" and who was a "legitimate" resident. This stems, in part, from the difficulty of pinpointing the land allegedly being invaded. Conflicts over blueprints were common. Numerous blueprints existed for most colonias proletarias, each legitimizing the claims of different residents. The multiplication of blueprints as well as censuses and property titles did not produce the legibility identified by James Scott as the driving goal of state action in regard to territory. It had the opposite effect: creating utter confusion. Defending Mercado, Suárez Ocaña denied that there was any invasion, explaining that the lots distributed by the Oficina de Colonias were not located in the park but on a strip of land adjacent to it, following the neighborhood's official blueprint.[46] The park in Ramos Millán, however, was probably not more than an empty strip of land itself, described by social workers as "a large lot bereft of any green areas."[47]

Throughout the 1940s and early 1950s, the authority of the Oficina de Colonias continued to be challenged by the Coalición de Colonos, an organization with the capacity to mobilize hundreds of families and with connections within the city and federal governments as well as branches of the PRI. Neither side was completely victorious, as evidenced by the cleavage between the "original" residents, who had contracts signed by the Oficina de Colonias, and residents represented by the Coalición de Colonos, who probably arrived after December 1950. A 1955 report on the neighborhood prepared by social workers referenced a group of "squatters" from Atlampa and Escuadrón 201 living in Ramos Millán (most likely the families defended by Flores and Plata Belmont).[48]

Colonias Proletarias and the Government of Ernesto P. Uruchurtu

Colonia Ramos Millán was one of the last colonias proletarias sponsored by the city government. In the early 1950s the forces that gave rise to this housing model crumbled. The DDF dramatically reduced the establishment of new colonias proletarias. The Supreme Court hindered the establishment of colonias proletarias. And the ideals of social justice that justified the establishment of colonias proletarias in the first place lost sway. The colonias proletarias established in the 1930s and 1940s benefited from infrastructure improvements during the 1940s and 1950s, eventually receiving municipal services and land titles. But references to colonias proletarias began to shift. Initially hailed as the building blocks of a working-class metropolis, they were increasingly viewed as squatter settlements breaking the law, defined by their marginality.

The man most responsible for these changes, at least at the municipal level, was Ernesto P. Uruchurtu, the regent that President Adolfo Ruiz Cortines appointed in December 1952 to replace Fernando Casas Alemán.[49] Uruchurtu held power till 1966, making his thirteen-year tenure the longest in the city's history. A powerful ruler known as the iron regent, Uruchurtu crafted alliances with the middle classes, small industrialists, commercial groups, and key unions and corporate groups.[50] His many successes as a regent were due to his authoritarian style, administrative efficiency, and capacity to attune his positions to the sensibility of the growing middle classes. Uruchurtu fixed the city's finances, led major infrastructure projects, and acquired fame as a moralizing figure, tough on corruption and bent on uplifting various realms of city life, from inaugurating gardens and markets to censoring immoral performances at theaters and nightclubs.

"Uruchurtu's model was Los Angeles," architect Teodoro González de León quipped dismissively. "He was a *norteño* who liked to visit Los Angeles every December."[51] Architects like González de León and Mario Pani describe Uruchurtu as a parochial and conservative figure whose goal was not to transform the city in accordance with an urban ideal but simply to make it "more livable."[52] If Uruchurtu did not have a grand urban vision, he did have an obsession: halting urban growth. In this he was not alone. The expansion of Mexico City elicited widespread anxieties by the 1950s, as expressed in pessimistic writings, paintings, and films warning of an impending demographic, social, and environmental catastrophe.[53] As historian Manuel Perló Cohen has argued, Uruchurtu led a three-pronged approach to fight growth: deindustrialization, reducing licenses for new neighborhoods, and combating land invasions and squatter settlements. The number of government-sanctioned neighborhoods was drastically reduced.[54] And the support for the creation of new colonias proletarias was reduced as well, resulting in a steep decline in their number.[55]

Uruchurtu's antigrowth policies were effective but had important unintended consequences. Crucially, informal neighborhoods continued to be built in two spaces that functioned as a sort of escape valve for growth. First, lands under the ejido system continued to be subdivided and sold outside of the law, a process that the government did not fully stop.[56] Second, dozens of neighborhoods continued to be built in the State of Mexico, which would become the new frontier of urban growth and the largest real-estate market in the Valley of Mexico, as exemplified by the expansion of Ciudad Netzahualcóyotl in the 1960s.

The change in policy toward colonias proletarias predated Uruchurtu's government. In 1948 the DDF reduced the number of acres purchased for the purpose of establishing colonias proletarias.[57] The new stance can also be read between the lines of Mexico City's new Planning Law, approved in 1953. The drafting and passing of the law took at least three years, from early 1950 to December 1953, thus covering the tenures of Casas Alemán and Uruchurtu. An early version of the law, drafted in 1950 or 1951, explicitly listed as a planning responsibility "the formation of colonias proletarias and the enlargement of the already existing ones."[58] This proposal might have been influenced by political leaders who advocated for more expropriations to create colonias proletarias.[59] But the final law made no reference to the matter.

In a "landmark decision" in 1951, the Supreme Court declared the use of eminent domain for the purpose of establishing colonias proletarias unconstitutional.[60] The number of colonias proletarias sanctioned by the government plummeted after this decision, as did the number of expropriations with the goal of establishing them.[61] Around the same time, in December 1951, a group of PRI representatives sent to Congress a Ley de Colonización Proletaria (Law of Proletarian Settlement) to push for the establishment of new colonias proletarias, which representatives described as an "effective mechanism for the expansion and progress of the city and its community."[62] The representatives lauded Fernando Casas Alemán for his support of settlers but deplored the lack of a "legal tool that would allow the state to fulfill its protective role" and help "humble settlers to fix the housing problem on their own."[63] The law was not approved. In retrospect, 1951 represents a promising year on the path toward a more explicit policy in favor of colonias proletarias. These possibilities existed because of the political leverage that colonias proletarias had, which would erode in the 1950s.

Upon his arrival in office in December 1952, Uruchurtu declared that the earlier official sanction of colonias proletarias had followed the rationale of placating ambitious political leaders who doggedly fought for recognition.[64] Uruchurtu's stance put him in conflict with the settlers and brokers with whom previous regents like Casas Alemán had deftly built alliances. In the months leading to the election of President Adolfo Ruiz Cortines in the summer of 1952, PRI representatives continued to push for a law to increase expropriations to form colonias proletarias and protect residents from developers.[65] Architects and planners rejected this position, favoring technocratic solutions to the housing problem instead. While these experts did not always call for explicit bans on colonias proletarias, they were increasingly preoccupied with the negative environmental consequences of unbridled growth, including concerns over "pathological urbanism," water provision, and environmental degradation.[66]

As I have argued, the confrontation between technocratic city officials set on restricting growth and politicians—allied with local brokers—supportive of colonias proletarias was demarcated decades before Uruchurtu arrived in power. But technocrats in the 1950s embraced a new environmentalist discourse fixated on the perennial *problema de las aguas* (water problem) in the Valley of Mexico.[67] In June 1951 the federal government created the Hydrological Commission of the Valley of Mexico, whose policy proposals Uruchurtu as regent would zealously follow. As the planners referenced earlier, commission members identified the Valley of Mexico as the proper scale of analysis for addressing the problem of water: its supply and disposal, its overabundance and scarcity.

By the 1950s, the hydraulic engineering projects of the Porfirian era were plainly under a strain. A flood paralyzed the capital for ten days in May 1951. Floods were exacerbated by soil subsidence, the sinking of low-lying parts of the city that were once under Lake Texcoco. Subsidence, in turn, was worsened by the construction of artesian wells that pumped water from the ground aquifer to service hundreds of thousands living in colonias proletarias. The desiccation of the lake and the deforestation of the valley created dust storms that choked the city for days on end. Environmental experts—to use an anachronistic term to describe biologist Enrique Beltrán and engineers Gonzalo Blanco Macías and Nabor Carrillo—realized that these problems were interconnected, that "flooding, deforestation, dust storms, water waste, and subsidence were tied together in a vicious circle."[68] Informal urbanization had become an existential environmental threat.

In the end, Mexico City's Planning Law of 1953 made no explicit reference to colonias proletarias. But it did include regulations against illegal subdivisions, a "legal lacuna" in earlier laws.[69] The new law required that developers install municipal services, donate land for the construction of markets, schools, and other public buildings, and make contributions in cash for the construction of these buildings and infrastructure. Uruchurtu was not involved in the drafting of these regulations, but in his hands they became key instruments for combating growth. In his first year as regent, Uruchurtu suspended subdivisions that did not abide by the new legal requirements; lots in these neighborhoods could not be sold, provided with alignment and construction licenses, or connected to the water and sewage system until their status was regularized. To do so, developers had to pay the taxes set forth in the 1941 Reglamento de Fraccionamientos, the 1953 Planning Law, and an additional tax to be connected to the water and sewage system.[70]

The Water Department was a key gatekeeper for sanctioning new subdivisions. When Uruchurtu came into office, half of the population lacked access to water and sewage services in their homes.[71] Water Department director Eduardo Molina rejected dozens of petitions for the formation of new subdivisions because his office was unable to provide them with water. In September 1954 Molina rejected the petition made by the residents of Colonia Ampliación Santa Lucía to be connected to the water network.[72] Colonia Agrícola Pantitlán was also denied access to the water network because Molina contended that its developers had "subdivided the land without regard to the most elemental planning notions, aggravating the problem of water scarcity."[73]

To circumvent these regulations, settlers claimed to live in colonias proletarias. In July 1955, for example, residents of Colonia El Rosedal requested an exemption from the 15 percent land donation owed to the government and the recently established water tax, obligations that planning codes imposed on regular subdivisions. The residents, teachers who bought their lots with a government loan, claimed that they lived in a colonia proletaria whose subdivision had been approved by the government. Despite having paid for the "urbanization, electrification, etc.," of the neighborhood, they contended that Public Works refused to grant them recognition.[74] Although records from the Oficina de Colonias show that El Rosedal was indeed a colonia proletaria, Public Works authorities had not approved its subdivision. Like countless other neighborhoods, El Rosedal was in an ambiguous legal zone, between full membership in the city and tolerated acceptance. For residents of these neighborhoods, this gray zone became harsher during Uruchurtu's tenure. Thousands petitioned for lots, land titles, municipal services, and exemptions for cooperation payments (mostly for water) in the 1950s, but the city government denied most of the requests because of the "serious water problem faced by the city."[75] Living in an informal neighborhood, by virtue of breaking planning codes or lacking land titles, pushed residents to a more precarious legal position, making them more vulnerable to government removals.

As an unintended outcome of this policy, hundreds of neighborhoods were established in the neighboring State of Mexico, which did not pass laws regulating subdivisions until 1958. In December 1962 a group of landless families settled in Colonia Cuchillo del Tesoro, in an area located between the State of Mexico and the Federal District. The DDF claimed that the lot was located in the Federal District and that the settlement was an invasion organized by Benigno Prado Valencia and Samuel Suárez Yañez. The "invaders" claimed that they had lawfully purchased the land and that it was located in the State of Mexico. Both governments established a commission to delimit the boundaries, resulting in a long and messy conflict that entangled bureaucrats and judges from both jurisdictions. "Colonia Cuchilla del

Tesoro, State of Mexico, is merely one battleground where the inextinguishable human instinct to obtain a lot shall triumph," wrote Prado Valencia and Suárez Yañez in a pamphlet defending their cause. Uruchurtu's ban on new subdivisions had "inundated the State of Mexico [with] a destitute population," they wrote. They acknowledged that the housing problem could not easily be fixed, but bans on growth were futile, because Mexicans "long for the security provided by a lot, rather than a nest in a housing project; we should postpone the construction of the latter and work toward the urbanization of the former."[76] Prado Valencia and Suárez Yáñez were counting on the common practice of regularizing possession in informal neighborhoods, which colonias proletarias institutionalized in the 1940s. But by the 1960s they faced stern opposition from Uruchurtu, the iron regent.

The Marginalization of Colonia Ramos Millán

In 1963 Ramos Millán became the object of scholarly inquiry in the form of a thesis written by Martha Regina Jiménez y Castilla, a student at the Universidad Nacional Autónoma de México (UNAM). "Bramadero: un caso ilustrativo de población marginal" offers a snapshot of Ramos Millán a decade after its foundation, during the government of Uruchurtu.[77] At the time, Mexican social scientists were engaged in a transnational dialogue on urbanism, leading to the intellectual and ideological construction of what historian Adrián Gorelik has called the "Latin American city": the idea that Latin American cities constituted a regional category, whose problems could eventually be solved through policy interventions.[78]

Until the 1950s, social scientists in the region were primarily preoccupied with indigeneity and the perennial agrarian question.[79] Planners, scholars, and policymakers traveled across the hemisphere to discuss housing, migration, and marginality in seminars and conferences. Sociologists Philip Hauser and José Medina Echeverría organized the seminar "Urbanization in Latin America" in Santiago, Chile, in 1959. It was attended by an emerging group of scholars of Latin American urbanization that included Gino Germani, José Matos Mar, and Andrew Pearse, who conducted the first urban sociological surveys in Buenos Aires, Lima, and Rio de Janeiro, respectively.[80] In this context, Mexican colonias proletarias came to be seen not as a local policy with a distinct history but as the Mexican version of the Latin American marginal squatter settlement, perhaps *the* problem that came to define the region as a whole.[81]

Jiménez y Castilla's work focused on the alleged "marginality" of Ramos Millán's rural migrants, whom she considered unprepared to make it in the city. She described three-fourths of the neighborhood's population as migrants facing a dramatic cultural conflict upon their arrival in Mexico City. While Mexico's capital offered labor opportunities and living conditions superior to those in the countryside, Jiménez y Castilla argued that "not all peasants achieved their goals," partly because of the competition with educated urbanites better prepared to undertake "technical activities."[82] The alienation and difficulties faced by migrants were often grossly exaggerated, if not entirely false.[83] Residents of Ramos Millán were integrated into the urban job market and were far from alienated, avidly following the press, radio broadcasts, and sporting events from a Golden Age of national, urban, and popular culture.[84]

Jiménez y Castilla's analysis is representative of the "myth of marginality" exposed by anthropologist Janice Perlman in the 1970s—the notion that Latin America's urban poor were living in chaotic squatter settlements, alienated from the national culture and economy because of their traditional culture.[85] While Jiménez y Castilla's admittedly obscure BA thesis from the 1960s was inconsequential, its analysis was telling. Marginality, modernization, and the folk-urban continuum—the entire theoretical framework within which Jiménez y Castilla was working—were criticized by Perlman, William Mangin, and other social scientists in the 1960s and 1970s.

It is intriguing that Jiménez y Castilla failed to mention that Ramos Millán was a government project. This omission is particularly striking since Ramos Millán had only been founded a decade earlier and was something of a showcase colonia proletaria. This erasure of Ramos Millán's proud political origins was made possible by the widespread stigmatization of colonias proletarias that characterized the Uruchurtu government. In the 1940s the phrase *colonia proletaria* carried a positive connotation, semantically linked to the Mexican Revolution. But its connotations turned increasingly negative over the following two decades, a token of stigma.

The legal category of colonias proletaria lost much of its significance after 1950, as court rulings and policy decisions rendered it mostly irrelevant. Instead, observers emphasized the poverty and infrastructural shortcomings of colonias proletarias, which were very real. Newspaper and scholarly articles described colonias proletarias as marginal settlements, disregarding the political context that gave rise to them as well as the fact that they were the result of a government policy. This stigmatization is illustrated by the widespread diffusion of the term *paracaidistas* (literally, parachutists) in reference to colonias proletarias. The term refers to the squatters and land invaders who were increasingly (and wrongly) believed to be the residents of colonias proletarias. In the words of a piece published in the weekly *Mañana* in 1955, colonias proletarias were "built by squatters who invaded a piece of land and constructed a shack." Invasions were led by "immoral leaders" who subdivided land and sold it to careless purchasers.[86] Another journalist described colonias proletarias as coming to life when "a group of humble and homeless families vegetating in dark and filthy vecindades assembled . . . invading surreptitiously, as an act of magic, a vacant and peripheral lot that was thus converted into a Court of Miracles."[87]

The line between invasions and legitimate settlements was thin, dependent on the political connections enjoyed by neighborhood leaders. And the morality of these leaders must be understood in the context of a tiered real-estate market structured by planning codes and political brokers operating in the gray space between legality and illegality. The political legitimacy enjoyed by colonias proletarias and their leaders faded during the 1950s and 1960s, as city officials and journalists increasingly emphasized that colonias proletarias were breaking the law: informality became their most important trait. In a knowledgeable 1977 scholarly article that critiqued negative portrayals of colonias proletarias, Peter Ward nonetheless explained that "colonias proletarias encompass squatter settlements [*paracaidistas*] and clandestine settlements."[88] This was not the case before 1950, as colonias proletarias were *by definition* sanctioned by the city government, but it was a widespread assumption by the 1970s.

Anxiety over squatters was embedded in broader fears of explosive urban growth. At least since the 1930s, demographers had called attention to the "urban elephantiasis" threatening Mexico City due to rural migration.[89] But haunting images of megacities, hordes of peasant immigrants, and endless squatter settlements multiplied in the 1950s. "It is a well-known fact that the Republic is macrocephalic," read a newspaper article. "Compared to a human body, it has a monstrous head and a rachitic body."[90] Gómez Mayorga best captured these anxieties in his 1957 antigrowth jeremiad *¿Qué hacer por la Ciudad de México?* If Mexico City's unruly growth was not halted, he warned, the city would swallow the whole country, which would then face starvation.[91] The housing problem, he noted in a different text, stemmed from the failure of architects and planners "to understand the social groups they wish to redeem and from the Marxist assumption that the [housing] problem was economic." Amplifying Porfirian undertones that never really went away, Gómez Mayorga wrote that architects needed to stop "talking about social differences and abusing the expression 'social justice,' for we might be pitifully oversimplifying matters and not seeing that people live not only how they can but how they choose."[92]

Was the crisis of colonias proletarias real or a figment of the imagination of middle-class observers? In 1955 a team of social workers surveyed

Colonia Ramos Millán to answer this question.[93] Surveyors registered poor living conditions but also noted improvements since its foundation five years earlier. According to the report, the subdivision of the neighborhood was well laid out (*bien trazada*), but it lacked water, pavement, sewage disposal, and public lighting. Residents lived in houses of varying degrees of quality, from brick and adobe constructions to shacks built with wood, cardboard sheets, and sheet metal. Most residents worked as bricklayers, gardeners, laundrywomen, servants, and factory workers. Ramos Millán featured a rich variety of businesses, which challenged contemporary notions of colonias proletarias as cultural deserts. There were thirty-five stores as well as barbershops, beauty parlors, woodworking shops, numerous *tortillerías* and nixtamal mills, and eighteen cantinas and *pulquerías*, or "centers of vice," where gambling and heavy drinking gave the police an excuse to conduct raids.[94] During the 1950s, Ramos Millán—like many other neighborhoods—was monitored, surveyed, and (slowly) provided with municipal services, only to be labeled as marginal a decade later.[95]

The improvements of the 1950s feature prominently in recent oral histories of the neighborhood.[96] Residents evoke a tight community that attended local screenings, wrestling and boxing matches, and national celebrations like Independence Day and Las Posadas in December. Residents also remember gang violence between youths from different sections of the neighborhood: Tlacotal, Bramadero, and the neighboring Juventino Rosas and Tlazintla. Ramos Millán was provided with water, a sewage system, and electricity by the early 1960s.[97] The government had also built schools (among them the Escuela Carlos Zapata Vela, now called Escuela Abraham Lincoln, still standing) and a market where a state-owned store sold produce at subsidized prices. The Ministry of Health ran pest control services, conducted sanitary surveys, and provided medical care and sanitary and maternity training for children and mothers.[98] Starting in 1956, it also sponsored a community center that provided daily meals and courses on "domestic economy," "beauty culture," baking, and decoration.[99]

By the time Jiménez y Castilla surveyed the neighborhood, the Instituto Nacional de la Vivienda (National Housing Institute, INV) had also built a small housing unit in Colonia Ramos Millán as part of its citywide program to improve colonias proletarias.[100] Many children born in the neighborhood in the early 1950s attended high school in the 1960s, evidence of the social mobility experienced by this cohort of Mexican baby boomers. And students from Colonia Ramos Millán's high school and (a few) college students—from the Instituto Politécnico Nacional—participated in the student movement of 1968. While the movement was mostly middle-class, many of its participants, especially high-school students, came from colonias proletarias. The participation of teenagers from colonias proletarias magnified and diversified the protests in terms of class and social geography.[101] Despite the descriptions of marginality, it is fair to say that Colonia Ramos Millán had been integrated into an uneven and deficient yet tangible and consequential welfare state. Its first residents settled in the neighborhood at a fortuitous time, during the Mexican Miracle, experiencing social mobility and an expansion of citizenship at rates that later generations would not enjoy.

Speaking in Monterrey in 1956, at Mexico's Seventh Sociological Congress, historian and lawyer Fernando Anaya Monroy lamented that Mexico City had developed in a "cancerous" manner. But there were reasons for hope: "colonias proletarias, housing projects, daycare centers, hospitals, and schools" were forging a new urban, "eloquent, and mestizo" nation.[102] Ramos Millán captures the perils and possibilities that urbanization posed during this decade. Historians continue to grapple with them. It is hard to say whether Colonia Ramos Millán was a representative colonia proletaria. As we have seen, it was something of a showcase. But the actors engaged in it, the battles fought there, and the government projects and social conflicts that characterized it were not atypical. Colonia Ramos Millán was the locus of agrarian reform, industrialization, architectural modernism, and a welfare state on the cheap. It was also the locus of a churning real-estate market, messy and antidemocratic broker politics, and geographical, social, and political inequalities. Colonias proletarias must be understood in this context of overlapping jurisdictions and ideological ambiguity.

Colonia Ramos Millán also captures the momentous 1950s transformation of Mexican society: the erosion of the radical promises of the revolution and the most important moment of economic growth in Mexican history; the authoritarian modernization of the city and the local political leaders that sustained it; the middle classes' fears of migrants and squatter settlements; and the forging of a national, urban, and popular culture in Mexico City's working-class neighborhoods. Colonia Ramos Millán was initially envisioned as a colonia proletaria with a cutting-edge Pani-designed housing project, but the reality was more inauspicious, more like the early photographs of the place. The division and allocation of land were conducted by characters like Conrado Mercado, Rafael Suárez Ocaña, and Salvador Flores, whose affiliation as government officials, neighborhood leaders, and party members was as blurry as the line between helping and exploiting residents.

During the 1950s, Ramos Millán was provided with schools, clinics, and markets by an administration bent on preventing the creation of more neighborhoods like it. Many of the families who continued to arrive were considered squatters for years. And so this colonia proletaria, a study in ironies and contradictions, developed at the interface between government oversight and bottom-up organizing, city codes and extralegal politics, progressive political languages and narrow and segmented interests. The process and end result were not pretty, just, or technically rational. But Ramos Millán somehow worked, at least for a while: as a real-estate market, as a way of reconciling conflicting and disparate political interests, and as an experiment in social welfare for those lucky enough to gain access to it. The experiment began to reach its limits in the 1950s, as evidenced by the semantic shift suffered by the word *proletarian*. It had become a pejorative term by the 1960s, closely linked to poverty and marginality. The term *colonias proletarias* shifted in meaning as well: from a viable rubric for urban growth in political, social, and urbanist terms to an urban pathology.

6

The Housing Problem in the Era of Modernization

Ernesto P. Uruchurtu's long tenure as regent (1952–1966) spanned most of the so-called Mexican Miracle: a period when the national economy expanded at a steadfast clip, steered by a strong developmentalist state.[1] Like the Porfirian capital half a century earlier, Mexico City was transformed by architectural landmarks and public works that projected—to Mexico and the world—social peace, modernization, and nationalism, culminating in the 1968 Olympic Games, the apotheosis of the postrevolutionary regime.[2] Buildings and public works included the new modernist campus of the Universidad Nacional (built in 1952), the Juárez housing project (also 1952), the Polytechnic University (1959), the Medical Center (1963), the Tlatelolco housing project, the National Museum of Anthropology [Museo Nacional de Antropología], the San Juan de Aragón housing project, the Anillo Periférico beltway (all inaugurated in 1964), and the subway system, whose first line opened in 1969.

Most of these works were spearheaded by the federal government. A few, like the subway, were opposed by Uruchurtu.[3] While these projects were not guided by a single urban vision—Uruchurtu's or anyone else's—together they transformed the scale, shape, and physiognomy of the city. While the Zócalo remained its belly button, the city was propelled outward, dislocating its Porfirian axes. The population doubled between 1950 and 1970, but growth was particularly rapid in the peripheral delegaciones, which quadrupled their population, surpassing the number of inhabitants of Mexico City proper. Growth was even more dramatic on the outskirts of the city, including in the State of Mexico. Ciudad Netzahualcóyotl, the largest informal settlement in the metropolitan area, reached a population of 1 million by 1970.

The euphoria evidenced by this frenzy of construction only added to the profound anxiety about housing, poverty, and unbridled growth shared by urban experts and the middle classes. Manifestations of modernist

Table 6.1. Population figures for Mexico City and the Federal District

Year	*Distrito Federal population*	*Mexico City population*	*Percentage of Mexico City in total population*	*Delegaciones population*	*Percentage of delegaciones in total population*
1930	1,229,068	1,029,068	83.69	200,508	16.31
1940	1,757,530	1,448,422	82.41	309,108	17.59
1950	3,050,442	2,234,795	73.26	815,647	26.74
1960	4,870,876	2,832,133	58.14	2,038,743	41.86
1970	6,874,165	2,902,969	42.22	3,937,499	57.28

Source: Ariel Rodríguez Kuri, "Ciudad oficial, 1930–1970," in *Historia política de la Ciudad de México*, 430.

development in the form of hospitals, universities, and housing projects made backwardness and misery even more shocking, hence the scandals elicited by filmmaker Luis Buñuel's *Los olvidados* (1950) and anthropologist Oscar Lewis's *The Children of Sánchez* (1961). By casting a spotlight on poverty among the city youth, both foreigners—a *gachupín* (Spaniard) and a gringo, to make matters worse—provoked a nationalist backlash that revealed the insecurities of Mexican elites about modernization and the achievements of the revolution.[4] It would be a platitude to describe 1950s Mexico City as a "city of contrasts" with "palaces and pigsties."[5] When was this not the case? But renderings of poverty and the "housing problem" in particular changed dramatically—more than the city itself—during the 1950s.

This chapter analyzes the research, categories, and policies that framed the "housing problem" between 1952 and 1964. The first section describes the term *herradura de tugurios* (horseshoe of slums), which during the Porfirian period described a chain of unsanitary dwellings around the city center. The term would continue to be used until the 1960s, decades after becoming outdated. The second section introduces a landmark housing study published in 1952, "The Housing Problem in Mexico City." This was the first time colonias proletarias were included in a survey of this kind. Surveyors viewed colonias proletarias as part of a housing typology, overplaying their informal character while dismissing their relationship with the government. The third section focuses on the opposition between inner-city slums (*tugurios*) and peripheral colonias proletarias, which were increasingly referred to as squatter settlements. This opposition was an intellectual construction that allowed planners and architects to pursue a two-pronged policy toward housing and urban development: "intensive/inward" and "extensive/outward."[6] Inner-city slums would be replaced with dense vertical housing projects through urban renewal. Colonias proletarias would be upgraded through targeted interventions or replaced with horizontal housing projects. This dual policy is exemplified by the housing projects described in the fourth section: Nonoalco-Tlatelolco, Mexico City's iconic urban renewal project, and San Juan de Aragón, a less iconic but no less important housing project on the eastern edge of the city.

In the 1950s housing policy went from a political question—a right claimed by settlers in the 1930s and 1940s and granted as a political favor—to a technical question, a pathology of underdevelopment amenable to expert solutions. The city became a laboratory where a new cadre of experts—planners, architects, anthropologists, economists, and others—sought to elucidate the perennial housing problem. Following a national shift associated with the presidency of Miguel Alemán (1946–1952), the ideologies of modernization and development acquired precedence over revolutionary promises of social justice. At the city level, Uruchurtu was bent on regulating growth and ending the creation of informal neighborhoods, which he partially achieved. The establishment of informal neighborhoods on private and public lands was curtailed, with the unintended consequence of an increase in settlements in communal and ejido agrarian lands and in the State of Mexico.[7]

Uruchurtu's antigrowth stance put him at odds with settlers and political actors clustered around the PRI. In the end, his vision was curbed by these groups, as evidenced by the political crisis that ended his tenure: the public scandal that followed the removal of a group of "squatters" south of the city. The 1970s saw the emergence of a reinvigorated settler movement and renewed government efforts to broker an alliance with them. By this time, opposition to the PRI had begun to make headway among various social and economic groups, while the State of Mexico became the main locus of informal urbanization in the metropolitan region.[8]

The "Horseshoe of Slums"

While Mexico City changed dramatically between the Porfirian era and 1950, the specters conjured by the "housing problem" barely changed at all, as evidenced by enduring representations of the slum in its imaginary geography. Starting at the turn of the twentieth century, the chain of working-class neighborhoods surrounding the northern and eastern parts of the city center became the most researched area in Mexico City, if not any city. Sanitary inspectors surveyed these neighborhoods beginning in the 1880s, describing them as filthy, barbaric, and ridden with criminals.[9] Criminologists, journalists, sociologists, and architects followed suit, surveying the area and connecting poverty to urban decay and unsanitary housing, which continued to be associated with fears of racial degeneracy.[10] In the 1930s the area began to be referred to as the "horseshoe of slums" (*herradura de tugurios*), a moniker exploited by planners and architects through the 1960s.

The term *slum* originated in nineteenth-century Britain to describe unsanitary and overcrowded industrial districts. It carried a heavy stigma but little analytical edge, as it was used for a wide variety of dwellings that public officials and middle-class observers—whose attitudes ranged from outright repulsion to paternalistic condescension—saw as lacking.[11] In translating *tugurios* as "slums," I am following US and Mexican social scientists who resorted to the word to make sense of processes they considered universal. Oscar Lewis, for instance, described the vecindad where he conducted his research as a "slum tenement." Lewis did not consider Mexico City a Latin American or Third World city but a universal one, whose "lower-class settlements" shared similarities with those in "London, Glasgow, Paris [and] Harlem."[12] Likewise, Mexican planners, architects, and social scientists read tugurios as familiar forms in the universal script of urbanization, a universality underscored by their occasional use of the English-term "slum."[13]

Beginning in 1933, the Banco Nacional Hipotecario y de Obras Públicas (National Bank of Mortgages and Public Works, BNHOP) led a study of housing conditions in the horseshoe of slums. The BNHOP began surveying housing in 1935, when its "Study of Mexico City" identified 100,000 overcrowded and insalubrious houses where half a million people lived. One of the participants in the survey was Adolfo Zamora, a lawyer who rose through the ranks of the organization, becoming its director in 1947. Like "slummers" around the world, Zamora succumbed to the "attraction of repulsion" of the underworld.[14] He wandered the streets of his adoptive city (he was born in Guatemala) for decades, "reading, full of emotion, the Braille code of its palaces and tugurios." Zamora proposed replacing these dwellings with sanitary housing in order to free residents from "tuberculosis, rickets, typhus, and all the vileness, depravity, and disease that are incubated in [these] pigsties."[15]

Zamora advocated for the construction of 50,000 dwellings and the destruction of 250 hectares of slums, an "active factor in the physical, moral, and industrial inferiority of the metropolitan population."[16] The BNHOP built 12,000 units between 1947 and 1952, a number dwarfed by the needs of the city but still a dramatic increase from the earlier period, when "no serious efforts to fix the problem of popular housing" were made.[17] As important as their quantity was the spectacular nature of these constructions. The Juárez and Miguel Alemán housing projects, designed by Mario Pani, were hailed as modernist landmarks, widely publicized in newspapers and journals, and remain icons of the Mexican Miracle.[18]

Amid this optimism, President Miguel Alemán convened a national conference on popular housing. Borrowing the bellicose rhetoric adopted by planners worldwide, Adolfo Zamora declared at the conference inauguration in 1950 that the "War against the Slum" had begun.[19] If the war started in 1950, preparations had begun much earlier. In addition to participating in the 1935 "Study of Mexico City," Zamora collaborated on a second survey in 1947. Led by architect Félix Sánchez, the "Investigation of the Housing Problem in Mexico City" continued to view the problem essentially as a matter of central *vecindades* and *tugurios*, terms often used interchangeably.[20] While *vecindad* designated a group of working-class homes around a courtyard, *tugurio* referred to a larger area of the city, usually more than a few blocks. This reveals a change in scale, a move from architectural to urban planning solutions to the housing problem.

In a remarkable omission, colonias proletarias were not included in the housing surveys of 1935 and 1947: they were off the map. The hypervisibility of the slums diverted the experts' gaze from the city margins. They were focused on the center.[21] The findings of the 1947 "Investigation of Mexico City" were represented in a series of plates that integrated maps, charts, and photographs of urban poverty. These images reproduce a familiar visual language used to portray conditions in slums across the world. Photographs featured children playing amid the rubble and garbage that plagued overcrowded vecindades. Many of these photographs, often shot from rooftops, provide the viewer with a sense of intimacy, fulfilling the voyeuristic urge of the middle classes. Depictions of urban poverty were juxtaposed with maps and blueprints that dated back to the turn of the century. Strikingly, the majority of these maps only included the area within the official boundaries of Mexico City, failing to display its peripheral delegaciones, where most colonias proletarias were located. That is where a quarter of the city population lived by 1950 and more than half by 1970.

Neither were colonias proletarias included in the studies conducted by US sociologist Norman Hayner in the 1940s. In a 1945 article, Hayner located Mexico City's slums north, east, and south of the city center, following Zamora's mapping of poverty.[22] Colonias proletarias were absent from his analysis, a blind spot shared by the public officials who guided him through the Mexican underworld.[23] Hayner did make passing references to colonias proletarias in *New Patterns in Old Mexico* (1966), which described them as neighborhoods "peripheral to established communities, initiated by so-called 'parachutists,' squatters who just 'fall' into these open spaces."[24] Tugurios were clearly marked. But few colonias proletarias were featured on the map included in Hayner's book, a remarkable omission given that by then they were the most widespread housing option for the working class.

Even more astonishingly, given the later publication date, colonias proletarias were absent from the map in an abridged version of Hayner's article, published in Spanish in 1964 in the *Revista Mexicana de Sociología*, Mexico's flagship sociological journal.[25] The weight of the city-center slums in representations of urban poverty is not visible only on maps. Oscar Lewis's *The Children of Sánchez*, published in 1961, was set in the horseshoe of slums, whose stigmatization had been cemented by decades of writings but whose demographic weight was clearly decreasing by that time. Lewis was aware of the growth of colonias proletarias and mentioned them in his book, but it was the barrio of Tepito that captured his attention.

In conclusion, the horseshoe of slums remained the most widespread representation of poverty and subpar housing until the early 1950s, years after its relative demographic weight had plummeted. In 1955 surveyors calculated that only 15 percent of the city's population lived in tugurios. At the same time, almost half of the population (46 percent) lived in colonias proletarias, the housing form rendered invisible in housing surveys from the 1940s.[26] It would seem natural to posit a relationship between invisibility and powerlessness. But the invisibility of colonias proletarias did not make them politically irrelevant—far from it. As I have argued, colonias proletarias enjoyed the most political leverage in the 1940s. In any case, the gulf between the imaginary geography of housing and the city that was taking shape in the late 1940s could not have been wider. The fears and fascination evoked by the slums for decades left little attention to be directed elsewhere.

The "Housing Problem" in 1952

Things began to change in 1952 when colonias proletarias were included as a category in the BNHOP's landmark survey: "The Housing Problem in Mexico City."[27] The seven-month research project was based on the work of an army of surveyors who distributed questionnaires, conducted interviews, and analyzed blueprints, cadastral maps, and aerial photographs.[28] Two goals animated the endeavor: providing a diagnosis of the housing problem and developing a plan to fix it. The survey, unsurprisingly, did not resolve the housing problem but did successfully reframe it. The survey categories became a fixture for decades.

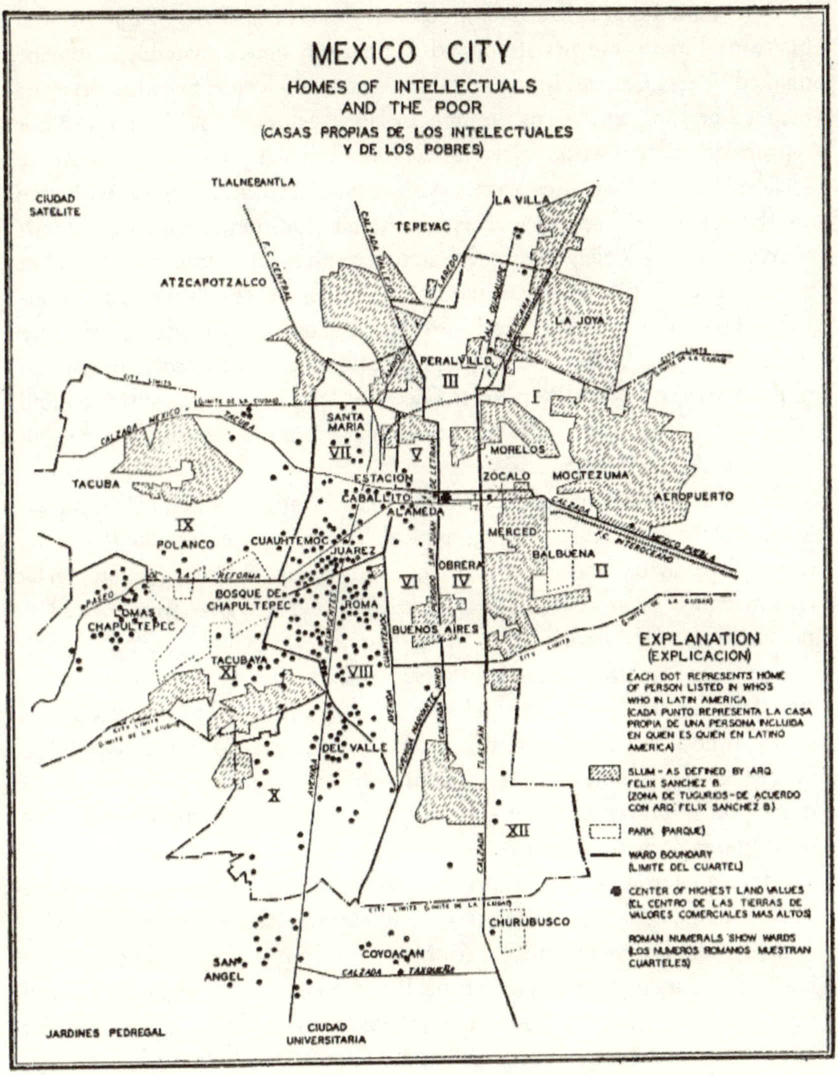

Figure 6.1. "Mexico City: Homes of Intellectuals and the Poor." *Revista Mexicana de Sociología* 26 (1964). Reprinted in 1964, this map reproduced the social geography of the city circa 1935–1940. The city is still divided into cuarteles, an increasingly anachronistic division that would be abandoned entirely in 1970. The slums are depicted in gray, but dozens of colonias proletarias farther east and north are quite literally left out of the picture. The "intellectuals" were listed in *Who's Who in Latin America*, a publication that included architects, artists, authors, and "public men" such as Carlos Contreras, Gerardo Murillo "Dr. Atl," Alberto Pani, and Jesús Galindo y Villa.

Several methodological assumptions distorted the analysis of Zamora and his team. First, surveyors attempted to freeze in time a dynamic landscape marked by regional and intra-urban movements of people. Second, surveyors mapped housing conditions throughout large sectors of the city but did not capture differences within city blocks. This approach produced a city where social class and land uses were clearly demarcated and aligned with one another. Finally, the survey analyzed the density, location, and physical conditions of colonias proletarias, understanding them as an architectural form but not as a legal, administrative, and political unit. Surveyors displayed an astonishing ignorance of the political history of the city. They made no reference to the Oficina de Colonias or the expropriations that gave rise to the colonias proletarias. The BNHOP erased the decades-long history of politicking and state sponsorship, understanding the colonias proletarias instead as the result of a post-1940 migratory crisis.

Surveyors considered the differences between tugurios and colonias proletarias to be historical and geographical. Tugurios were described as overcrowded, decaying, and unhygienic remnants of the old city, geographically circumscribed to its center. In contrast, colonias proletarias were viewed as the outcome of industrialization and a migratory crisis that went back ten to twelve years—an urban form akin to squatter or "parachutists" settlements.[29] Based on this assessment, later scholars wrongly continued to view the 1940s as the time when Mexico City's informal city exploded.[30] The opposition between tugurios and colonias proletarias blurred the complex processes of decay and improvement that different generations of neighborhoods were undergoing. Surveyors described colonias proletarias as unplanned neighborhoods created from scratch and lacking municipal services but did not realize that numerous colonias proletarias eventually received water, drainage systems, and public amenities and became integrated into the city. Others deteriorated, becoming tugurios over time. But Zamora and his team made a still photograph rather than a film, leading them to underestimate the progressive nature of colonias proletarias as well as their possible resemblance to tugurios.

Following the rigid tenets of the Congrès Internationaux d'Architecture Moderne, the survey divided Mexico City according to four functions: housing, work, social services, and circulation. At least since the 1930s, planners embraced zoning categories both to describe the city and to make plans for it. By accepting this understanding of space and social function, surveyors set an implicit benchmark according to which social classes, housing forms, and clearly delimitated neighborhoods aligned with each other. Porous boundaries between social classes and housing forms abounded, which was seen as a problem. The survey disapprovingly noted that "small peddlers, bums, prostitutes, beggars, and [other] lumpen sectors were intermingled with industrial workers and the lower petite bourgeoisie."[31] Housing officials were eager to format complex urban configurations under such headings as "industrial zones" and "low-income housing."[32]

This spatial homogeneity did not exist in a city where multiple uses and housing forms coexisted in a single block. According to surveyors, this coexistence had been produced by the recent transformations of the city, which had not reached the "rigid forms" of more advanced metropoles. Because "different residential areas did not have a single housing form," surveyors categorized city blocks as "homogenous" based on the predominant housing form.[33] This decision was the result of the research tools at the disposal of surveyors (sample surveys and questionnaires distributed by a small team) as well as the shortcomings they faced, such as the lack of a complete cadastral plan of the city. But the decision to map the city as a mosaic of discrete and homogenous zones also reveals the influence of prescriptive models such as those diffused by the CIAM and the Chicago School of Sociology.

Finally, "The Housing Problem in Mexico City" analyzed colonias proletarias not as a political and administrative unit but rather as an architectural and urban form. They were, to adopt a classic definition, a pathological component of the *urbs* but not part of the postrevolutionary *civitas*. The term *colonia proletaria* always had a double meaning: administrative and morphological. By considering only the latter, surveyors told just half of the story. The survey made fleeting mention of the government's role in the establishment of colonias proletarias by referencing the "improper" grants of public land that gave rise to them. But it did not describe the sui generis urban code regulating them, the patronage networks buttressing them, and the official recognition that the city government awarded them.[34] In fact, the original program for the study did not distinguish between colonias proletarias and squatter settlements.[35] Colonias proletarias were thus rendered informal. This was not their most noticeable trait (which was their poor infrastructure), but it was so obvious that it barely merited mention. Rather than address the linkages between colonias proletarias and the Mexican political system, surveyors examined the neighborhoods' infrastructure, the material conditions of their houses, and their relationship with the larger city. Were colonias proletarias connected to the city center? Did they have access to schools and markets? What was their population density?[36] In asking such questions, the survey construed colonias proletarias as an urban pathology, not as constitutive of Mexico City's political and government structures. It turned them into a problem amenable to technical solutions, rather than one that could be solved through political negotiations.

Tugurios and Colonias Proletarias

Despite these inaccuracies, the categories of the 1952 survey continued to be used for decades by researchers and city officials to develop public policies: urban renewal projects in the city center, on the one hand, and of upgrading the peripheries through targeted interventions in colonias proletarias and the construction of horizontal housing projects, on the other: building cities "within" the city and "outside" of the city, as architect Mario Pani described these integrated approaches.[37] While colonias proletarias gained visibility in the 1950s, the specter of tugurios did not disappear. Both housing forms became mirror problems, a generative heuristic developed by planners, architects, sociologists, anthropologists, and social workers.

This binary crystallized a vast and shifting landscape. It became a powerful opposition that addressed larger questions about the relationship between society and urban forms. While tugurios were old, colonias proletarias were new. While tugurios were in or close to the city center, colonias proletarias were located in the peripheries. While residents of tugurios paid rent, inhabitants of colonias proletarias owned their own lots or were buying them through monthly payments. Tugurios were overcrowded and close to markets, schools, and other urban facilities. Colonias proletarias were sparsely populated, unpaved, and unconnected to the water and drainage network. While overcrowded tugurios bred incest, crime, and corruption, residents of colonias proletarias suffered from social anomie because they lacked communal spaces. Unsurprisingly, these stark oppositions would inspire different policies for the two spaces.

We owe the best descriptions of tugurios to Oscar Lewis.[38] Both his work and its reception reveal key features about these spaces and their stigmatization. Lewis conducted fieldwork throughout the city during the 1950s, from the wealthy Lomas de Chapultepec to the middle-class Juárez housing project. However, the bulk of his research was conducted in the horseshoe of slums, specifically in Colonia Morelos and the barrio of Tepito (both neighborhoods are side by side), which Lewis documented in unparalleled detail. In March 1960 a team of Lewis's students conducted a thorough census of the area. Surveying the neighborhood block-by-block, students registered "building types," "uses," and "locations" in the most systematic descriptions of 1950s Mexico City available: a universe of shops, workshops, offices, clinics, inns, small restaurants, *pulquerías*, and, of course, vecindades in all shapes and sizes. One can almost imagine that Jane Jacobs, whose book *The Death and Life of Great American Cities* was published in the same year as Lewis's

The Children of Sánchez (both edited by Random House's Jason Epstein), would have appreciated the place.[39]

Lewis was struck by a richness amid the poverty, what sociologists might later call social capital. This perspective, evident in Lewis's archive but not always foregrounded in his published work, is all the more noticeable because it contradicts his infamous "culture of poverty" thesis: that the urban poor were enmeshed in a cycle of poverty from which they could not escape.[40] While Lewis rose to prominence in the United States as the maligned author of this thesis, many readers in Mexico insightfully reinterpreted his work as evidence of the positive features of neighborhoods like Colonia Morelos and Tepito. Carlos Monsiváis, for instance, described Tepito as a place where solidarity and misery coexisted.[41] The layers of history and social relationships of the barrio contrasted with the "anonymous" and "impersonal" "megalopolis" emerging in the postwar period, exemplified by residents of housing projects who barely spoke with each other, according to Lewis.[42] Writing in the 1970s, sociologist Susan Eckstein similarly portrayed the area around Tepito in a not altogether negative light. Bustling with activity, its "buildings, streets, small shops, and local markets [were] filled with people selling a wide array of goods to customers from diverse parts of the city." Eckstein characterized this "inner-city slum" as a stable community with traditions, local heroes, and "a core of residents who were born and raised locally" and did "not wish to leave."[43]

To find evidence of the "social capital" of Mexico City's working-class neighborhoods is to read Lewis's archive against the grain. But many readers focused on the poverty and social ills plaguing the neighborhoods he described as well as the difference between the culture of their residents and the culture of the middle classes. In the 1950s, when Lewis conducted his research, the Instituto Nacional de la Vivienda commissioned social workers to survey 750 blocks according to "building conditions, land use, industrial or commercial record number, number of people employed in the locale, and housing type."[44]

Established in 1954, the INV continued the research conducted by the BNHOP in the previous decade, often with the same personnel (architect Félix Sánchez was the key figure representing the continuity between the two institutions). Negative descriptions of tugurios dominate the surveys conducted by INV officials, whose deeply pessimistic interpretation left no room for ambivalence. INV officials deplored the area's "tremendous promiscuity": the mix of residential, commercial, and industrial uses made it a prime target for urban renewal.[45] The conclusions of the research team were depressing:

the widespread existence of tugurios "warranted a radical policy of elimination and replacement by new housing."[46] At times, the reports from the INV seem to anticipate Lewis's "culture of poverty" thesis. A section devoted to La Merced, the central market area, depicted its typical residents, who "do not lead a hygienic life [and] . . . are dominated by their instincts." INV officials described the "typical Merced man":

> Possesses few emotions and inhabits a fantasy world. Prone to depression. Holds a trade by routine, without deriving pleasure from it. He is intellectually and economically disordered, because he does not pursue a goal and does not wish to improve himself; because his social role is practically nonexistent. He is irresponsible in his duties, neglecting himself and his family. Lacks moral principles and spiritually displays little propensity for idealism, fewer artistic tendencies, and almost no scientific ideas . . . he is constantly at risk of falling prey to demagogues, shopkeepers, leaders, etc.[47]

In 1965 anthropologist Enrique Valencia published a study of the area, which he described as Mexico's first "urban sociology." Using sociologist Ernest Burgess's concentric zone model, Valencia called La Merced a "transition zone" marked by its proximity to the city center, the degeneration of its urban fabric, and its migrant population.[48] Valencia was also influenced by Lewis and the studies conducted by the BNHOP and the INV, which he used profusely. His study is extraordinarily rich, combining analyses of migration, the economy, and the colonial architecture of the area, which he was determined to preserve. At the same time, Valencia identified the same pathologies that Lewis and others noted: delinquency, vagrancy, overcrowding, poverty, and vice. Echoing INV officials, he recommended a surgical urban regeneration that protected historical monuments and relocated residents into neighborhoods with better conditions. By the 1960s, urban renewal had become *the* solution to the problem of the tugurio.

An INV proposal to bring Robert Moses, "head of New York's urban renewal plan," to Mexico City as an advisor exemplifies the growing influence of this model.[49] Discussed in the late 1950s, at the peak of Moses's influence, this idea was not surprising.[50] New York, after all, had played a prominent role as a policy model for Mexico and other cities, from Carlos Contreras's stint in the city in the 1920s to the invitation extended to Rudolph Giuliani as an advisor in the fight against crime in the early 2000s.[51] But the list of INV officials who penned the proposal is intriguing. It includes architect David Cymet Lerer, the foremost expert on colonias proletarias; Teodoro González de León, who would later rise to prominence as the architect of El Colegio de

México; and, most surprisingly, the anthropologist Guillermo Bonfil Batalla. In the 1970s Bonfil Batalla rejected *indigenismo*, the state-led developmentalist project to uplift and assimilate Mexico's Indigenous population.[52] He argued for the existence of a Mexican civilization with Indigenous roots subjugated by a "foreign" Western culture. A small section of the book reinterpreted Mexico City's vecindades as an expression of communal solidarity, in stark contrast to the housing projects built in the 1950s and 1960s. Ironically, many of these projects were inspired by communitarian ideals and possessed communal spaces like nurseries and sports facilities. As explained in previous chapters, they were sometimes criticized by proletarian families as "Soviet-inspired" solutions to the housing problem. Nonetheless, apartments in housing projects were designed for individual families, upholding the family as the social unit par excellence. In the end, Moses did not visit Mexico, so perhaps the invitation is little more than an archival curiosity.[53] Yet the coalescence of this varied group of intellectuals captures a fascination with urban renewal as the solution to Mexico City's housing problem, a solution that blended architecture and planning, anthropology and sociology, all united in faith in the state and science as means to uplift society.

While the INV commissioned one research team to study tugurios, another focused on colonias proletarias, described as "the peripheral cordon of the city . . . improvised settlements built on large empty lots with low real-estate values," poor planning, and inadequate urban services, "disarticulated from the functional organism of the city."[54] Two young architects from the Instituto Politécnico Nacional (Polytechnic University, IPN), David Cymet Lerer and Guillermo Ortiz Flores, spearheaded the research. The IPN combined the practices of architecture and engineering, producing a pragmatic and politically progressive approach to the housing question. Founded by a group of radical architects in the 1930s mentioned in chapter 2—Juan O'Gorman, Juan Legarreta, and José Luis Cuevas, among others—it became a key institution that "promoted a strong concern with the problems of society." Reinaldo Pérez Rayón—a graduate of the IPN who designed its modernist campus in the late 1950s—explained that the school "democratized the career of architecture."[55] Pérez Rayón became director of the Master Plan Office in the 1950s, when he invited Cymet Lerer and Ortiz Flores to collaborate on solving the problem of colonias proletarias.

Cymet Lerer and Ortiz Flores published their findings in a 1955 study, *El problema de las colonias proletarias, Ciudad de México*. Both were influenced by planners like Carlos Lazo, who served as minister of public works during the presidency of Alemán and embodied the developmentalist ethos of the period. "The problem with Lazo," Reinaldo Pérez Rayón joked, "is that he is not planning the country but the universe."[56] Following Lazo's principles of integral planning, Cymet Lerer and Ortiz Flores approached the problem of colonias proletarias "from the general to the particular, from the nation to the region, and from the region to the city."[57] They began their study with an analysis of the subsoil, hydrology, and environment of the Valley of Mexico, followed by an exploration of the history, economy, infrastructure, and migration patterns driving the growth of the city.

Cymet Lerer and Ortiz Flores marshaled countless statistics, but their understanding of Mexico City followed a well-known metanarrative based on the history of North Atlantic metropoles and inspired by authors like Lewis Mumford. "Masses of peasants abandon the land and become workers in dark factories," they asserted, exaggerating the magnitude of the industrial economy. "A cancer has invaded the urban organism." The same metanarratives clouded their understanding of colonias proletarias, whose origins they traced back to the 1930s.[58] The authors made references to the sui generis governance of colonias proletarias but viewed these neighborhoods as the product of a recent migratory crisis, clearly visible after 1940, rather than as the outcome of a long history of claims-making that went back to the revolutionary years.

Relying on data from the Oficina de Colonias, Cymet Lerer and Ortiz Flores counted 279 colonias proletarias, in which a quarter of the population of Mexico City lived (736,035).[59] Poor infrastructure was their most urgent problem: 85 percent of colonias proletarias lacked paved streets; 57 percent had no schools; 72 percent did not have a market; 80 percent lacked green areas; 45 percent did not have a sewage system; and 35 percent had no water. They suffered a dearth of communal spaces and insufficient integration with the city. Cymet Lerer and Ortiz Flores presented colonias proletarias as sparsely populated. Their descriptions were rich in images associated with the countryside: wild dogs, pigsties, dusty streets. In a later work Ortiz Flores lamented that the "landscape" was "devoid of water and trees, resembling a desert."[60]

Cymet Lerer and Ortiz Flores joined the INV after graduation and led a research team.[61] They concluded that colonias proletarias lacked not only municipal services but also "work centers, markets, schools, churches, parks, community centers, and an adequate street system: the facilities necessary for the enjoyment of 'a normal life.'"[62] Ironically, they found colonias proletarias to be deficient in community, precisely what tugurios, for better or worse, already had.[63] "Creating spaces where communal life can take place is key for regenerating colonias proletarias," another INV report stated. The question of community was often posed numerically, as a matter of scale.

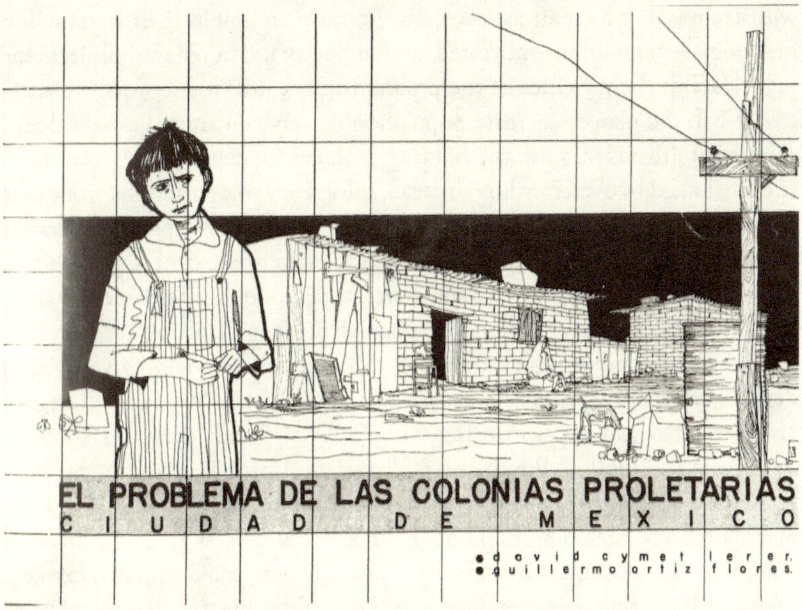

Figure 6.2. Title page of David Cymet Lerer and Guillermo Ortiz Flores's *El problema de las colonias proletarias, Ciudad de México.*

The INV calculated that 3,000 residents constituted a neighborhood unit, whose communal organs should include a residential zone, a commercial zone for daily shopping, a daycare center, and a playground. Four neighborhoods—or 12,000 residents—added up to the next "communal grouping," which required a market, an elementary school, a church, and artisanal shops. Finally, the largest grouping was a 60,000-resident barrio, to be provided with a larger market, a secondary school, a sports park, an industrial zone, and a wide avenue.[64]

The postwar period is often remembered for its utopian cities and housing projects—Brasilia, Islamabad, Tlatelolco—built by planners and architects full of hubris. But neighborhoods were also at the center of a different kind of utopian imagining, articulated around everyday life and facilities such as schools, community centers, and health clinics. Neighborhoods across the world became the "basic building block" of ideal cities, and colonias proletarias could be reframed as one version of it.[65]

In 1958 the INV proposed a four-point program for colonias proletarias: demolishing houses that were beyond repair, improving the condition of salvageable houses, increasing population density, and providing householders with technical and credit assistance to improve and build their homes. The first point—demolition—mirrored contemporary urban renewal projects for tugurios. But the novelties of the program represented a noteworthy transition. First, the plan to increase population density constituted a radical and counterintuitive idea, since the housing problem for decades had been inextricably linked to overcrowding. Instead, the agency recognized the work that residents had invested in colonias proletarias, which it viewed as a foundation for further improvements. The INV sought to establish a partnership with residents of colonias proletarias to build structurally sound, affordable houses.[66] To this end, it distributed building manuals with information on materials and construction techniques, designed to foster collaboration between residents, architects, engineers, and social workers.[67] Inspired by these ideas, the government began experimenting with "self-help" and "sites and services" projects in the 1960s.[68] The INV established an "integral improvement" program for Colonia Agrícola Oriental, developed as a "possible model" for other neighborhoods, including building a thousand houses as well as providing guidance and subsidized materials so that residents could improve existing homes.[69] These actions represented a departure from the decade-long policies of ever more stringent building codes that established "artificially high [housing] standards."[70]

In 1965 US planner Bernard J. Frieden described colonias proletarias as "the most significant [solution] to the housing problem of Mexico City."[71] Unthinkable a decade earlier, this assessment dovetailed with a tectonic intellectual shift summarized by anthropologist William Mangin: the proposition that squatter settlements were not a problem but rather a solution to the housing question in Latin America. Mangin conducted his fieldwork in the *barriadas* (shantytowns) of Lima, sometimes in collaboration with British architect John F. C. Turner, who famously praised the advantages of self-construction and the power of communities to collaborate in building their homes and neighborhoods.[72] By the 1960s, Mexican colonias proletarias were understood as part of a larger family of Latin American squatter settlements that included, in Mangin's analysis, "*barriadas brujas* in Panama, *ranchos* in Venezuela, *barriadas* in Peru, *callampas* in Chile, *cantegriles* in Uruguay, *favelas* in Brazil and, in other places, marginal areas, clandestine urbanizations, *barrios* of invasion, parachutists, phantom towns, etc."[73] It did not matter that colonias proletarias rarely originated from squatter invasions and had been sanctioned or actively supported by the government. By the 1960s, they had become the Mexican version of Latin America's "slums of hope."[74]

Scholars often viewed peripheral squatter settlements as an urban frontier: an empty space to be colonized through the toil of settlers. But just as the myth of the frontier in the United States erased Native American histories, the idea of the urban periphery as an empty space transformed by industrious settlers was blind to the political and juridical entanglements that had shaped these neighborhoods.[75] As we have seen, colonias proletarias experienced a remarkable degree of institutionalization during the 1940s. The de facto planning regime that oversaw them during their heyday in the 1940s was less the product of an expert understanding of the housing problem than the outcome of a political crucible in the postrevolutionary city.

In sum, tugurios and colonias proletarias became two sides of the same coin, complementary diagnoses for the housing problem of a city experiencing momentous change. The differences between the two housing forms appear, in retrospect, less significant than the fact that both were studied by a multidisciplinary cadre of experts confident of their capacity to fix the housing problem. However, these experts also shared blind spots. In particular, they were incapable of acknowledging the postrevolutionary political history of colonias proletarias; the relationship between settlers, brokers, and state officials; and the active government support for colonias proletarias in the 1940s.

Housing and Decentralization: Tlatelolco and San Juan de Aragón

The complementary goals of urban renewal in the city center and the improvement of colonias proletarias on the periphery became a widely accepted hermeneutic that translated into two modes of urban development: the renewal of slums and the "organized decentralization" of the city through housing projects.[76] Mario Pani had pushed for the construction of peripheral housing projects (unidades vecinales) as an alternative to overcrowded central "slums" since the 1940s. As the former were built, the theory went, the latter would slowly be emptied, allowing for the regeneration of the city center.[77] "Growth will never be prevented by mere regulations," Pani wrote. "It can only be stopped by creating or furthering, outside of [the city], attractive work centers for the new immigrant population."[78] The integrated objectives of urban renewal in the center and densifying the periphery through "organized decentralization" were pursued by several actors—architects, city officials, and political brokers—in the 1950s and 1960s. These groups were not always coordinated, but their actions were guided by a unified urban vision.

Renderings of the inner city as a surrounded by horseshoe of slums led to several "bulldozer" urban renewal projects. Most were not completed, but urban renewal justified the razing of hundreds of city blocks, the displacement

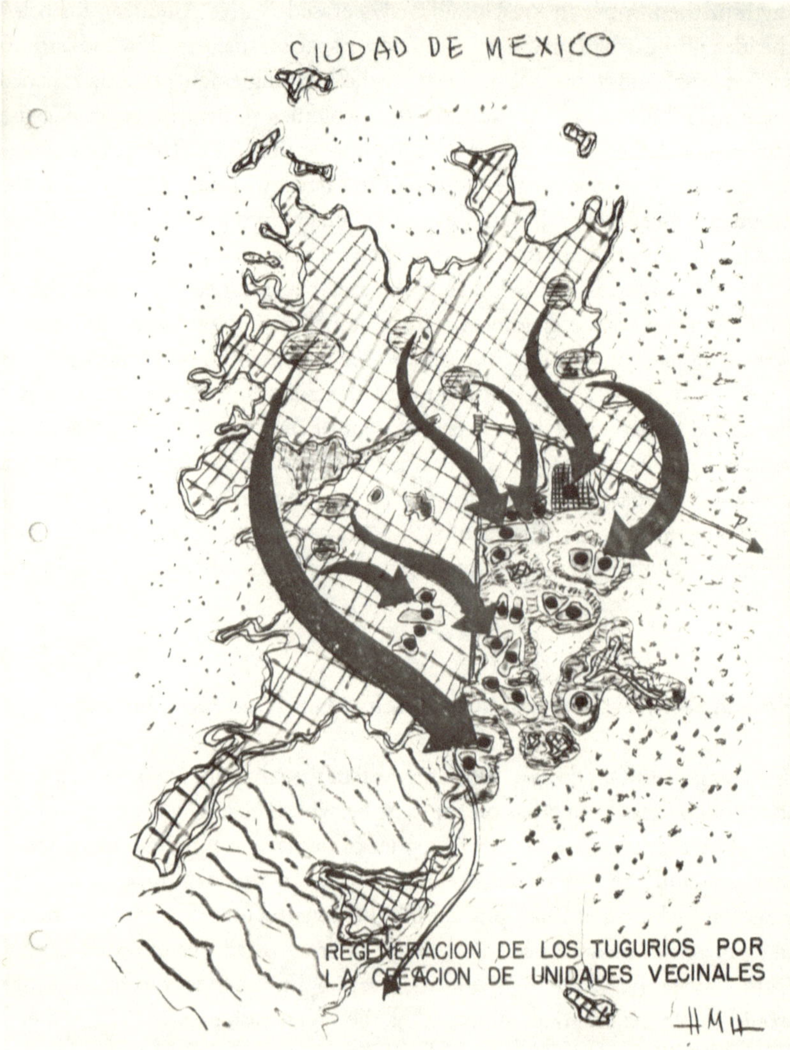

Figure 6.3. "Regeneración de los tugurios por la creación de unidades vecinales." AHCDMX, Obras Públicas, box 658, file 1. Undated, this sketch by Mario Pani reveals his vision of building housing projects in the southeast to house displaced residents from slum areas.

of thousands of families, and the construction of a handful of housing projects.[79] The Nonoalco-Tlatelolco complex (henceforth Tlatelolco) was the most ambitious and emblematic. Tlatelolco covers 950,000 square meters in a rectangular plot 1.5 kilometers north of the city center: the east-west axis is roughly 2 kilometers long; the south-north one is around 500 meters. The complex is situated in what used to be the northern end of the horseshoe of slums: a federally owned industrial zone covered by tenements and crossed by railroad tracks, roads, and overpasses.

Inaugurated in 1964 by President Adolfo López Mateos (1958–1964), Tlatelolco was composed of 102 buildings where 70,000 to 80,000 residents would live in 11,916 apartments. The complex also included 45 "social service buildings," among them daycare centers (13); elementary (9), secondary (2), and high schools (1); and social clubs, clinics, museums, movie theaters, and other amenities. As in Pani's earlier housing projects, the construction of multistory apartment buildings—with heights ranging from four to twenty-two floors—created open spaces for gardens, sports facilities, and public plazas, including the Plaza of the Three Cultures, the heart of the project and a historical landmark in its own right. The plaza integrated modernist residential towers with a sixteenth-century convent and the pre-Columbian ruins of Tlatelolco. Like the contemporary plans for colonias proletarias mentioned earlier, the project was divided into three superblocks—human-scale barrios where residents could conduct their daily affairs. The scale was massive. If Tlatelolco had been a city at the time of its inauguration, it would rank 23rd in Mexico, with a population size similar to Toluca's.[80]

Though it would become indelibly associated with the student massacre of October 2, 1968, just a few years after its inauguration, Tlatelolco originally symbolized a muscular developmentalist state and the postwar economic boom. "The cobweb of railroad tracks that strangled the city for decades," wrote chronicler Arturo Sotomayor in 1968, "is no longer a perfidious web but geometry pointing us to the future."[81] The ideals of modernism and modernization were communicated by Pani and his team through architectural gestures and mass media like photographs, film, and the printed word. Multiple issues of *Arquitectura/México*, the journal Pani edited, featured Tlatelolco, from its early plans to its apotheotic inauguration.[82] In the years preceding the construction, the journal editors published blueprints, zoning studies, and housing surveys to persuade readers of the dire housing conditions in the area. Editors marshaled economic statistics to convince investors of the financial soundness of the project, arguing that the regeneration of the urban fabric would raise real-estate values. This propaganda effort culminated in a lavish double issue of *Arquitectura/México* published in 1966. The black-and-white photographs by Armando Salas Portugal that illustrated the feature reproduced the leitmotif put forward by Pani and others for more than a decade: the contrast between overcrowded, insalubrious, and disorderly slums and the rational, modern, and luminous housing complexes.[83]

This propaganda effort was strengthened because the area had been portrayed as a slum for over half a century. The infamous reputation of Nonoalco as the underbelly of modernization was cemented by decades of literary, photographic, and film representations. Porfirian sanitary officials depicted San Miguel Nonoalco and Atlampa as "barbaric" barrios.[84] Decades later, Fernando del Paso described the area in detail in his modernist novel *José Trigo*, published in 1966 but written a few years earlier, before the construction of Tlatelolco (the novel even included a neighborhood map). The housing complex would stand in a "crucial spot," a journalist reported in 1960, that "has been, since its beginnings, a reflection of misery and insalubrity blocking the circulation of arteries vital to the life of the metropolis."[85] Another journalist mentioned Nonoalco as a site that acquired "global fame" through Oscar Lewis's *Five Families* (1959, published in Mexico in 1961 as *Antropología de la pobreza*).[86] The publishing of *The Children of Sánchez* in Mexico in 1964 would elicit a scandal, prompting the Sociedad Mexicana de Geografía y Estadística to accuse Lewis and his publisher of the crime of "social dissolution" and defamation of the Mexican people.[87] The work of Lewis and other chroniclers of urban poverty, however, was also used to justify the construction of Tlatelolco.

A closer look at Pani's Tlatelolco master plan reveals how state renderings distorted the lived experience of residents. An early version targeted a triangular block in the northwest section of the project for demolition: Colonia Ampliación Guerrero was described as "wreckable."[88] According to its residents, however, it was a respectable neighborhood in the process of improvement. Residents of Ampliación Guerrero had a long history of politicking and negotiating with city authorities. After receiving eviction notices in the spring of 1960, they organized a Junta de Defensa de Colonos (Settler Defense Board) to fight against removal from their homes.[89] In a series of letters to local and federal authorities, residents explained that they settled in the neighborhood in 1920, when they began a slow but steady process of urban improvement.[90] The leader of the junta, Pedro Martínez Serrano (a man with a long history of engagement with city authorities), claimed that Colonia Ampliación Guerrero was fully equipped with urban services and that its residents held property titles: they were not squatting on federal land as reported in the newspapers. Residents rejected descriptions of their homes as "barracks and pigsties," offering as evidence photographs of their homes and their neighborhood.[91] The photographs show one-story and two-story houses

Figure 6.4. "Expediente de la Colonia Ampliación Guerrero (1 imagen)." AHCDMX, Obras Públicas, box 658, file 1. This photograph was included in a petition sent by the residents of Colonia Ampliación Guerrero to Ernesto Uruchurtu and President Adolfo López Mateos in 1960.

in lively colors. The neighborhood is fully upgraded, with lampposts, pavement, sidewalks, and small shops.

Press reports from March 1960 stated that the "squatters who had invaded federal lands were in the process of being removed by city authorities."[92] But the press also spoke sympathetically of the plight of families who settled "over forty years ago and . . . are now forced to sell the homes that they built after years of sacrifices."[93] Residents also counted on the support of Congressman Manuel Moreno Cárdenas, who joined their rallies and assisted in their fight against the BNHOP. Their mobilization was successful: the final project did not include Colonia Ampliación Guerrero, which remains standing across

Figure 6.5. "Expediente Manuel Moreno Cárdenas (1 imagen)." AHCDMX, Obras Públicas, box 658, file 1. This photograph of the barrio of Atlampa was sent by deputy Manuel Moreno Cárdenas to regent Ernesto Uruchurtu in December 1960.

from Tlatelolco, divided from the massive complex by Manuel González Avenue.

Tlatelolco laid bare the webs of political patronage in which residents lived. Public works that were part of the grand project, such as the expansion of Reforma and San Juan de Letrán (the main thoroughfares that ran through Tlatelolco), displaced thousands of residents from Colonia Guerrero and Colonia Panamericana, neighborhoods that were part of the horseshoe of slums.[94] According to city planners, these and other neighborhoods were in a state of "anarchy and abandonment" (a description that must be taken with a grain of salt in light of the assessment of Ampliación Guerrero).[95] Furthermore, they were plagued by property conflicts that rendered removals and compensations extremely fraught. The transfer of displaced residents was negotiated by city authorities, representatives, and local brokers. Moreno Cárdenas, for example, who had defended the claims of the Junta de Defensa de Colonos to remain in Colonia Ampliación Guerrero, also negotiated the transfer of residents from the barrio of Atlampa to Santa Cruz Meyehualco, a housing project built by the city government in Iztapalapa in 1963.[96]

Conditions in these neighborhoods, located on the margins of railroad tracks, were dire compared to those in Colonia Ampliación Guerrero.

Pani envisioned "making a city within the city" and "outside of the city" as complementary projects: urban renewal in the center and the construction of housing units on the periphery.[97] Both goals were also premised on and further deepened class inequalities in the city: working-class residents from Nonoalco and Atlampa were displaced from the area that would house middle-class families in the dazzling project of Tlatelolco. Pani and his colleagues were largely unaware of the politicking entailed by these population transfers. But it is worth noting that they were relying on the work of political actors like Moreno Cárdenas. As described in the previous chapter, the Coalición de Colonos was also active in Atlampa during the 1950s, negotiating the resettlement of residents to colonias proletarias like Gabriel Ramos Millán (the site for Pani's unexecuted Unidad de Vivienda Tlacotal y Bramadero).

Families displaced from the horseshoe of slums were not only resettled to colonias proletarias like Gabriel Ramos Millán and Agrícola Oriental. Thousands were given spots in Santa Cruz Mayehualco (inaugurated in 1963) and San Juan de Aragón (inaugurated in 1964), two housing projects built around the same time as Tlatelolco. Santa Cruz Mayehualco consisted of 3,000 houses. Around 300 were sold to ragpickers who had been living in a garbage dump adjacent to the development;[98] the rest were distributed among thousands of families displaced by public works in the city center.[99] A humble project, Santa Cruz Mayehualco was barely referenced in contemporary architectural journals, except to mention its residents, the ragpickers of the nearby dump.[100]

San Juan de Aragón was a much more ambitious undertaking as well as a study in contrasts with Tlatelolco.[101] The two projects differed in terms of their design, location, and prospective residents. San Juan de Aragón included 16,558 units, making it larger than Tlatelolco. It was aimed at both middle-class and working-class residents, whereas Tlatelolco was designed with a privileged, salaried middle class in mind.[102] While Tlatelolco was central and highly visible, San Juan de Aragón was located on the outskirts of the city, on former ejido lands in the northeast and east, close to colonias proletarias and the beltway that the city inaugurated in 1964. Unlike the high-rises built by Pani, San Juan de Aragón consisted of one-story and two-story single-family houses.[103] Tlatelolco was a national showcase, designed by Pani but sponsored by federal ministries and bankrolled by national institutions like the BNHOP and the Instituto de Seguridad y Servicios Sociales de los Trabajadores del Estado (Institute of Social Security and Services for State Workers, ISSSTE). While San Juan de Aragón was partly funded by international capital, the project was spearheaded by Uruchurtu, who often locked horns with Pani.[104] Nonetheless, the projects can be viewed as complementary. Intensive development and extensive development were part of a singular urban vision that required relocating populations across the city.

San Juan de Aragón was designed by Enrique Cervantes Sánchez, commissioned by Uruchurtu to build single-family homes rather than high-rise apartments.[105] The project scaled up from a basic urban cell (*unidad plaza*), composed of 12 to 16 houses, to an intermediate grouping (*unidad calle*), composed of 60 to 100 houses, to a superblock where 2,500 to 5,000 residents would live and share a "kindergarten, school, commercial spaces, civic plaza, and leisure spaces for adults and children."[106] Superblocks included up to seven unidades vecinales, with a public zoo at the center. This was not a vertical but a horizontal utopia—a utopia of the neighborhood, to borrow historian Rosemary Wakeman's notion—and a much more pragmatic one.[107] The cost of San Juan de Aragón was half that of Tlatelolco, although the two projects housed a similar number of residents. The decision to build single-family homes rather than high-rises represented a departure from the modernist utopias of the period, espousing instead the ideals of middle-class domesticity centered around the single-family home.

The decision to build single-family houses with communal facilities reflected a developmentalist vision aimed at uplifting an uncultured population. San Juan de Aragón was built for both middle-class bureaucrats and displaced families of a lower socioeconomic status.[108] Since the project was designed for families with "low education and culture, it is convenient to isolate them in order to avoid the fights and troubles that a closer proximity could create," one architect stated, contradicting the communal ethos that supposedly inspired the place.[109] San Juan de Aragón housed families previously living in "the irregular settlement of the Cerro de Tepeyac" as well as the horseshoe of slums.[110] Authorities were eager to prevent the deterioration identified in earlier housing projects, attributed to residents' "cultural level."[111] In order to prevent families from altering their homes, contracts ordered that purchasers use their property for residential purposes and exclusively for themselves and their dependents. Contracts also stipulated that residents could not alter their homes, use them for the sale of alcohol or other illicit activities, or "raise animals prejudicial to hygiene and the maintenance of the property, such as pigs, asses, cows, rabbits, and others."[112] Housewives were prohibited from drying their laundry in their front yards. They protested against this restriction because many made a living as laundry workers.[113] On the flip side of these prohibitions were the social programs to uplift the residents of the projects (including medical assistance, literacy campaigns, special programs for women, and collective marriage ceremonies), which were also implemented in colonias proletarias.[114]

There are important differences among Tlatelolco, San Juan de Aragón, and the colonias proletarias I have described throughout this book (which also display important variations). But it is also worth noting the similarities between these housing forms and how they complemented each other. Tlatelolco and San Juan de Aragón were state projects, financed with national and international capital and designed by well-known architects working in coordination with a flurry of government agencies. In contrast, colonias proletarias were the outcome of the interplay between city officials, developers, and settlers, often working at the margins of the law. But both housing forms became part of a singular urban vision in the 1950s and 1960s.

The construction of housing projects (in the city center and its peripheries) and the upgrading of colonias proletarias were inspired by development, modernization, and urban decentralization, ideals pursued by planners, architects, and other urban experts. Accomplishing these goals required a combination of technical and political actions. On the one hand, a new cadre of experts surveyed the city with new methods (sample surveys, ethnographies) and categories (slums and colonias proletarias), leading them to devise urban policies and build housing projects. On the other, actions like the razing of a slum or the transfer of a group of squatters from the city center to a peripheral colonia proletaria or housing project entailed negotiations involving city officials, political brokers like representative Moreno Cárdenas, and neighborhood associations like the Coalición de Colonos or the Junta de Defensa de Colonos of Colonia Ampliación Guerrero.

The opposition between housing projects and colonias proletarias—like that between formal and informal urbanization—derives from entrenched scholarly binaries and popular perceptions. While housing projects like San Juan de Aragón have been mostly studied by historians of architecture, colonias proletarias have been analyzed by geographers, sociologists, and political scientists, who refer to them as modalities of informal housing or *urbanismo popular*. But the lines between the two housing forms, as I have argued throughout this book, are blurry and shifting.[115] Colonia Michoacana, for example, was designed by radical architect Juan Legarreta as an experimental state-sponsored utopia for workers. Parts of the project were never completed, but residents built their homes in blocks that were part of the original layout, and the neighborhood was registered as a colonia proletaria by the 1950s.[116] The colonia proletaria Gabriel Ramos Millán was originally envisioned as one of twenty-one housing complexes in the southeast of the city, according to Mario Pani's ambitious plan. Once the government purchased the land, however, the neighborhood was settled through the coordination of political brokers amid property conflicts. The first years in the housing complex of San Juan de Aragón were marked by legal conflicts and hardships similar to those in colonias proletarias. Property disputes were common, and residents had to negotiate with authorities for the provision of titles to secure their possession.[117] Residents requested permits to build wooden fences and improvise a marketplace, works that remained unfinished upon the inauguration of the complex.[118] Adopting a legal and political model more than a hundred years old, residents formed a Junta de Mejoras Materiales to work on neighborhood improvements, a development that the city authorities welcomed.

The housing policies analyzed in this chapter addressed a series of urban pathologies: unsanitary housing, an overextended city, decaying slums, sprawling peripheries, and a poor and uneducated population. As these anxieties of modernization reached a fever pitch in the 1950s, they became subsumed under the problem of informality. As Uruchurtu (and others) deployed planning laws to curb the establishment of informal neighborhoods, terms like *squatters* and *squatter settlements* were used to stigmatize (often unfairly) peoples and spaces deemed outside of the law, like the lawful residents of Colonia Ampliación Guerrero, whose neighborhood was labeled as a wreckable slum. The "problem of informality" gained prominence during the administration of Uruchurtu, as fantasies of modernization were haunted by the specters of migrant squatter settlements and explosive growth sensationalized and widely disseminated by the press. But the webs of patronage that entangled residents, members of Congress, the Oficina de Colonias, and organizations like the Coalición de Colonos continued to influence daily life in colonias proletarias.[119] This duality explains some of the contradictions of the period: the simultaneous upgrading of colonias and the regent's stern opposition to the establishment of new neighborhoods.

The technocratic sectors of the local and federal governments intent on controlling growth and the political actors that profited from supporting colonias proletarias reached a "détente" during Uruchurtu's thirteen-year administration.[120] But Uruchurtu's opposition to informal neighborhoods put him on a collision course with neighborhood associations and the party officials representing them. In September 1966 the DDF evicted 4,000 residents of Pedregal del Ajusco and Santa Úrsula, neighborhoods built on ejido lands south of the city, near the Aztec Stadium, one of the main venues for the 1968 Olympics and the 1970 World Cup. The subdivision of ejido lands was illegal, but developers and colonia leaders had sold lots in the area since the early 1950s.[121] The eviction followed an expropriation decree to build a road to the

Aztec Stadium but was also justified for safety reasons, with the government explaining that "squatters" were living in hazardous terrain, close to an explosives factory. On September 12, 1966, city workers and police forces evicted the residents and demolished around 400 houses amid pleas and protests.

Actions like these were common during the administration of the powerful iron regent, but their aftermath was far from typical. Several journalists reported on the eviction, and the coverage proved damning. It was reported that two children and a pregnant woman died in the operation. The outcry was loud: settlers, reporters, and politicians joined forces against the regent. Representatives from all parties in Congress condemned the razing and distanced themselves from Uruchurtu, who was forced to resign. The concatenation of events was so fast, the attack against Uruchurtu so seemingly coordinated, and the eviction so clumsily timed that Manuel Perló Cohen has plausibly suggested that the regent did not order the razing and that the political crisis was manufactured by his enemies.[122] Regardless, the conflict between Uruchurtu and political leaders supporting urban residents predated September 1966. The downfall of the regent is only comprehensible in the context of the opposition between Uruchurtu and the PRI over the issue of urban growth. This was just the latest iteration of a fight that went back to the 1920s, between city technocrats and political brokers, modernization and revolution.

Conclusion

The changes in Mexico City after 1964 defy an easy narrative. The scale of the city increased by orders of magnitude across nearly every indicator. Indeed, writing of "the city" blurs the reality of multiple cities subsumed under the urban sprawl of the capital. Despite the frenzied construction of high-rises along its most iconic avenues, most of the city remains "chata y cacariza" (flat and pockmarked), as architect Pedro Ramírez Vázquez once described it.[1] Today the megalopolis extends over 2,362 square kilometers, spread across sixteen *alcaldías* (formerly delegaciones) within Mexico City, fifty-nine municipalities in the State of Mexico, and one municipality in the State of Hidalgo. (In 2016 the Distrito Federal officially became known as the Ciudad de México.) The four central alcaldías—the area that made up the Porfirian city—cover 139 square kilometers, a mere one-twentieth of the metropolitan area.

The metropolitan area had 5 million inhabitants in 1960: 2.8 million in the central city, 2 million in the peripheral delegaciones, and approximately 300,000 in the neighboring State of Mexico. By 1980, it had 14.4 million inhabitants: 2.6 million in the central city, 6.2 million in the peripheral delegaciones, and 5.6 million in the State of Mexico. Today 1.8 million live in the central city, 7.4 million in the peripheral alcaldías, and 12.6 million in the States of Mexico and Hidalgo, adding up to 21.8 million.[2] The data can be endlessly dissected, but a clear pattern emerges. While the central city has lost population, growth in the State of Mexico has been relentless. Just as the peripheral delegaciones surpassed the population of Mexico City by 1970, the State of Mexico surpassed the Federal District by 2000.

The periphery has always been the site of the most frantic growth. In the 1920s and 1930s this included neighborhoods such as Colonia Ex-Hipódromo Peralvillo. In the 1940s and 1950s it expanded to places like

Gertrudis Sánchez and Gabriel Ramos Millán. Starting in the 1960s, the State of Mexico became the main site of informal urbanization, and is where most working-class residents continue to live. Every morning, millions of workers from the State of Mexico commute for hours to work as street vendors, janitors, and construction workers in Mexico City. "Would Mexico City survive for one day without the cheap labor of these *mexiquenses*?"[3]

Luis Echeverría won the presidency in 1970, amid mounting political trouble. The repression of the student movement on October 2, 1968—at the Plaza of the Three Cultures in Tlatelolco—followed a decade-long series of protests in the capital by physicians, teachers, and railroad workers (among others). On the housing front, the late 1960s saw renewed efforts by settlers to advance their interests in the aftermath of Uruchurtu's restrictive policies. In 1967 the Federación de Organizaciones Proletarias del Distrito Federal (Federation of Proletarian Organizations of the Federal District, FOPDF), which included 400 colonias and 3 million members, convened its first extraordinary congress. The FOPDF sought to unite settlers as a political bloc under the aegis of the CNOP.[4] Like previous organizations, the FOPDF petitioned the city and federal government to upgrade municipal services in colonias proletarias (increasingly referred to as colonias populares), to regularize land tenure in conflict-ridden neighborhoods, and to curb land invasions. In the eyes of contemporary observers, the PRI had become a powerful machine of co-optation and domination.[5]

Over the next two decades, however, the relationship between settlers and the PRI began to fray. A series of political crises focused on housing shook the capital and other cities in the 1970s. In 1969 residents of Ciudad Netzahualcóyotl in the State of Mexico organized a payment strike against developers who had defrauded them. Like their predecessors from earlier decades described in this book, developers had sold land that they did not own, failed to distribute the municipal services they promised, and resorted to violence to dispossess lot purchasers. Settlers created the Movimiento Restaurador de Colonos (Settlers' Restoration Movement, MRC) to fight back and demanded that the federal government expropriate the land, formalize its possession, and prosecute fraudulent developers.

Conflicts over property and municipal services exploded in Monterrey, Chihuahua, and Cuernavaca, among other cities. Thousands of settlers rejected collaborating with government authorities and embraced transnational leftist ideologies like Maoism, communism, and Liberation Theology. Many acted in collaboration with radical students, laypeople, and priests who believed that the Mexican bourgeois state was spiraling into its final crisis and that an urban revolution was imminent.[6] For all their differences, settlers asserted their independence from the Mexican state and rejected (to varying degrees) the legitimacy of the PRI.

In response to these challenges, Echeverría overhauled federal housing policy, prioritizing the construction of housing for formal workers and increasing "public intervention in low-income housing and land issues."[7] As part of a "democratic opening," Echeverría encouraged settlers to organize and make demands on his administration, partially reestablishing the alliance between the federal government, the PRI, and settlers that had been strained by Uruchurtu.[8] While many organizations rejected co-optation, as noted, others negotiated with the government. Echeverría led an ambitious program of land regularization in neighborhoods suffering from property conflicts. Previously conducted by the Oficina de Colonias, regularization was now in the hands of an efflorescence of national, local, and agrarian bureaucracies, often in competition with one another.[9]

The most consequential was the Comisión para la Regularización de la Tenencia de la Tierra (Commission for the Regularization of Land Tenure, CORETT), which regularized hundreds of thousands of lots in ejidos, which by the 1970s had become the most important site of informal urbanization. Regularizations entailed payment (by the homeowner who purchased ejido land) in exchange for a land title. This meant that purchasers paid twice for their lot: first to ejido authorities (a transaction that was outside the law) to purchase their lots and then to CORETT to regularize their possession. Agrarian authorities that sold the land illegally were not held responsible. The arrangement was a political success, in no small measure because it failed to prosecute ejido authorities, who continued to enjoy revolutionary legitimacy.[10] The president also brokered an agreement with residents of Ciudad Netzahualcóyotl. Echeverría deactivated the conflict by creating a fiduciary land trust to collect payments, distribute municipal services, and award land titles. The legal conflict was resolved through political negotiation, much to the dismay of settlers who expected criminal prosecution against fraudulent developers.[11] In light of the history examined in this book, it is not surprising that political pragmatism trumped the rule of law and developers were not held accountable.

As "informality" entered the global urban lingo in the 1970s, irregular urbanization rose to national prominence, coming to be viewed as Mexico City's "most urgent urban problem."[12] Indeed, scholars often consider this the decade when informality became a public crisis, with the previous decades having only hinted at what was to come.[13] As I have argued, though, anxieties over housing outside of the law, in the form of either unsanitary dwellings or anarchic urbanization, had been present since the turn of the twentieth century. Beginning in the 1950s and especially after 1970, however, the problem of informality was construed most notably as a problem of property.[14] In this context, regularization became "an *end in its own right*," as Peter Ward has argued, "a medium of negotiation and social control in so far as it constituted a cheap resource that could be granted and withheld by the authorities."[15] However, settlers continued to demand municipal services and other urban facilities, as they always did. Property titles were always sought as part and parcel of a broader integration into the city.[16]

Notwithstanding the stridency of the housing question during the Echeverría administration, both the perception of informality as a crisis and the regularization policies of the 1970s followed entrenched historical patterns: the state's bastard child has always ended up as a part of the family. Throughout the century, authorities remained torn between contradictory technical and political goals: regulating the modern city versus gaining legitimacy by fulfilling revolutionary housing promises. Informal housing remained at the center of a political battle between authorities, developers, and settlers. Land outside of the law never ceased to represent a profitable commodity as well as prized political capital, leveraged by brokers interfacing between settlers and the state.[17] Resolving property conflicts in informal neighborhoods continued to allow the government to gain legitimacy on the cheap by providing land titles and distributing municipal services in exchange for a fee. Finally, informal neighborhoods remained crucibles of citizenship for working-class residents, who became entangled with brokers and the Mexican political system as they asserted their right to housing.

The 1980s proved to be a momentous decade. Hundreds of settler organizations coalesced in the Movimiento Urbano Popular (Popular Urban Movement, MUP), a national federation that demanded housing and democratization while rejecting the authority of the PRI.[18] The MUP celebrated its first national congress in Monterrey in May 1980. The following year, forty associations from the Valley of Mexico—including both Mexico City and the State of Mexico—organized a regional branch, the Coordinadora Nacional del Movimiento Urbano Popular (National Coordinating Body of the Urban Popular Movement, CONAMUP). Most of its members came from settlements in the eastern and southern peripheries of the city, such as Netzahualcóyotl, Iztapalapa, and Tlalpan, but others were from central areas like Colonia Guerrero.[19]

This upsurge of autonomous organizing took place amid the multifaceted crisis of the 1980s.[20] The 1982 debt crisis and the austerity policies put in place in its aftermath undermined the legitimacy of the postrevolutionary political arrangement. The power of the PRI in the capital eroded as well, challenged by the growth of the MUP and other settler and tenant federations. In September 1985 a magnitude 8.1 earthquake struck the capital, killing thousands and leaving hundreds of thousands in the street. Most victims (*damnificados*) resided in central areas of the city, both in middle-class colonias such as Roma, Juárez, and the Tlatelolco housing project and in popular colonias like Morelos and Guerrero. City residents spontaneously organized, first to rescue victims from the wreckage and then to negotiate with the government the expropriation of damaged lots and the reconstruction of lost homes.[21] Many organizations ended up joining the leftist opposition parties that steadily increased their share of the vote during the 1980s and then coalesced around the Frente Democrático Nacional (National Democratic Front, FDN), the electoral coalition headed by Cuauhtémoc Cárdenas, who led a splinter group from the PRI in opposition to the party's neoliberal turn. The FDN carried the city vote in the 1988 national election and would have won the presidency had the government not committed massive electoral fraud.

The 1985 earthquake has been interpreted as the birth of Mexican "civil society," a heroic episode in a teleological "transition to democracy."[22] The history of the MUP is not as well known, even though some participants wrote accounts of their experience.[23] Countless members of the MUP and other settler and tenant organizations entered democratic politics and joined opposition parties in the 1980s and 1990s, including the left-wing Partido de la Revolución Democrática (Party of the Democratic Revolution, PRD), the party that succeeded the FDN and won the city government in 1997, in the first local election since the creation of the DDF in 1929.[24] The city—especially its eastern, working-class delegaciones—has remained a bastion of the Left, now represented by the Movimiento de Regeneración Nacional (Movement of National Regeneration, MORENA). The current mayor, Clara Brugada (elected in 2024), cut her political teeth in MUP politics in the 1980s. These experiences are yet to be fully integrated into Mexico's post-1968 history.[25]

Although informal housing continues to exist, the politics of informality have transformed in response to recent developments: the stagnation of the national economy and the plummeting of real wages since the 1980s; the lowering of birth rates and the rise of migration to the United States; neoliberal reforms; the transition to democracy; and the disintegration of the postrevolutionary political order, which over the past twenty years has been accompanied by harrowing levels of violence. Growth rates in Mexico City's metropolitan area have decreased since the 1980s, resulting in a relative decline in the city's demographic, economic, and political weight at the national level. While self-construction on the periphery continues to take place, it has become a much less viable mode of acquiring a house since the 1980s.[26]

The claims to housing discussed in this book were made in a particular historical period: during the postrevolutionary decades, when the revolutionary promise of social citizenship empowered urban popular groups, before the decades of modernization and growth that came to a halt with the debt crisis of 1982. The informal peripheries analyzed here have become central areas, fully consolidated and integrated into the city with significantly lower rates of poverty than neighborhoods in the State of Mexico.[27] But they were hard hit by the 1980s economic crisis, leading researchers to conclude that the "slums of hope" of the 1950s enjoyed a particularly auspicious set of circumstances that would not necessarily repeat itself.[28] It remains to be seen whether the trajectory of integration and consolidation described here will continue.

Beginning in 2001, the federal government transformed its housing policy, extending millions of cheap mortgages to low-income earners. Construction companies built and sold millions of minuscule houses on the periphery of the capital and other cities, integrating millions of poor urban dwellers into the international financial system. Located far from workplaces and urban amenities, these houses are constructed with cheap materials, lack public spaces, and suffer high rates of crime. But unlike mid-century colonias proletarias, which were similarly described in the 1950s, these are not progressive but rapidly decaying neighborhoods, many of which have been abandoned by their indebted residents.[29]

Informal urbanization continues, but it is smaller in scale and, in the case of Mexico City, mostly takes place on the environmentally protected land (*suelo de conservación*) south of the city. Indeed, environmentalism has become the dominant expert discourse demarcating the informal city, a century after the rise of sanitation.[30] Settlements on conservation lands in Mexico City have not benefited from large-scale regularization programs. Neither have they become fully integrated. Many remain in a legal limbo, overseen by countless planning and environmental offices.[31] Indeed, the rise of the environmental movement and neoliberal reforms is concomitant with the erosion of the postrevolutionary regime. The residents of contemporary informal neighborhoods do not wield the same power as their predecessors a century ago. Informality continues to exist, as does inequality. Modernization and revolution are over.

Acknowledgments

This book has been a long time in the making. I completed it during the dog days of the Texas summer, but it is the culmination of years of work and life entwined in cities, readings, friendships, and losses. Whatever merits this book might have, they are due to those who helped me along the way. I am now pleased to thank them.

Several institutions supported the completion of this book since its first life as a dissertation. The University of Chicago and the Mexican Consejo Nacional de la Ciencia y la Tecnología funded my doctoral studies. The Center for Latin American Studies and the History Department at the University of Chicago supported research trips to Mexico City, as did the Instituto de Investigaciones Históricas at the UNAM. I was the recipient of a Mellon Advanced Studies Fellowship as well as a fellowship from the Center for US-Mexican Studies and a Mellon Postdoctoral Fellowship at the University of California, San Diego. I also enjoyed a semester leave and steady support from Trinity University, my current institution.

The mentorship I received at the University of Chicago was exceptional. Throughout years of friendship, Mauricio Tenorio Trillo has taught me that history writing requires both rigor and imagination and has shown me that the voices of historians ought to be enriched by their life and broader intellectual exploration. Brodwyn Fischer has been the sharpest of mentors, and her probing questions have informed my work for many years now. This is a first attempt at answering some of those questions. I also learned from Emilio Kourí, Dain Borges, and Paul Cheney. Years before, my professors at El Colegio de México allowed me to envision a life surrounded by books: Soledad Loaeza, Juan Gustavo Galindo, Fernando Escalante, and the late Martha Elena Venier, whose presence I could feel as I wrote this book in my second language.

Chicago also gave me a community of colleagues and friends clustered around the Latin American History Workshop and Jimmy's, two dear institutions: Diana Schwartz Francisco, Marcel Anduiza, Aiala Levy, Casey Lurtz, Dan Webb, Nicole Beckman, Yuna Blajer, Keegan Boyer, Tessa Murphy, Jackie Sumner, Miles Loomis, Jorge Campos, Chris Moore, Pablo Palomino, Colin Rydell, Jamie Gentry, and Natalie Arsenault. Erin E. McCullugh was my partner for many of those years. This book carries the memory of our happy time together. I first studied the history of Mexico City with Luis Fernando Granados, a wonderful historian, writer, and friend, sorely missed since his untimely passing.

I spent two years at the University of California, San Diego, where I enjoyed the companionship of Melissa Flocca, Greg Mallinger, Tania Islas, Tom Passananti, Alfredo Corchado, Jan Feiling, Kirk Kirkland, Sharon Rose, Pamela Radcliff, Nancy Postero, and Matt Vitz, a fine interlocutor for many years now. Nancy Kwak has always been a model of scholarly solidarity, of which I have long been a beneficiary. Georgia Hartman was a true friend while we both lived in La Jolla; the conference on housing that we organized in May 2017 taught me much of what I know about collaboration and interdisciplinarity, words that academics often use but seldom put into practice.

My ideas about informality are indebted to my work with the research collaborative La Ville Informelle au Vingtième Siècle, led by Charlotte Vorms. I thank her, as well as Laurent Coudroy de Lille, Francesco Bartolini, Françoise de Barros, Eva Camelli, Luciano Villani, Brodwyn Fischer, Emanuel Giannotti, Jim House, Adriana Massidda, Serge Ollivier, Valeria Snitcofsky, Rafael Soares Gonçalves, and Antonio Azuela, first mentor and now dear friend and coauthor. Our seminars together in Paris, Rio de Janeiro, and Mexico City have been a life gift.

Sergio Miranda Pacheco has supported me for over a decade now. Thanks also to Alejandra Leal, Alejandro de Antuñano, Paula López Caballero, Manuel Perló Cohen, Mariana Hijar, Georg Leidenberger, Rodrigo Meneses Reyes, Simeon Newman, Corina Zeltsmann, and Cristóbal Jácome-Moreno. I cannot thank all the archivists and librarians who helped me along the way, but I should mention Ricardo Méndez and the late architect Rafael Cordero, at the Archivo Histórico de la Ciudad de México.

Trinity University has been my professional home since 2019. It is a pleasure to work with Todd Barnet, Jimmy Butts, Jason Johnson, Erin Kramer, Ken Loiselle, David Lesch, Sarah Luginbill, Gina Tam, and Lauren Turek. Anene Ejikeme, Nicole Marafioti, and the late Carey Latimore guided me as department chairs, making sure I had everything I needed to complete this book. Kind, curious, and passionate, my students truly make this the best job.

Luis Horacio Aceves and Rodrigo Saavedra have been there from the very start. I pitched countless ideas to Paul González and Guillermo Ávila as we ran around the Viveros park on crisp Sunday mornings, followed by borsch, vodkas, and Baltika beers at our cherished Kolobok. My aunt, Tere Villarreal, and my late grandmother, Elena Villarreal, hosted me while I conducted the bulk of my research in Mexico City.

Enrique Dávila and I became historians together, and I count our rambling conversations as one of life's pleasures. I have learned from him more than I can express here. Had I not met José Juan Pérez Meléndez and Chris Lesser, my time in Chicago would have been unbelievably dimmer and less happy. Both have been like a family and have deeply shaped what I think friendship can be.

José Juan Pérez Meléndez, Chris Lesser, Cristóbal Jácome-Moreno, and Nancy Kwak read parts of this book as I made final revisions. I worked with Sarah Selvidge as a developmental editor. She was sharp and wise and pushed me to write the best book I could write. It was a pleasure to work with Kerry Webb and her team at the University of Texas Press. I thank her, her colleagues at the press, and the peer reviewers who read this manuscript and provided invaluable feedback.

Across South Texas, Gosia, Andrew, and Wojtek Stypko have welcomed me into their family with open hearts. My sister, Magdalena, is the kindest person I know and a lifelong accomplice. She and her family—Jorge, Santiago, and Elena—give me more joy than they know.

I met Anna during a global pandemic—when the world fell into disarray. But my world has never felt safer, more teeming with promise. Anna, I can't wait for the future together. I can only hope to make you as happy as you have made me.

My final words are for my parents, Pilar Villarreal and Emilio de Antuñano Maurer (whose love for architecture inspired this book). You have always encouraged me to pursue my passions, even when they have led me far away. I hope you know that your love has nourished these pages and know how grateful I am for it.

Notes

Introduction

1. Gómez Mayorga, "El plano de la ciudad," 16.

2. I am adapting a definition I used in Azuela and de Antuñano, "Four Regimes of Informality."

3. I follow Varley's arguments rejecting the "notion of informal settlement[s] as challenging the state" in "Postcolonialising Informality," 8.

4. I usually use "settlers" when referring to residents of informal neighborhoods organized politically and operating at a city-wide level. I use "residents" when I refer to the same groups in specific neighborhoods.

5. Different examples of the "problematization of informality" across Latin America, southern Europe, and North Africa are discussed in Vorms and Fischer, *Informal Cities*.

6. Most recent work on urban informality explicitly addresses the fraught history of the term. Authors have criticized the clear-cut distinction between the formal and the informal city posited by scholars in the 1970s, proposing instead a dynamic relationship between the two sectors. In politics the term "informal" has been used both to stigmatize residents outside of the law and to celebrate their creativity and resistance. Recent works addressing the term include Fischer and Vorms, "Introduction: Informal Urbanism as History"; Varley, "Postcolonialising Informality"; de Caldeira, "Peripheral Urbanization"; Gilbert and de Jong, "Entanglements of Periphery and Informality in Mexico City"; Roy, "Why India Cannot Plan Its Cities"; and Quiroz Rothe, "Introducción." Another common criticism is that the term "informality" has been used too broadly to describe extremely diverse geographies and histories, reifying concepts such as the "Third World" or the "Global South." Two influential texts criticized for this reason are United Nations–Habitat, *The Challenge of Slums*; and Davis, *Planet of Slums*.

7. Hart, "Informal Income Opportunities and Urban Employment in Ghana."

8. The 2003 UN–Habitat report *The Challenge of Slums* was exemplary in its conflation of legal and architectural levels of analysis. The report listed "lack of basic services, substandard housing or illegal and inadequate building structures, [and] insecure tenure; irregular or informal settlements" as characteristics of slums. Its authors

understood "informal" as describing two different phenomena: (1) houses or neighborhoods in defiance of urban regulations or lacking property titles; and (2) self-built houses or neighborhoods that share geographical and morphological traits that are different from those of a normative city. Gyger points out the distinction between the two phenomena in *Improvised Cities*. On the conflation between legal and social categories, see Azuela, *La ciudad, la propiedad privada y el derecho*. For criticisms of the report, see Mayne, *Slums*; and Gilbert, "The Return of the Slum."

9. Roy, "Transnational Trespassings." On the utility of urban informality for analyzing housing in the United States, see Kwak, "California Formalising"; and Ward, *Colonias and Public Policy in Mexico and Texas*.

10. Gorelik has historicized the "Latin American city" as a problem to be solved by scholars and policymakers, an intellectual and policy category that crystallized between 1940 and 1970, in *La ciudad latinoamericana*. For similar intellectual histories, see also Connolly, "La ciudad y el hábitat popular"; Fischer, "A Century in Present Tense"; Valladares, *A invenção da favela*; and Gyger, *Improvised Cities*.

11. Duhau, *Habitat popular y política urbana*, 90. On Ciudad Netzahualcóyotl, see Yee, *Informal Metropolis*; and Vélez-Ibañez, *Rituals of Marginality*.

12. This was one of the central premises of the work conducted by the research group La Ville Informelle au XXème Siècle, which has influenced my ideas in ways I cannot express in a note.

13. José Antonio Rivera, Miguel García et al. to Consejo de Salubridad, January 31, 1907, AHSS, Fondo Salubridad Pública, Sección Salubridad en el Distrito Federal, box 1, file 36. Drawing from Rama's *La ciudad letrada*, many authors trace the genesis of the Latin American informal city to the colonial period. See Hernández and Kellett, "Introduction: Reimagining the Informal in Latin America"; and Connolly, "Latin American Informal Urbanism." I delve into this chronology in chapter 1.

14. "Urbanismo oficial," 21.

15. A. Rivera Torres, "Es muy grave para nuestra metrópoli el éxodo campesino," *Excélsior*, October 9, 1955. Architect Teodoro González de León, remembering in the 1990s, identified the 1950s as the decade of Mexico City's downfall. "The city could not contain demographic growth, urban services could not keep up with the expansion of the city, marginal areas appeared." "Entrevista realizada a Teodoro González de León por Graciela de Garay, el día 15 de agosto de 1991 en la Ciudad de México," Archivo de la Palabra del Instituto de Investigaciones Dr. José María Luis Mora.

16. BNHOP, "El problema de la habitación en la Ciudad de México."

17. Ibargüengoitia, *La casa de usted y otros viajes*, 94–95.

18. The trope of the dystopic megacity was often inflected with irony and humor in Mexico, as exemplified by chroniclers like Guillermo Sheridan and Carlos Monsiváis, who famously described 1990s Mexico City as "postapocalyptic" in *Los rituales del caos*.

19. Throughout this book I refer to residents of informal neighborhoods as popular groups, working-class families, and the urban poor. I use some of these formulations as analytic categories; others are categories deployed by historical actors. None of them is neutral. The terms "popular groups" and *colonias populares* are used in opposition to "elite" or "middle-class" peoples and spaces. On the phrase *colonias populares*, see Connolly, "La ciudad y el hábitat popular." Although Mexico City had a relatively small working class (at least in comparison with metropoles of the North Atlantic or São Paulo), I sometimes use the term following its usage by city residents who adopted

categories like "proletarian" and "worker" to partake in the proud postrevolutionary discursive universe. Finally, terms such as "urban poor," "marginal sector," and "squatters" (*paracaidistas*) were used by state officials and elite groups to stigmatize residents of informal neighborhoods. I refer to these terms when analyzing the discourse of these elite groups.

20. The latest iteration of this ethnocentrism is visible in complaints against informal street vendors for occupying citizen public spaces. See Crossa, *Luchando por un espacio en la Ciudad de México*; Leal, "'You Cannot Be Here'"; and Moctezuma, *El desvanecimiento de lo popular*. My musings on urban informality and its relationship with an ideal history of the West are inspired by Robinson, *Ordinary Cities*; and Chakrabarty, *Provincializing Europe*.

21. Fischer and Vorms, "Introduction: Informal Urbanism as History," 11.

22. This is not a novel idea, at least for historians of Mexico, who have long explored how the discretionary use of laws bolstered the power of the state. See Escalante Gonzalbo, *Ciudadanos imaginarios* and *México*. Urban scholars over the past twenty years have theorized that the selective nonapplication of the law is a fundamental tool for governance and planning. See Azuela, *La ciudad, la propiedad privada y el derecho*; Roy, *City Requiem, Calcutta*; Fischer, "Historicising Informal Governance in 20th Century Brazil"; Yiftachel, "Theoretical Notes on 'Gray Cities'"; and Chaterjee, *The Politics of the Governed*.

23. Describing similar dynamics in Indian cities, Roy has characterized informality not as an unregulated space but as a "state of deregulation . . . where the ownership, use, and purpose of land cannot be fixed and mapped according to any prescribed set of regulations or the law" in "Why India Cannot Plan Its Cities," 80. I am borrowing the term "spatial fixation" from Craib, *Cartographic Mexico*.

24. Escalante Gonzalbo, *Ciudadanos imaginarios*, 292.

25. I put the term in quotation marks because an important contribution of this literature has been to reflect on the geopolitics of knowledge inscribed in the term "Global South."

26. This argument was made by Varley in "Postcolonialising Informality?" My work is indebted to the research of Antonio Azuela, René Coulomb, Angela Giglia, Martha Schteingart, Emilio Duhau, Priscilla Connolly, Peter Ward, María Soledad Cruz Rodríguez, Alicia Zicccardi, and other authors I cite throughout this book (and with whom I sometimes disagree). Both "irregular settlements" and "popular neighborhoods" became increasingly common phrases in the 1970s, the decade when the term "informal" was coined. Both allude, implicitly or explicitly, to the illegal or extralegal character of the neighborhoods in question. "Human settlements" were incorporated into the Mexican Constitution in a 1976 reform that expanded the planning powers of the Mexican state. The use of "settlements" also follows the United Nations Conference on Human Settlements and Sustainable Urban Development (Habitat I) held in Vancouver, Canada, in 1976. Whereas the term "irregular settlements" stresses the breaking of city codes, *colonias populares* has a more positive connotation, emphasizing the nonelite character and popular culture of these neighborhoods. See Connolly, "Vaivenes tempranos del urbanismo popular en América Latina."

27. Cornelius, *Politics and the Migrant Poor in Mexico City*. For a scholarly study published in 1956 that documented this relationship, see Cornejo Cabrera, "La colonia proletaria Escuadrón 201." As chapter 2 describes, informal neighborhoods were

created as early as the 1920s through land grants distributed to working-class families by the federal government. On the relationship between the state and settlers in this decade, see Urbina Martínez, "Años veinte, organización vecinal y desarrollo urbano."

28. Most work on the built environment has focused on self-construction and the progressive nature of settlements built in this way. See Ward, "Self-Help Housing in Mexico City"; Frieden, "The Search for Housing Policy in Mexico City"; and Harth-Deneke, "The Colonias Proletarias of Mexico City." Much of this was influenced by the seminal work conducted by architect John F. C. Turner and anthropologist William Mangin, whose work I analyze in chapter 6. On social networks in informal settlements, see Lomnitz, *¿Cómo sobreviven los marginados?*; and de la Rocha, *Los recursos de la pobreza*. On the importance of self-construction within the political economy, see Ward, *Mexico City*. On the relationship between informal neighborhoods and the Mexican political system, see Loaeza, "Perspectivas para una historia política del Distrito Federal en el siglo XX"; Perló Cohen, *Estado, vivienda y estructura urbana en el cardenismo*; and Rodríguez Kuri, "Ciudad oficial."

29. For a recent summary of this position, see Duhau, "The Informal City."

30. For economic critiques of self-construction, see Ward, *Self-Help Housing*; Pradilla, "Notas acerca del problema de la vivienda"; Schteingart, "Sector inmobiliario capitalista y formas de apropiación del suelo urbano"; and Alonso, *Lucha urbana y acumulación de capital*. Political critiques include Alonso, *Los movimientos sociales en el Valle de México*; Perló Cohen, "Política y vivienda en México, 1910–1952"; and Vélez-Ibañez, *Rituals of Marginality*.

31. This historiography is growing. For recent works, see Urbina Martínez, "De discursos y realidades"; Yee, *Informal Metropolis*; and Quiroz Rothe, "Introducción." Earlier works include Cisneros Sosa, *Aproximaciones a la historia del urbanismo popular*; and Sánchez Mejorada, *Rezagos de la modernidad*. For a comparative historical approach, see Vorms and Fischer, *Informal Cities*.

32. For example, Martha Schteingart—a reputable housing scholar—wrote in 1990 that "the percentage of city residents living under conditions [of urban informality] increased . . . from 2.3 in 1947 to 22% in 1955 (when these settlements became a permanent feature) to around 50% in 1976." "Prácticas de producción y reproducción en el sector informal en México," 157. For similar chronologies, see Connolly, "Uncontrolled Settlements and Self-Build"; and Miranda Pacheco, "La vivienda popular del milagro mexicano en la Ciudad de México."

33. As I explain in chapter 6, the first surveys that quantified colonias proletarias—which we can anachronistically label informal—were published in 1952.

34. In pointing out this paradox, I am inspired by Cruz Rodríguez, *Crecimiento urbano y procesos sociales en el Distrito Federal (1920–1928)*.

35. These neighborhood associations, however, predated the revolution and had a long history of claims-making. For a longer history of their role in urbanization, see Jiménez, *Making an Urban Public*.

36. Loaeza, "Perspectivas para una historia política del Distrito Federal en el siglo XX," 122–123.

37. Henri Lefebvre's formulation of the right to the city has been very influential among urban scholars in Latin America. See Granados, *Uso y valor de Henri Lefebvre*. Citizenship in an urban context, more broadly, has also been an important theme in Latin America's urban history. See Holston, *Insurgent Citizenship*; Fischer, *A Poverty of Rights*; and Pineo and Baer, *Cities of Hope*.

38. Gorelik, *La ciudad latinoamericana.* On Mexico City as a lab for the study of migration and poverty, see de Antuñano, "Mexico City as an Urban Laboratory."

39. The latter group was composed of US scholars who conducted ethnographic research in the 1970s. See Eckstein, *The Poverty of Revolution*; and Cornelius, *Politics and the Migrant Poor in Mexico City.* See also Loaeza, "Perspectivas para una historia política del Distrito Federal en el siglo XX." Scholars emphasizing the domination of the urban masses were inspired by Marxism and revisionist histories of the Mexican Revolution and accordingly viewed the Mexican regime as betraying the revolution in order to support capitalist urbanization. See Ramírez Saiz, *El movimiento urbano popular en México*; Alonso, *Los movimientos sociales en el Valle de México*; and Perló Cohen, "Política y vivienda en México, 1910–1952."

40. The housing project of Tlatelolco (1964) was built after the razing of thousands of houses in the city center. Two years later, the city regent, Ernesto P. Uruchurtu, ordered the razing of two informal neighborhoods, an action that led to his political downfall. Both events are analyzed in chapter 6.

41. Snitcofsky, *Historia de las villas en la ciudad de Buenos Aires.* For comparative histories of informal urbanization in Latin America, see Vorms and Fischer, *Informal Cities*; and Calvo Isaza, *Urbanización y revolución en América Latina.*

42. Primo Villa Michel, director of the Instituto Nacional de la Vivienda, distributed copies of the *Plan de emergencia* in 1958 to architect Félix Sánchez, who led the most important housing surveys of the city as head of the Banco Nacional Hipotecario y de Obras Públicas. Primo Villa Michel to Félix Sánchez, April 14, 1958, AGN, INV, box 1.

43. Cited in Calvo Isaza, *Urbanización y revolución en América Latina*, 323.

44. For useful starting points, see Calvo Isaza, *Urbanización y revolución en América Latina*; Yee, *Informal Metropolis*; Moctezuma Barragán, *Despertares*; and Ramírez de Garay, "El sismo de 1985 en la Ciudad de México."

45. On the relationship between agrarian property and urban informality, see Azuela, *La ciudad, la propiedad privada y el derecho*; Varley, "¿Propiedad de la revolución?"; Durand, *La ciudad invade al ejido*; and Cruz Rodríguez, *Propiedad, poblamiento y periferia rural en la zona metropolitana de la Ciudad de Mexico.*

46. I conducted the bulk of my research in Mexico's Archivo General de la Nación (General Archive of the Nation, AGN) and the Archivo Histórico de la Ciudad de México (Historical Archive of Mexico City, AHCDMX). The AGN holds thousands of petitions from neighborhood associations to federal authorities, a key source for understanding city politics. The AHCDMX holds government sources like planning committee minutes, technical studies, and official blueprints. Many of these sources remain poorly catalogued and are still insufficiently mined by historians. I have also conducted research in Mexico's Archivo General Agrario (General Agrarian Archive, AGA) and the archives of the Instituto Nacional de la Vivienda (National Housing Institute, INV), which I have used to document the urbanization of agrarian holdings in Mexico City and the country's housing policy.

Chapter 1: Sanitary Informality in the Porfirian City

1. On the significance of this population density from a geographical and economic perspective, see Bataillon, *La ciudad y el campo en el México central*; and Tutino, *The Mexican Heartland.*

2. This is particularly true for the period before 1950, when most demographic growth was driven by internal migration. Starting in that year, increases in the birth rate accounted for most of the city's growth. Unikel, *El desarrollo urbano de México*, 44.

3. In the words of geographer Claude Bataillon in "México," Mexico City was always a "métis" (mestizo) capital city that offered remarkable social mobility.

4. Morse, "Cities as People."

5. My analysis of the sanitary city is indebted to Agostoni, *Monuments of Progress*; Vitz, *A City on a Lake*; Miranda Pacheco, "Urbe inmunda"; and Tenorio Trillo, *I Speak of the City*. On the transnational movement to sanitize cities, see Platt; *Shock Cities*; Nightingale, *Segregation*; and Vitz, *Globalizing Urban Environmental History*.

6. Ibargüengoitia, *La casa de usted y otros viajes*, 146.

7. Cited in Mundy, *The Death of Aztec Tenochtitlán, the Life of Mexico City*, 1.

8. I borrow the term "Zócalo-centric" from Granados, "Nuestra urbe."

9. Townsend, *Fifth Sun*, 20–24.

10. Escalante Gonzalbo and Alcántara Gallegos, "La Ciudad de México desde su fundación hasta la conquista española," 19.

11. The relationship between the grid and the colonization project has been explored in classic works: Kagan, *Urban Images of the Hispanic World, 1493–1794*; Rama, *La ciudad letrada*; and O'Gorman, "Reflexiones sobre la distribución colonial de la Ciudad de México."

12. Kagan, *Urban Images of the Hispanic World, 1493–1794*, 9.

13. Lira, *Comunidades indígenas frente a la Ciudad de México.*

14. Cervantes de Salazar, *Life in the Imperial and Loyal City of Mexico in New Spain*, 51. My understanding of this invisibility of the Indian city owes much to Mundy, *The Death of Aztec Tenochtitlan, the Life of Mexico City*; and Connolly, "Latin American Informal Urbanism."

15. Tutino, *The Mexican Heartland.*

16. Candiani, *Dreaming of Dry Land.*

17. Escalante Gonzalbo and Alcántara Gallegos, "La Ciudad de México desde su fundación hasta la conquista española"; Lira, *Comunidades indígenas frente a la Ciudad de México*; and O'Hara, *A Flock Divided.*

18. Granados, "Cosmopolitan Indians and Mesoamerican Barrios in Bourbon Mexico City."

19. Torres Puga, "La ciudad novohispana."

20. For urban analyses of the Bourbon reforms, see Viqueira, *¿Relajados o reprimidos?*; Sánchez de Tagle, *Los dueños de la calle*; and Voekel, "Peeing on the Palace."

21. Ortiz Escamilla, "Política y poder en una época revolucionaria," 188–189.

22. "Los miserables de entonces tienen aún herederos, que . . . se arrastran a sus orillas, llevando una existencia, que abrevian por fortuna, el aire malsano, el hambre y la intemperie . . . que el centro dorado de México está rodeado por un cinturón de miseria y fango." Cited in González Rodríguez, *Los bajos fondos*, 20.

23. Hardy cited in González Rodríguez, *Los bajos fondos*, 18.

24. García Cubas, *Geografía e historia del Distrito Federal*, 22.

25. Prantl and Grosso, *La Ciudad de México*, 696.

26. Granados, "De la ciudad capitalista a la ciudad colonial." The extent to which class differences in Mexico are related to racial categories (or skin color) and racial differences are subsumed under class differences remains a matter of debate. Navarrete, "Blanquitud vs. blancura, mestizaje y privilegio en México de los siglos XIX a XXI."

27. For population numbers, see Pérez Toledo, "Formas de gobierno local, modelos constitucionales y cuerpo electoral, 1824–1867," 225.

28. Tenorio Trillo, *I Speak of the City*.

29. Galindo y Villa, *Historia sumaria de la Ciudad de México*, 210.

30. "Nuestras costumbres son más complicadas, nos ha salido el sexto, el séptimo, el octavo sentido y el cielo sabe cuántos más; tenemos sutilezas y refinamientos que no es posible retratar, por lo tornadizos y efímeros que son." Cited in Quirarte, *Elogio de la calle*, 296–297.

31. Galindo y Villa, *Historia sumaria de la Ciudad de México*, 210.

32. Rodriguez Kuri, *La experiencia olvidada*, 92.

33. Histories that illustrate this process include Miranda Pacheco, *Tacubaya*; and Urbina Martínez, "De discursos y realidades."

34. Robles Pezuela, *Memoria presentada a S. M. el Emperador*, 103. See also Jiménez Muñoz, *La traza del poder*, 24.

35. I am following McMichael's morphological analysis of these neighborhoods in "The Urban Development of Mexico City, 1850–1930." For information on developers, see Jimenez Muñoz, *La traza del poder*; and Morales, "La expansión de la Ciudad de México en el siglo XIX."

36. Pallares, "Lo que significa el fraccionamiento de Hipódromo de la Condesa," 41.

37. McMichael, "The Urban Development of Mexico City, 1850–1930," 148.

38. Morales and Gayón Córdova, "Casas y viviendas de la Ciudad de México."

39. Lear, *Workers, Neighbors, and Citizens*, 36.

40. Pallares, "Lo que significa el fraccionamiento de Hipódromo de la Condesa," 42.

41. "La colonia," *El Arquitecto* 1 (1923): 2.

42. "No hubo urbanización previa y de allí vienen las calles en laberinto; no hubo drenaje, ni se establecieron cloacas ni desagües, y de allí viene lo inmundo; no hubo alumbrado público, y de aquí viene el que el crimen." "La cuna del crimen," *El Imparcial*, July 6, 1905. The fears of crime and unsanitary conditions that crystallized in places like Colonia La Bolsa are analyzed by Piccato, *City of Suspects*.

43. Konove, *Black Market Capital*, 145.

44. "Acuerdo que fijó las reglas para la admisión de nuevas colonias y calles en la Ciudad de México" and "Lista de las colonias autorizadas en el Distrito Federal," *Boletín Oficial del Consejo Superior de Gobierno del Distrito Federal* 7, no. 35, October 30, 1906.

45. See Buffington and Piccato, *True Stories of Crime in Modern Mexico*; and Lozano, *De la opinión a la noticia*.

46. I cite the places that Heriberto Frías mentioned in his description of penny-press journalists. "Va a los talleres, entra a las fábricas, charla en los cuarteles, visita las cárceles, recorre los hospitales, ríe en los teatros, pasa por los burdeles, frecuenta las iglesias y cantinas, escucha en las antesalas ministeriales, come en los banquetes solemnes y goza en los almuercitos de los barrios pobres." Cited in Speckman Guerra, *Crimen y castigo*, 174.

47. De Murga, "Atisbos sociológicos."

48. Jackson, *Crabgrass Frontier*, 14–16.

49. Pani, *La higiene en México*, 119.

50. Cited in Platt, *Shock Cities*, 17.

51. Macedo, *La criminalidad en México*, 7.

52. Guerrero, *La génesis del crimen en México*, 158, 160.

53. Guerrero, *La génesis del crimen en México*, 165, 177.

54. Redfield, "The Folk Society," 293–294.

55. My analysis in the last three paragraphs is indebted to Rodríguez Kuri, "Urbanización y secularización en México"; Tenorio Trillo, *Elogio de la impureza*; Knight, "Racism, Revolution, and Indigenismo"; López Caballero, *Indígenas de la nación*; Rosemblatt, *The Science and Politics of Race in Mexico and the United States, 1910–1950*; and Gorelik, *La ciudad latinoamericana.*

56. De Murga, "Atisbos sociológicos," 486.

57. This point has been made by intellectual and cultural historians during the last three decades. My main inspirations are Abbott, *The System of Professions*; Lepenies, *Between Literature and Science*; and Tenorio Trillo, *I Speak of the City.*

58. Agostoni, *Monuments of Progress*, 55.

59. Cited in Vitz, *A City on a Lake*, 27.

60. As Vitz writes in *A City on a Lake*, "miasmas coexisted with germs in Mexican science—and popular culture in the twentieth century. The gradual acceptance of germ theory, however, strengthened sanitarians' resolve by pinpointing the cause of illness" (27). See also Agostoni, *Monuments of Progress*; and Miranda Pacheco, "Urbe inmunda."

61. Agostoni, *Monuments of Progress*, chapter 5. My summary of these projects is also based on Vitz, *A City on a Lake*, chapter 1; and Rodríguez Kuri, *Historia del desasosiego*, chapter 5.

62. "Fin de una obra magna," *La Voz de México*, March 23, 1900.

63. The construction of a drainage system and a potable water system and paving of the streets usually took place in tandem for greater efficiency.

64. Many of these legal devices were compiled by Ortiz Molina, *Prontuario.* On Porfirian urban laws and regulations, see Rodríguez Kuri, *La experiencia olvidada*; Alexander, *City on Fire*; Weber, *Death Is All around Us*; Vitz, *A City on a Lake*; Agostoni, *Monuments of Progress*; Montaño, *Electrifying Mexico*; Bliss, *Compromised Positions*; Briseño, *Candil de la calle, oscuridad de la casa*; and Aboites, *El agua de la nación.*

65. Jiménez Muñoz has documented the relationship between the city's financial and political elite in *La traza del poder.*

66. For a contemporary assessment of these differences, see Miguel Ángel de Quevedo, "El programa sanitario y de salubridad pública en el Valle y la Ciudad de México," *Boletín Oficial* 7, no. 46 (December 7, 1906).

67. "[P]or diversos rumbos de la capital se establecieron varias de esas llamadas colonias, sin que para ello se hubiera recabado la aprobación de la propia autoridad; pero al mismo tiempo las casas construidas en esos lugares iban habitándose, constituyéndose focos de insalubridad o guaridas de bandidos que, a las sombras de la noche, por falta de alumbrado público, se lanzaban a la consumación de numerosos delitos." Jesús Galindo y Villa, "Las colonias en la municipalidad de México y en el Distrito Federal," *Boletín Oficial* 7, no. 35 (October 30, 1906): 549.

68. On these historiographic debates from the perspective of Latin American urban history, see Jiménez, *Making an Urban Public.*

69. In the words of a contemporary newspaper article, if left to their own devices, developers "constructed in the largest possible area of their lots and divided their houses in unhygienic pigsties that they rented at high prices and under tyrannical conditions." "Los cuartos bajos y las accesorias: inodoros y caños de desagüe," *El Universal*, June 1, 1899.

70. Rodríguez Kuri, *La experiencia olvidada*, 72–80.

71. "El Consejo Superior de Salubridad a través del tiempo," *Boletín Oficial del Consejo Superior de Gobierno del Distrito Federal* 7, no. 40 (November 16, 1906): 633–636.

72. Agostoni, *Monuments of Progress*, 23.

73. "Las habitaciones para el pueblo," *El Imparcial*, March 13, 1902.

74. Cossio, "Algunas noticias sobre las colonias de esta capital."

75. "Acuerdo que fijó las reglas para la admisión de nuevas colonias y calles en la Ciudad de México" (approved in April 1903). Reproduced in *Boletín Oficial del Consejo Superior de Gobierno del Distrito Federal* 7, no. 35 (October 30, 1906).

76. On the 1903 code, see Berra, "La expansión de la Ciudad de México y los conflictos urbanos, 1900–1930," 188–189; Urbina Martínez, "De discursos y realidades," 57–59; and Jiménez Muñoz, *La traza del poder*, 34–35.

77. This was the conclusion reached by a 1908 Public Works report penned by Antonio Torres Torrija. Cited in Jiménez Muñoz, *La traza del poder*, 53. According to a different report, several colonias (including Díaz de León, Valle Gómez, La Bolsa, La Viga, and Scheibe) were not authorized by the municipal government, which did not accept any responsibility for them. See Yúdico, "Las colonias de la capital."

78. Agostoni, *Monuments of Progress*, 58.

79. Consejo Superior de Salubridad, *Informes rendidos por los inspectores sanitarios de cuartel y los de distrito al Consejo Superior de Salubridad*, 11–12.

80. Cited in Agostoni, *Monuments of Progress*, 74.

81. "Por desgracia, en materia de higiene entre la acción gubernativa y la individual, hay una enorme distancia. Tendremos a la ciudad saneada; pero seguiremos conservando al individuo sin higiene; agua para lavarse, pero gente que no se lava." "Nuestros problemas higiénicos," *El Imparcial*, June 23, 1902.

82. For an ultimately failed project to upgrade conditions in the barrio, see Konove, "Making a Modern Barrio."

83. Arechiga Córdoba, "De acueductos, acequias y atarjeas," 160.

84. Consejo Superior de Salubridad, *Informes rendidos por los inspectores sanitarios de cuartel y los de distrito al Consejo Superior de Salubridad*, 39.

85. Consejo Superior de Salubridad, *Informes rendidos por los inspectores sanitarios de cuartel y los de distrito al Consejo Superior de Salubridad*, 44.

86. Pani, *La higiene en México*, 7.

87. Martínez Delgado, *La experiencia urbana*, 47. He was writing about Aguascalientes, but most Mexican cities experienced the same change. See also Rodríguez Kuri, *Historia del desasosiego*; and Jiménez, *Making an Urban Public*.

88. "No atranquen, que faltamos nosotros," *El Diablito Bromista* 2, no. 249, May 31, 1908.

89. AHCDMX, Fondo Ayuntamiento, Colonias, vol. 520, files 48 and 58.

90. "El Gobierno del Distrito Federal remite ejemplares del contrato celebrado entre la Secretaría de Fomento y el Sr. Carlos David Gheest para establecer una o más colonias al oriente de esta capital. García Teruel y Pablo Macedo solicitan establecer una Colonia en los terrenos del Rastro," AHCDMX, Fondo Ayuntamiento, Colonias, vol. 519, file 12.

91. "[E]n caso de que no puedan llenarse todos los requisitos legales, *lo práctico sería entrar en alguna transacción con sus propietarios, a fin de llenar, siquiera, algunos de los requisitos*" (emphasis added). "El Ayuntamiento de Guadalupe Hidalgo hace conocer

la moción del concejal Luis de la Brena en que se pide se gestione ante quien corresponda la recepción de las colonias que existen sin autorización como son la de Valle y Gómez, la de la Calzada de Vallejo o Peralvillo y la de Porfirio Díaz, hoy calles de Vicente Villada," AHCDMX, Fondo Ayuntamiento, Consejo Superior de Gobierno, Colonias, vol. 593, file 33.

92. "El Ayuntamiento de Guadalupe Hidalgo hace conocer la moción del concejal Luis de la Brena en que se pide se gestione ante quien corresponda la recepción de las colonias que existen sin autorización como son la de Valle y Gómez, la de la Calzada de Vallejo o Peralvillo y la de Porfirio Díaz, hoy calles de Vicente Villada," AHCDMX, Fondo Ayuntamiento, Consejo Superior de Gobierno, Colonias, vol. 593, file 33.

93. Yúdico, "Las colonias de la capital."

94. Connolly, "Latin American Informal Urbanism," 28.

Chapter 2: Revolution in the Hinterland, Revolution in the City

1. "Actas del Consejo Consultivo," April 2, 1930, Biblioteca del Archivo Histórico de la Ciudad de México. Throughout the chapter I cite both Puig Casauranc's presentation at the Consejo Consultivo and the report derived from it, published in *Obras Públicas* the same month.

2. Puig Casauranc, "Por qué y en qué extensión faltan los servicios de urbanización en el Distrito Federal," 223, 227, 225.

3. "Actas del Consejo Consultivo," April 2, 1930, Biblioteca del Archivo Histórico de la Ciudad de México.

4. For a classic interpretation of brokers, see Cornelius, *Politics and the Migrant Poor in Mexico City*. For a more recent historical analysis of urban caciques, see Yee, *Informal Metropolis*. My understanding of brokers is also influenced by Escalante Gonzalbo, *Ciudadanos imaginarios* and *México: El peso del pasado*.

5. Lear, *Workers, Neighbors, and Citizens*, 1. The relationship between the city's popular classes and the federal government is analyzed by Davis in *Urban Leviathan*.

6. On the changes that the revolution brought to the political culture of the city, see Rodríguez Kuri, *Historia del desasosiego*.

7. My understanding of this period owes a lot to Lear, *Workers, Neighbors, and Citizens*, chapters 7 and 8; and Perló Cohen, "Política y vivienda en México, 1910–1952."

8. Vitz, *A City on a Lake*, 83.

9. Wood, "*Viva la Revolución Social!*," 106.

10. Lear, *Workers, Neighbors, and Citizens*, 355–358.

11. Jiménez Muñoz, *La traza del poder*, 320.

12. Fuentes, *La región más transparente del aire*, 89.

13. "Todo incompleto en la metropoli," *Obras Públicas* 1, no. 4 (April 1930): 223.

14. Mercado Revilla, "Colonia Obrera," 173–174.

15. "Acuerdo sobre la Colonia en los potreros llamados de 'El Cuartelito'" (1899); reproduced in *Boletín Oficial del Consejo Superior de Gobierno* 7, no. 35 (October 30, 1906): 551.

16. "Hágase saber al público que el Ayuntamiento de la Capital no ha autorizado . . . la creación de una nueva Colonia. . . . Por lo mismo, no dará servicio municipal alguno, y los propietarios, para cumplir con las disposiciones del Código Sanitario, tendrán

que proveer sus casas de desagües, de agua potable, y demás condiciones." AHCDMX, Fondo Ayuntamiento, Colonias, vol. 519, file 22.

17. Bribiesca, *Memoria del H. Ayuntamiento en 1908*, 299.

18. Puig Casauranc, "Por qué y en qué extensión faltan los servicios de urbanización en el Distrito Federal," 226.

19. Cited in Mercado Revilla, "Colonia Obrera," 172.

20. This decree is cited in Cruz Rodríguez, *Crecimiento urbano y procesos sociales en el Distrito Federal*, 129–130. See also Urbina Martínez, "Años veinte, organización vecinal y desarrollo urbano."

21. Sindicato de la Colonia Obrera de Bolívar to Plutarco Elías Calles, October 22, 1925, AGN, O/C, box 114, file 242-M1-C. Improvement works in the neighborhood were later led by an ad hoc, government-sanctioned Junta de Mejoras Materiales.

22. Sindicato de la Colonia Obrera de Bolívar to Plutarco Elías Calles, October 22, 1925, AGN, O/C, box 114, file 242-M1-C.

23. Federación de Organizaciones de Colonos del Distrito Federal to President Abelardo Rodríguez, May 1, 1934, AGN, LCR, box 883, file 545.2/4.

24. "[S]i bien es cierto que los libramos de la tiranía del casero, en cambio, nuestra vida es angustiosa: sin escuelas, luz, pavimento, etc., pues de todo carecemos hasta de policía que es en extremo deficiente." Sindicato de la Colonia Obrera de Bolívar to Plutarco Elías Calles, October 22, 1925, AGN, O/C, box 114, file 242-M1-C.

25. Records from the Junta de Mejoras Materiales can be found in AGN, Dirección General de Gobierno, file 2.331.9.(29)-151.

26. City residents created improvement boards as early as 1872, when the board of Colonia Santa María la Ribera petitioned the municipal government for support for the upkeep of the school. As Rodríguez Kuri points out in *La experiencia olvidada* (96), this was a middle-class organization working on behalf of the city's middle-class neighborhood par excellence. Other early juntas de mejoras materiales, in more modest neighborhoods, are mentioned by Aréchiga Córdoba, "Saneamiento e higiene pública en la Ciudad de México," 286–297.

27. Urbina Martínez, "Los colonos se organizan"; Vázquez Ramírez, *Organización y resistencia popular en la Ciudad de México durante la crisis de 1929–1932.*

28. Sindicato de Colonos y Vecinos de Portales to President Lázaro Cárdenas, August 25, 1935, AGN, LCR, file 418.2/1.

29. "Fraccionamiento de Los Portales," *Mexican Herald*, May 1, 1915.

30. Sindicato de Colonos y Vecinos de Portales to President Lázaro Cárdenas, August 25, 1935, AGN, LCR, file 418.2/1.

31. On the social character of the Mexican Constitution, see Cossío Díaz and Ortega Soriano, *La herencia del constitutionalismo social mexicano y sus desafíos.*

32. Federación de Organizaciones de Colonos del Distrito Federal to President Abelardo Rodríguez, May 1, 1934, AGN, LCR, box 883, file 545.2/4.

33. "El artículo 27 de la Constitución General de la República y el artículo 735 del Código Civil, marcan al Ejecutivo de la Unión la resolución del problema de la tierra, máxime que la Nación no tiene que hacer ningún desembolso por estar ya pagada la tierra por los colonos." Sindicato de Colonos y Vecinos de Portales to Lázaro Cárdenas, August 25, 1935, AGN, LCR, file 418.2/1.

34. Beginning in 1929, they registered with the federal Ministry of Government and then later with the Ministry of the Economy and the local Oficina de

Cooperación. Residents also affiliated with the Partido Nacional Revolucionario, the political party that coalesced the various revolutionary factions after the assassination of Álvaro Obregón in 1928. On the affiliation with the PNR, see Urbina Martínez, "Los colonos se organizan," 178.

35. Vecinos de la Colonia Moderna to Gral. Francisco R. Serrano, August 1926, AGN, O/C, box 95, file 241-D2-C11.

36. Diputado Samuel Villarreal to Despacho de Gobernación, September 2, 1930, AGN, DGG, box 2711, file 331.9.(29)100.

37. For example, a federal representative—diputado José Muñoz Cota—led the Federación Mexicana de Colonos Proletarios in the 1930s. AGN, LCR, box 883, file 545.2/4.

38. More than sixty associations of urban residents coexisted in Mexico City in the 1930s, organized under the umbrella of larger federations such as the Federación de Organizaciones de Colonos del Distrito Federal (Federation of Settlers' Organizations of the Federal District), the Confederación Mexicana de Colonos Proletarios (Mexican Confederation of Proletarian Settlers), the Confederación de Colonos de México (Mexican Settler Confederation), and the Frente Único de Colonos de la República (United Front of Settlers of the Republic). Jiménez Muñoz, *La traza del poder*, 255–259. See also Cruz Rodríguez, *Crecimiento urbano y procesos sociales*; Berra, "La expansión de la Ciudad de México y los conflictos urbanos, 1900–1930"; and Perló Cohen, "Política y vivienda en México, 1910–1952."

39. Hernández Rodríguez, *Historia mínima del PRI*, 1–2.

40. Both neighborhoods have been the object of scholarly investigations. On Colonia Ex–Hipódromo Peralvillo, see Ziccardi, "La Sociedad Cooperativa 'Plutarco Elías Calles'"; and Vitz, *A City on a Lake*, 167–171. On La Vaquita, see Zamorano Villarreal, *Vivienda mínima obrera en el México posrevolucionario*.

41. Ziccardi, "La Sociedad Cooperativa 'Plutarco Elías Calles,'" 34.

42. Perló Cohen, "Política y vivienda en México, 1910–1952."

43. Berra, "La expansión de la Ciudad de México y los conflictos urbanos, 1900–1930," 212.

44. Empleados de la Dirección General de Correos to President Álvaro Obregón, December 8, 1921, AGN, O/C, 711-C-51.

45. Paperwork from the mid-1920s can be found in AGN, O/C, box 55, file 121-H-C-78.

46. Colonia Postal was built in 1925 and received partial urban services in 1929. Puig Causaranc, "Por qué y en qué extensión faltan los servicios de urbanización en el Distrito Federal," 231. Colonia Federal continued to suffer from poor urbanization until at least the 1950s, when its residents were petitioning for urban services. AHCDMX, DDF, OP, 471.2

47. "Colonia de Empleados y Obreros en el Ex–Hipódromo Peralvillo," AGN, O/C, file 711-C-51, bundle 3.

48. Zárraga was a professor at the San Carlos Academy of Architecture. On his influence on O'Gorman, see O'Rourke, *Modern Architecture in Mexico City*, 217–219.

49. Elfego Lugo to Fernando Torreblanca, October 1922, AGN, O/C, 711-C-51.

50. For similar proposals made during this period, see Jesús Monserrat to President Álvaro Obregón, November 30, 1922; and Jesús Cueva to President Álvaro Obregón,

December 12, 1922, both in AGN, O/C, file 711-C-51. See also González Navarro, *Población y sociedad en México*, 198–200.

51. *Diario de Debates de la Cámara de Diputados*, December 21, 1922.

52. Jesús Rodríguez Tinoco to Álvaro Obregón, February 16, 1923, AGN, O/C, file 711-C-51.

53. In the following years, Abitia sought government patronage and funding as a film producer. A paper trail of his trajectory can be found in AGN, O/C, file 803-A-26.

54. [Secretario Particular of] Plutarco Elías Calles to Jesús Abitia, January 5, 1925, AGN, O/C, file 711-C-51.

55. Margarito Ramírez to Plutarco Elías Calles, October 14, 1925, AGN, O/C, file 711-C-51.

56. "La sesión de ayer del Congreso Estudiantil," *El Pueblo*, March 18, 1918.

57. Urbina Martínez, "Algunas formas de negociación de los sectores populares ante los juzgados civiles de la Ciudad de México en las primeras décadas del siglo XX."

58. For accusations against Navarro, see Margarito Ramírez to Plutarco Elías Calles, October 14, 1925, AGN, O/C, file 711-C-51.

59. Piccato, *Historia mínima de la violencia en México*, chapter 4.

60. Vitz, *A City on a Lake*, 172–174.

61. The Junta de Mejoras Materiales experienced several changes over the following years. It was renamed the Sociedad Urbanizadora y Colonizadora del Ex-Hipódromo de Peralvillo and then the Sociedad Cooperativa Plutarco Elias Calles.

62. On the Junta de Mejoras Materiales and its relationship with Abitia, see Memorandum a Plutarco Elías Calles, November 30, 1926, AGN, O/C, file 711-C-51; and Guillermo Záraga, "Memorandum sobre la Colonia Ex-Hipódromo Peralvillo," June 17, 1927, AGN, O/C, file 711-C-51.

63. José Arcipresto to Ramiro Martínez, November 5, 1926, AGN, O/C, file 711-C-51.

64. Guillermo Záraga, "Memorandum sobre la Colonia Ex-Hipódromo Peralvillo," June 17, 1927, AGN, O/C, file 711-C-51.

65. "Memorandum que manifiesta las causas que motivaron que el dpto. de Bienes Nacionales se hiciera cargo de la administración de la Colonia del Ex–Hipódromo de Peralvillo," December 30, 1935, AGN, LCR, box 359, file 418.2/31.

66. In July 1935, for example, residents of Colonia Pro-Hogar accused Alfonso Ruiz Velasco of stealing their contributions to the cooperative of the neighborhood. "Manifiesto al C. Presidente de la República, al C. Jefe del Departamento Central, C. Secretario de Economía Nacional, Presidente del P.N.R y a todos los Revolucionarios, de verdad, del país y al Público General," July 27, 1935, AGN, LCR, file 418.2/8. Like countless other neighborhoods, Colonia Pro-Hogar was divided into two cooperatives, one of which was led by Ruiz Velasco.

67. The investigation was led by the Dirección General de Cooperativas y Comercio. Cited in Ziccardi, "La Sociedad Cooperativa 'Plutarco Elías Calles,'" 33.

68. Ziccardi, "La Sociedad Cooperativa 'Plutarco Elías Calles,'" 35.

69. Puig Casauranc, "Por qué y en qué extensión faltan los servicios de urbanización en el Distrito Federal," 228.

70. On these projects, see Selvidge, "Modernism and Miracles," chapter 2; Zamorano Villarreal, *Vivienda mínima obrera en el México posrevolucionario*; and Olsen,

Artifacts of Revolution, chapter 3. On the ferment in which progressive architectural ideas took root, see also Leidenberger, "Las 'pláticas' de los arquitectos de 1933 y el giro racionalista y social en el México posrevolucionario."

71. Olsen, *Artifacts of Revolution*, 88–96.

72. DDF, *El Departamento del Distrito Federal y la habitación para obreros y empleados*, 16–17. Zamorano Villarreal stresses the relationship between state-funded housing and contemporary planning guidelines developed by architect Carlos Contreras in *Vivienda mínima obrera en el México posrevolucionario*, 113–114.

73. Cited in González Navarro, *Población y sociedad en México*, 199.

74. Zamorano Villarreal, *Vivienda mínima obrera en el México posrevolucionario*, 131, 136, 156.

75. For example, plans to create a public park in Colonia Hernán Cortés threatened to dispossess residents living in the area, who protested against the project. AGN, LC, Box 359, file 418.2/73. In another instance, residents of Colonia Sector Popular Obrero in 1951 rejected government plans to establish residential blocks in lands earmarked for a public park. See Presidencia del Comité Directivo de la Asociación Pro-Mejoramiento de la Colonia Sector Popular to Fernando Casas Alemán, January 31, 1951, AHCDMX, OP, box 161, bundle 3. Chapters 3 and 4 also document instances where lands earmarked for public parks were invaded by landless families.

76. "Trató de cometer un despojo un fraccionador, al frente de un grupo de gente armada," *El Nacional*, July 15, 1934.

77. "Editorial," *Hogar y Trabajo*, November 30, 1941. I thank Claudia Zamorano Villarreal for kindly sharing this source.

78. "Un brutal atropello a los vecinos de la Colonia Monterrey de esta ciudad," *El Nacional*, September 6, 1940.

79. Details of the contract are found in AHCDMX, OP, box 163, bundle 1.

80. Rodríguez Kuri, *La experiencia olvidada*, 21. See also Miranda Pacheco, *La creación del Departamento del Distrito Federal.*

81. Cited in Sánchez Ruiz, "El contexto que rodeó a las propuestas de planificación del arquitecto Carlos Contreras," 21.

82. Almada, "Ideas sobre la organización conveniente de la Dirección de Obras Públicas del Distrito Federal," 2.

83. DDF, *Atlas general del Distrito Federal.*

84. Puig Casauranc, "Por qué y en qué extensión faltan los servicios de urbanización en el Distrito Federal," 227.

85. "Actas del Consejo Consultivo," June 5, 1929, Biblioteca del Archivo Histórico de la Ciudad de México.

86. "Reglamento de cooperación por particulares, a las obras públicas en el Distrito Federal," *Diario Oficial de la Federación*, December 15, 1931; "Una nueva concesión al pueblo," *El Nacional*, December 14, 1931.

87. DDF, *Memoria del Departamento del Distrito Federal* (1932–1933), chapter 9, "Cooperación."

88. DDF, *Informe que rinde el C. Jefe del Departamento del Distrito Federal de la obra realizada durante el año de 1934*, 205.

89. DDF, *Informe presidencial* (1933). See also "Actas del Consejo Consultivo," March 9, 1933, Biblioteca del Archivo Histórico de la Ciudad de México.

90. "La nueva orientación del Departamento al dotar de agua potable, drenaje y pavimentos a las colonias pobres de la Capital . . . se justifica no solamente por la tendencia de la Revolución de suprimir privilegios y desigualdades . . . en el orden práctico encontramos que tales desigualdades o preferencias a ciertas zonas . . . tienen trascendentales consecuencias para la colectividad." DDF, *Memoria del Departamento del Distrito Federal* (1935), 12.

91. Such was the government description in 1941. DDF, *Memoria del Departamento del Distrito Federal* (1941), 116.

92. For critiques of Romero, see "Actas del Consejo Consultivo," March 9, 1933, Biblioteca del Archivo Histórico de la Ciudad de México. For an account of his use of violence, see "Trató de cometer un despojo un fraccionador, al frente de un grupo de gente armada," *El Nacional*, July 15, 1934.

93. Agrupación Fraternal de la Colonia Emilio Carranza to Lázaro Cárdenas, March 15, 1936, AGN, LCR, file 545.2/4.

94. Shortly after the creation of the office, Manuel Rodríguez Gutiérrez surveyed the condition of working-class neighborhoods, as the federal government informed residents of Colonia Portales in a 1934 letter. J. Rodríguez de la Fuente to Liga de Defensa de Colonos y Vecinos de Portales, December 28, 1934, AGN, LCR, file 418.2/1. A commission was formed in the mid-1930s by Rafael de Villa (Oficina de Cooperación), engineer Luis Ángeles (Oficina de Fraccionamientos), and licenciado Ortiz Mena (Oficina Consultiva). The commission was mentioned in Unión General de Colonos del Distrito Federal to President Lázaro Cárdenas, September 24, 1936, AGN, LCR, 545.2/4.

95. "Obstáculo a la Unión de Colonos: Villa removido," *El Nacional*, October 28, 1938.

96. DDF, *Memoria del Departamento del Distrito Federal* (1939), 249.

97. DDF, *Memoria del Departamento del Distrito Federal* (1940), 78–80.

98. DDF, *Memoria del Departamento del Distrito Federal*, (1938), 156–157.

99. Such was the assessment of a 1935 report by the Ministry of the Economy, cited in Ziccardi, "La Sociedad Cooperativa 'Plutarco Elías Calles,'" 33. See also "Funcionan sin autorización," *El Nacional*, December 15, 1935.

100. "Funcionan sin autorización," *El Nacional*, December 15, 1935.

101. Kennedy, "Two Globalizations of Law & Legal Thought: 1850–1968." See also Marino, "Institucionalización de la Reforma Agraria (1915–1937)."

102. See Meneses Reyes, "Los efectos materiales del constitucionalismo mexicano"; and Azuela and Saavedra, "Uso, desgaste y reuso de la expropiación en la Ciudad de México."

103. Cruz Rodríguez, *Crecimiento urbano y procesos sociales en el Distrito Federal*, 161.

104. Particularly in Tláhuac, Tlalpan, Iztapalapa, and Gustavo A. Madero. Cruz Rodríguez, *Crecimiento urbano y procesos sociales en el Distrito Federal*, 162–167.

105. This was the case of Colonia Portales (mentioned earlier), the Narvarte estate, and the ranches of Tlacotal and Bramadero, which I discuss in chapter 5. On the relationship between agrarian expropriations and urbanization, see Varley, "¿Propiedad de la revolución?"; and Montaño, *La tierra de Ixtapalapa*.

106. "En cuanto a la llamada urbanización, es absolutamente falso que exista, ya que no hay ni siquiera trazadas las calles ni hay obras de saneamiento, ni luz, ni agua,

ni policía, etc., etc. que pudiera indicar que en esa tierra va a fundarse algún centro de población. Los vecinos que suscribimos somos gente pobre y nos dedicamos a la agricultura con el producto de la que sostenemos a nuestras familias y si algunos nos hemos dedicado a trabajos distintos ha sido por la falta de tierra de cultivo." Víctor Bobadillo et al., October 25, 1929, AGA, Colonia Independencia, 23–974–6.

107. Presidente de la Comisión Local Agraria del Distrito Federal to Presidente de la Comisión Nacional Agraria, May 20, 1920, AGA, Magdalena Mixihuca, 23–899–1.

108. Juan Pardavé to Comisión Nacional Agraria, May 20, 1921, AGA, Magdalena Mixihuca, 23–899–1.

109. This was the case of Salvador Flores, the leader of the Coalición de Colonos, who began his career as an agrarian leader (see chapter 4). Accusations of agrarian leaders selling ejido lands and becoming actors in city politics abound. For one example, see the case of Manuel Guadarrama in Colonia Santiago Atzacoalco. AGA, Santiago Atzacoalco, 23–913–1.

110. The government of the State of Yucatán expropriated land in 1918 to distribute to a cooperative society of railroad workers. The government of the State of Veracruz ordered expropriations to build social housing in cities in 1926 and 1930. Both expropriations were declared invalid by the Supreme Court of Justice. Herrera-Martín, "Judicial Review of Expropriation," 150–154.

111. López Romero, "Un espacio para acceder a la ciudad."

112. Díaz y Díaz, *Ensayos sobre la propiedad*, 149.

113. México: Secretaría de Gobernación, *Código civil para el Distrito y territorios federales*, article 832.

114. Keiser, "Social Conceptions of Property and Labour."

115. *Diario de los Debates de la Cámara de Senadores*, year 1, regular session, Thirty-sixth Legislature, vol. 1, no. 23, "Sesión ordinaria celebrada el 8 de diciembre de 1934."

116. *Diario de los Debates de la Cámara de Senadores*, 7–8.

117. "La expropiación por razones de utilidad social, se caracteriza por la tendencia a satisfacer, de un modo directo o inmediato, las necesidades de determinada clase social, pero mediata o indirectamente, las de la colectividad. . . . Así acontece tanto en el fraccionamiento de los grandes latifundios o en su colonización, en beneficio de las clases campesinas, como en el fraccionamiento y urbanización de terrenos destinados a construir habitaciones baratas e higiénicas para obreros." Suprema Corte de la Nación, "Expropriación por causa de utilidad pública," in *Semanario Judicial de la Federación*, vol. 45, p. 4798, https://sjf2.scjn.gob.mx/detalle/tesis/335405 (revised July 2025).

118. Meneses Reyes, "Los efectos materiales del constitucionalismo mexicano."

119. Francisco Mújica to Lázaro Cárdenas, May 7, 1935, AGN, LCR, file 545.3/3.

120. The words, published in *Excélsior*, were cited in a report that described opposition to the law. "Ley de Expropiación," AGN, LCR, box 886, file 545.2/61, bundle 3.

121. Liga Nacional de Sociedades Cooperativas to Lázaro Cárdenas, November 6, 1936, AGN, LCR, box 886, file 545.2/61, bundle 3.

122. This point was originally made by Azuela and Cruz, "La institucionalización de las colonias populares y la política urbana en la Ciudad de México (1940–1946)."

123. Until 1992 ejido lands had a use but not an exchange value. They could not be sold, rented, mortgaged, or taxed and were outside of the (formal) real-estate market. On the ejido mode of property, see Azuela, *La ciudad, la propiedad privada y el derecho*, 106–127.

124. The ejido is often believed to be an Indigenous remnant. But the postrevolutionary ejido was a thoroughly modern political institution, inspired by contemporary critiques of liberalism, a historic interpretation of the Porfirian regime and the revolution, and a specific historic conjuncture when revolutionary intellectuals and politicians attempted to placate mobilized peasants demanding land. See Kourí, "Interpreting the Expropriation of Indian Pueblo Lands in Porfirian Mexico"; and Azuela, "Avatares de un cronotopo."

Chapter 3: Planning and Informality

1. Ward, *Mexico City*, 114.

2. Ward has also argued in *Welfare Politics in Mexico* that the city government did not develop a master plan supported by "an institutionalized apparatus" until the 1980s, finally moving from "paper plans to a process of planning" (47).

3. "Demoliciones gratis por el enemigo público," 22.

4. For a critique of this dualistic urban analysis, see de Caldeira, "Peripheral Urbanization"; and Gilbert and de Jong, "Entanglements of Periphery and Informality in Mexico City."

5. Sánchez Mejorada, "Discurso leído por el Señor Ingeniero Javier Sánchez Mejorada," 77.

6. Enrique Schultz was the other drafter. Sánchez Ruiz, *Planificación y urbanismo de la revolución mexicana*, 222. This federal law served as a template for Mexico City's local planning laws, passed in 1933 and 1936. See "Ley de Planificación y Zonificación del Distrito Federal y Territorios de la Baja California," *Diario Oficial*, January 17, 1933; and "Ley de Planificación y Zonificación para el Distrito Federal," *Diario Oficial*, June 12, 1936.

7. Cited in Contreras, *Informe final del XVI Congreso Internacional de Planificación y de la Habitación*, 84–85.

8. Violich, *Cities of Latin America*, 90.

9. "Entrevista realizada a Reinaldo Pérez Rayón, realizada por Graciela de Garay, el día 2 de octubre de 1991 en la Ciudad de México," Archivo de la Palabra del Instituto de Investigaciones Dr. José María Luis Mora.

10. Garza, *La urbanización de México en el siglo XX*, 39.

11. Most histories of urban planning have been written by historians of architecture and focus on prominent planners and projects. See, for instance, Sánchez Ruiz, *Planificación y urbanismo de la revolución mexicana*; Carranza, *Architecture as Revolution*; Valenzuela Aguilera, *Urbanistas y visionarios*; Vargas Salguero, Larrucea, and Chanfón Olmos, *Arquitectura de la revolución y revolución de la arquitectura*; Peraza Guzmán and Cruz González Franco, *Segunda modernidad urbano arquitectónica*; and Escudero, *Una ciudad noble y lógica*. Alternative approaches to planning, which pay closer attention to the bureaucratic process of planning and have influenced my own work, include Ronda and Ugalde, "Planeación urbana en la Ciudad de México en los cincuenta"; and Zenteno Martínez, "La Comisión Mixta de Planificación."

12. Historians of urban planning have traced the current of ideas flowing from Ebenezer Howard's late nineteenth-century "garden city" and modernist planning (whose most famous practitioner was Charles Édouard Jeanneret, better known as

Le Corbusier), which had its heyday in the 1950s. See Hall, *Cities of Tomorrow*; and Fishmann, *Urban Utopias in the Twentieth Century*.

13. Scott, *Seeing Like a State*. Useful critiques and conversations with Scott include Valverde, "Seeing Like a City"; Mitchell, *Rule of Experts*; and Holston, *The Modernist City*.

14. Pani, *La higiene en México*.

15. I analyze this process in Azuela and de Antuñano, "Four Regimes of Informality."

16. Escudero, *Una ciudad noble y lógica*, 30–51.

17. Violich, *Cities of Latin America*, 162. On the influence of US institutions on Latin American planners, see Gorelik, "Pan-American Routes"; and Almandoz, "Urbanization and Urbanism in Latin America."

18. Contreras, "La planificación de la República Mexicana," *El Universal*, March 15, 1925. A translated and edited version of his article was published in the journal of the American City Planning Institute the same year: "National Planning Project for the Republic of Mexico."

19. Contreras, "Asociación Nacional para la Planificación de la República Mexicana," cited in Sánchez Ruiz, *Planificación y urbanismo visionarios de Carlos Contreras*, 58.

20. Abbott, *The System of Professions*.

21. "Editorial," *Planificación* 1, no. 3 (November 1927): 3. A similar aphorism—"Survey before plan"—was coined by Scottish biologist, geographer, and city planner Patrick Geddes.

22. "Editorial," *Planificación* 1, no. 7 (March 1928): 4–6.

23. Estrada Berg and Quijano, "Comité del Plano Regional de la Ciudad de México y sus Alrededores."

24. See Jacques Lambert, "Rapport du 24 juin 1932 sur la nécessite et les bases d'un Règlement d'urbanisation pour Mexico" (1932); and "Premier rapport sur l'aménagement du Zocalo 'Plaza de la Constitucion'" (1932), AGN, GR, box 36, file 23.

25. Contreras acknowledged the "advice and splendid assistance" that Bassett and other members of the Regional Plan of New York and Its Environs offered him while in New York: "National Planning Project for the Republic of Mexico," 97. The New York plan was frequently mentioned during the 1920s and 1930s; see, for example, Loyo, "Una oficina municipal de estadística e investigación."

26. Toussaint, *Planos de la Ciudad de México*, 9, 19. On the relationship between planning and the history of architecture, see Escudero, "La ciudad posrevolucionaria en tres planos"; and Almandoz, "Urban Planning and Historiography in Latin America."

27. Choay, *The Modern City*, 17 (emphasis in the original).

28. My understanding of scale, projection, and symbolization as distortions of reality is inspired by de Sousa Santos, "Law."

29. Antúnez Echegaray, "La foto-topografía aérea y sus aplicaciones prácticas."

30. Contreras, "Plan Development of Mexico City."

31. Contreras, *Informe final del XVI Congreso Internacional de Planificación y de la Habitación*, 89–95.

32. "Maravillosa maqueta de la Ciudad de México," *El Universal*, August 16, 1938. Architect Miguel Ángel de Quevedo led the enterprise. Gómez and Ángel de Quevedo, *Testimonios vivos*, 155–156.

33. "Una brillante exposición en Bellas Artes," *El Universal*, August 17, 1938.

34. "La fijación de todas las zonas urbanas," *El Universal*, March 30, 1939.

35. Article 5 of the 1936 Ley de Planificación y Zonificación del Distrito Federal listed the duties and obligations of the Planning Commission. According to the law, it was Mexico City's highest planning body, with authority over Public Works and other committees and offices. However, bureaucratic skirmishes between the Planning Commission and other planning organs were frequent. "Decreto por el cual se demarcan las atribuciones que, en material de planificación y zonificación, competen a la Comisión del ramo y a la Dirección General de Obras Públicas," *Diario Oficial*, October 14, 1941. On the Planning Commission, see Ronda and Ugalde, "Planeación urbana en la Ciudad de México en los cincuenta."

36. As mentioned earlier, Violich identified thirteen offices tasked with planning in 1939. Architect Enrique Guerrero enumerated ten bodies dealing with urban planning a few years later in "Urbanismo oficial."

37. Salvador Arroyo to Guillermo Aguilar Álvarez, October 13, 1945, AHCDMX, OP, box 254, bundle 1.

38. Escudero, *Una ciudad noble y lógica*, 191–195.

39. Contreras, *El plano regulador*, 15, 16, 17–18.

40. Escudero, "La ciudad posrevolucionaria en tres planos"; Sánchez Ruiz, *Planificación y urbanismo visionarios de Carlos Contreras.*

41. On the work of this commission, see "Informe que rinde el Comité del Plano Regulador integrado por el arquitecto Carlos Contreras, ingeniero José A. Cuevas y arquitecto Carlos Tarditi, a la Comisión de Planificiación del Distrito Federal," 59. The commission was originally named the Comité del Plano Regulador, before it changed its name around 1937. Information on these short-lived offices is scarce and conflicting, but there is a clear continuity between the two of them, which were largely formed by the same group. I am basing this chronology on dates mentioned by the members of the Comisión del Plano Regulador in minutes from 1939 and 1940. "Acta de la sesión celebrada por la Comisión del Plano Regulador el día 3 de marzo de 1939," AHCDMX, OP, box 161, 1.

42. Aguirre, "Plazas públicas para deportes en el Distrito Federal," 115.

43. On Loyo and Mexico's population policy, see Silva, "Forking Paths," 135–145.

44. Loyo, *Notas sobre la evolución demográfica de la Ciudad de México*, 9.

45. Contreras, "Plan Development of Mexico City," 4–5.

46. Federico O'Reilly and Juan Antonio Lainé, "Estudio para formular previsiones sobre el probable crecimiento futuro de la población del Distrito Federal" (August 1940), AGN, CL, box 49, file 222.

47. Gómez Mayorga's views on growth are best synthesized in his 1958 book *¿Qué hacer por la Ciudad de México?* For an interpretation of the character, see Rodríguez Kuri, "Hacia México 1968," 57–58.

48. Meyer, "La Ciudad de México," 99; "Población de las principales colonias de la Ciudad de México, según el censo de 6 de marzo de 1940," in DDP, *Memoria del Departamento del Distrito Federal* (1941).

49. "El problema de la habitación en la Ciudad de México," *Estudios* 6 (1952): 4.

50. Meyer, "La Ciudad de México."

51. Three-fourths of the land in the Federal District was dedicated to agrarian uses in 1906. See de Gortari and Hernández Franyuti, *La Ciudad de México y el Distrito Federal*, 4:73–96.

52. Iztacalco: 11,212 to 33,945; Iztapalapa: 25,393 to 76,621; Azcapotzalco: 32,313 to 93,176; Gustavo A. Madero 41,567 to 204,833. Mexico: Dirección General de Estadística, *6º censo de población: 1940*.

53. Instituto Nacional de la Vivienda, *Colonias proletarias: problemas y soluciones*; Instituto Nacional de la Vivienda, *Herradura de tugurios*. I analyze these diagnoses in chapter 6.

54. Adolfo Zamora, "Informe sobre las labores desarrolladas por la Oficina de Estudios Municipales, del 1936 al de 1941," AGN, CL, box 89, file 8.

55. Banco Nacional Hipotecario y de Obras Públicas, *4 ponencias para el Primer Congreso Nacional de Habitaciones Obreras* (Mexico City: Oficina de Estudios Municipales, 1939). Pamphlet located in AGN, CL, box 89, file 8. See also Alatriste, "Apuntes para la solución de la habitación proletaria en la Ciudad de México" (1936), Centro de Estudios de Historia de México, Fondo Luis Montes de Oca, folder 343, file 32004.

56. "Acta de la sesión celebrada por la Comisión del Plano Regulador el día 31 de marzo de 1939," AHCDMX, OP, box 161, bundle 1.

57. DDF, *Memoria del Departamento del Distrito Federal* (1940), 100; "Reglamento de las fracciones I, V, y VII del artículo 3º de la Ley de Planificación y Zonificación del Distrito Federal," *Gaceta Oficial del Departamento del Distrito Federal* 1, no. 1, March 31, 1941.

58. Article 2: "Reglamento de las fracciones I, V, y VII del artículo 3º de la Ley de Planificación y Zonificación del Distrito Federal," *Gaceta Oficial del Departamento del Distrito Federal* 1, no. 1, March 31, 1941.

59. Article 1: "Reglamento de las fracciones I, V, y VII del artículo 3º de la Ley de Planificación y Zonificación del Distrito Federal," *Gaceta Oficial del Departamento del Distrito Federal* 1, no. 1, March 31, 1941.

60. For the exceptions, see "Excepción al Reglamento de las Fracciones I, V, y VII del artículo 3º de la Ley de Planificación y Zonificación del D.F.," *Gaceta Oficial del Departamento del Distrito Federal* 1, no. 12, September 15, 1941. The 1941 code was the "Reglamento sobre fraccionamiento de terrenos en el Distrito Federal," which stipulated the obligations of developers in order to subdivide new neighborhoods. The code also ordered that land divisions would have to follow guidelines set by the master plan, which was still not completed in 1941.

61. "Comisión del Plano Regulador," March 17, 1939, AHCDMX, OP, box 161, bundle 1.

62. On the ideas undergirding this belief, see Babb, *Managing Mexico*; Gauss, *Made in Mexico*; and Rodríguez Kuri, "Secretos de la idiosincrasia."

63. Antonio Ruiz Galindo, "The Basic Ideas of the Industrial City 'D. M. Nacional,'" *Social Sciences in Mexico* 1, no. 2 (Fall 1947): 40.

64. Garza, *El proceso de industrialización de la Ciudad de México (1821–1970)*, 139.

65. Gauss, *Made in Mexico*, 99.

66. Cymet Lerer and Ortiz Flores, *El problema de las colonias proletarias, Ciudad de México*, 50.

67. On the planning of these areas, see Candelario Galicia, "Industrial Vallejo." See also Maffitt, "From the Ashes of the Poet Kings."

68. "Se iniciaron los trabajos para la zonificación de la ciudad," *El Universal*, April 16, 1940.

69. Cymet Lerer and Ortiz Flores, *El problema de las colonias proletarias, Ciudad de México*, 50–51.

70. "Acta de la sesión celebrada por la Comisión del Plano Regulador el 24 de abril de 1939," AHCDMX, OP, box 161, bundle 1.

71. This was the case of the residents of Santa María la Ribera and Romero Rubio in the 1930s. "Las fábricas en la ciudad," *El Universal*, May 15, 1937; "Se iniciaron los trabajos para la zonificación de la ciudad," *El Universal*, April 16, 1940.

72. "Acta de la sesión celebrada por la Comisión del Plano Regulador el 24 de abril de 1939," AHCDMX, OP, box 161, bundle 1.

73. "Zonificación industrial en la metrópoli," *El Nacional*, August 3, 1939. On the decentralization of the industry over the 1920s and 1930s, see Candelario Galicia, "Industrial Vallejo," 113–117.

74. Contreras's comments in "Acta de la sesión celebrada por la Comisión del Plano Regulador el 24 de abril de 1939," AHCDMX, OP, box 161, bundle 1.

75. "Acta de la sesión celebrada por la Comisión del Plano Regulador el 17 de marzo de 1939," AHCDMX, OP, box 161, bundle 1.

76. Atlampa, El Rastro, San Lázaro and La Viga, Colonia Hidalgo, Colonia Algarín, Colonia del Valle, Colonia Anahuác, Colonia Santa Julia, Becerra, Refinería de Petróleo, Calzada de Guadalupe, and the Ford industrial plant. "Comisión de Planificación," November 13, 1940, AHCDMX, Planoteca, box 285, file 4.

77. "Todas las facilidades para la industria del Distrito Federal," *Gaceta Oficial del Departamento del Distrito Federal*, September 15, 1941.

78. "Anteproyecto de las terminales ferroviarias de México," no page (plate 6).

79. "Reglamento de las fracciones I, V, y VII del artículo 3º de la Ley de Planificación y Zonificación del Distrito Federal," *Gaceta Oficial del Departamento del Distrito Federal*, March 31, 1941.

80. For example, the Sociedad de Fraccionamientos Industriales explained, in the midst of a land conflict with an agrarian community, that an industrial decree was interpreted by them as a "frank invitation from the government to the entrepreneurs of the country to . . . industrialize the area." "Dictamen que presenta la consultoria #4, a cargo del C. Ing. Jesús Molina Urquidez, en el expediente de restitución de ejidos al poblado de Ixtacalco, delegación de Ixtacalco, del Distrito Federal," AGA, Ixtacalco, 24–910–15.

81. See, for example, Salvador Arroyo to Jefe de la Oficina de Planeación, February 20, 1947, AHCDMX, OP, box 254, bundle 1.

82. Cuevas et al., "Sugestiones que hace la Sociedad de Arquitectos Mexicanos a la Dirección de Obras Públicas del Gobierno del Distrito Federal para la formulación de la nueva Ley de Planificación y Zonificación del D.F.," 12.

83. García Cortés, "Plani-Destrucción," *El Universal*, January 17, 1954.

84. "Ley de Planificación y Zonificación para el Distrito Federal," *Diario Oficial*, June 12, 1936.

85. To make things worse, the tramway system was outdated by decades. According to a 1941 Public Works report, tramways only covered the extension of the city circa 1900–1905, when its population totaled 370,000. "Informe que rinde a la comisión mixta que estudia el problema de tranvías de la Ciudad de México la subcomisión designada para estudiar el aspecto técnico del citado problema" (1941), AHCDMX, OP, box 468, bundle 3.

86. Schulz, "Breve reseña acerca de los trabajos relacionados con la planificación de la Ciudad de México."

87. Escudero, *Una ciudad noble y lógica*, 234.

88. Gómez Mayorga, *¿Qué hacer por la Ciudad de México?*, 61.

89. For an early assessment of autoconstrucción, see INV, *Características, problemas y programa de acción en beneficio de las colonias proletarias*. For later analyses, see Ward, "The Practice and Potential of Self-Help Housing in Mexico City"; and Connolly, "Uncontrolled Settlements and Self-Build." I review these debates about the progressive nature of housing in colonias proletarias in chapter 6.

90. For a summary of this view, see Connolly, "Uncontrolled Settlements and Self-Build," 152–153.

91. "Comisión Reguladora del Crecimiento de la Ciudad," March 18, 1947, AHCDMX, OP, box 598, bundle 2.

92. "Comisión Reguladora del Crecimiento de la Ciudad," March 18, 1947, AHCDMX, OP, box 598, bundle 2.

93. "[D]espués viene el relleno que formará el conjunto del plano regulador." "Comisión Reguladora del Crecimiento de la Ciudad," March 18, 1947, AHCDMX, OP, box 598, bundle 2.

94. Gómez Mayorga, "El plano de la ciudad," 16.

95. "Romita, pueblo aislado dentro de una gran urbe," *El Universal*, February 13, 1944. Planning studies on Romita are referenced in DDF, *Memoria del Departamento del Distrito Federal* (1942).

96. "En contra de las expropiaciones sin causa: en contra de la anarquía," *El Universal*, October 27, 1941.

97. DDF, *Memoria del Departamento del Distrito Federal, del 1 de septiembre de 1942 al 31 de agosto de 1943*.

98. "Nos hemos encontrado una cantidad de colonias que han surgido recientemente y que están construyendo donde quieren y que piden al propio licenciado servicios de agua y saneamiento sin tomar en consideración las dificultades para llevarlo a cabo y nos pide se haga la planificación rápida; quizás se logre el aumento de personal para poder resolver estos casos dentro del Distrito Federal lo que es preferible a la anarquía que reina." "Comisión Reguladora del Crecimiento de la Ciudad," July 29, 1947, AHCDMX, OP, box 598, file 2.

99. Ingeniero Leopoldo Villa to Delegado de Villa Gustavo A. Madero, February 20, 1947, AHCDMX, OP, box 254, 1.

100. "[P]orque se encuentran varias personas presentes que se sienten afectadas con la planificación de la colonia Capultitlán y quieren exponer sus puntos de vista." "Comisión Reguladora del Crecimiento de la Ciudad," July 29, 1947, AHCDMX, OP, box 598, file 2.

101. "Comisión Reguladora del Crecimiento de la Ciudad," August 21, 1946, AHCDMX, Planoteca, box 258, file 4. For more examples of resident associations requesting official blueprints, see the cases of "Colonia Urbana Marte," AHCDMX, OP, box 471, bundle 2; and "Olivar del Conde," AHCDMX, OP, box 658, bundle 1.

102. "Comisión Reguladora del Crecimiento de la Ciudad," Acta 21 (no date, ca. 1947), AHCDMX, OP, box 598, bundle 2.

103. Duhau and Giglia, *Las reglas del desorden*, 347. De Soto summarizes the process of informal urbanization in *The Other Path*: "In informal settlements, the

various stages of traditional urban development are reversed. First, the informals occupy the land, then they build on it, next they install infrastructures, and only at the end do they acquire ownership" (17).

104. Ward, "The Practice and Potential of Self-Help Housing in Mexico City," 178.

105. "Las gentes no hacen caso pues construyen en donde quieren y como quieren y después vienen los conflictos; si es difícil planear una colonia, más difícil es ajustar esa planeación." "Comisión Reguladora del Crecimiento de la Ciudad," July 29, 1947, AHCDMX, OP, box 598, bundle 2.

106. "Ex-Escuela de Tiro," AHCDMX, OP, box 658, bundle 1.

107. Juan Guzmán to Fernando Ramírez, sub-jefe de la Oficina de Colonias, AGN, MAC, file 418.2/97.

108. Juan Guzmán to Fernando Ramírez, sub-jefe de la Oficina de Colonias, AGN, MAC, file 418.2/97.

109. Juan Guzmán to Manuel Ávila Camacho, August 18, 1941, AGN, MAC, file 418.2/97.

110. DDF, *Memoria del Departamento del Distrito Federal, del 1 de septiembre de 1942 al 31 de agosto de 1943*, 84.

111. The date of approval of the official blueprint can be found in Coalición de Colonos del D.F. to Manuel Ávila Camacho, AGN, MAC, file 418.2/97.

112. Oscar Villegas, Alberto Villa et al. to Manuel Ávila Camacho, AGN, MAC, file 418.2/97.

113. Enriqueta Vera, Alberto Villa et al. to Manuel Ávila Camacho, September 9, 1944, AGN, MAC, file 418.2/97.

114. More specifically, the 1942 Reglamento de Construcciones. Guillermo Aguilar Álvarez to Alberto Villa, Oscar Villegas et al., September 26, 1944, AGN, MAC, file 418.2/97.

115. Enriqueta Vera, Alberto Villa et al. to Manuel Ávila Camacho, September 9, 1944, "Colonia Gertrudis G. Sánchez," AGN, MAC, file 418.2/97.

116. INV, *Características, problemas y programa de acción en beneficio de las colonias proletarias*, 18, 24.

117. Rama, *La ciudad letrada.*

118. Gómez Mayorga, "El plano de la ciudad."

119. "La fijación de todas las zonas urbanas," *El Universal*, March 30, 1939.

Chapter 4: A Proletarian Metropolis

1. Key works on colonias proletarias include Perló Cohen, "Política y vivienda en México, 1910–1952"; Azuela and Cruz, "La institucionalización de las colonias populares y la política urbana en la Ciudad de México (1940–1946)"; and Sánchez Mejorada, *Rezagos de la modernidad*. Contemporary surveys by architects include Cymet Lerer and Ortiz Flores, *El problema de las colonias proletarias, Ciudad de México*; and Harth-Deneke, "The Colonias Proletarias of Mexico City."

2. It is hard to provide an exact number because different government offices collected their own records. Most scholars rely on the data that Cymet Lerer and Ortiz Flores assembled in *El problema de las colonias proletarias, Ciudad de México*

(1955), adding up to 279 neighborhoods. As professional architects employed by the Department of Public Works, Cymet Lerer and Ortiz Flores were technocrat experts, although their knowledge of the politics of colonias was less solid. The Oficina de Colonias, which actually sanctioned them, listed 304 colonias proletarias in the early 1950s, according to an undated census. AHCDMX, Gobernación, box 217. Cornejo Cabrera counted 280 colonias proletarias in 1957 in "La colonia proletaria Escuadrón 201," 167. Cornelius calculated 620 in 1970 (a number provided by PRI officials) in *Politics and the Migrant Poor in Mexico City*, 30, fn. 14.

3. Cornelius, *Politics and the Migrant Poor in Mexico City*, 30, fn. 14.

4. Connolly, "Latin American Informal Urbanism," 36.

5. Stanford, "A propósito de la creación del Instituto Nacional de la Vivienda: este es el problema," *Mañana*, June 11, 1955. Article clipping in AGN, INV, box 12.

6. If we categorize them in this way, we can identify numerous colonias proletarias not sanctioned by the Oficina de Colonias.

7. I am borrowing Holston's words in reference to São Paulo's peripheries in *Insurgent Citizenship*, 4.

8. Meneses Reyes, "Los efectos materiales del constitucionalismo mexicano."

9. Schmitter's classic definition in "Still the Century of Corporatism?" understands corporatism as a practice of interest representation that can serve regimes with very different ideologies. Critical interpretations of the Mexican political system as corporatist—and authoritarian—became common in the 1970s. See Reyna and Weinert, *Authoritarianism in Mexico*. For a recent historical interpretation of Mexican corporatism, see Robinet, "¿Los orígenes trasnacionales del 'corporativismo mexicano'?"

10. Kennedy, "Two Globalizations of Law & Legal Thought"; Rodgers, "In Search of Progressivism."

11. "El Derecho es una 'forma' instrumental que ha de ponerse al servicio—¡y sólo al servicio!—de las necesidades y aspiraciones de la vida de los hombres en los complicados entrelazamientos que se producen en el inextricable fenómeno de la solidaridad humana." Senorio, "Lo social como contenido del derecho," 87. The publication of this article in the *Revista Mexicana de Sociología*, Mexico's first sociological journal, further emphasizes the links between social legal thought and the social sciences.

12. *Diario de Debates de la Cámara de Diputados*, Forty-first Legislature, year 3, regular session, December 30, 1951, diary 37.

13. Antonio Azuela pointed out to me the significance of this preamble. It was drafted by Ignacio García Tellez, a lawyer who became dean of the Universidad Nacional in 1929 and later led the Department of Education and the Institute of Social Security. See Keiser, "Social Conceptions of Property and Labour."

14. Lombardo Toledano represented Mexico at the 1925 Ninth International Congress of Housing and Urban Planning in New York, where he met Carlos Contreras.

15. Rodríguez Kuri, "Ciudad oficial, 1930–1970," 419.

16. Cited in Bleynat, *Vendor's Capitalism*, 98.

17. Davis, *Urban Leviathan*, 68. See also Cisneros Sosa, *La ciudad que construimos*, 57.

18. José Ángel Espinoza, "Ponencia en pro de un régimen de gobierno integral para la Ciudad de México," December 26, 1947, AGN, CL, box 49, file 224.

19. "Reglamento de asociaciones pro-mejoramiento de las colonias del Distrito Federal," *Diario Oficial*, March 28, 1941.

20. The blurry line between protecting and controlling urban residents is visible in Eckstein, "The State and the Urban Poor"; and Perló Cohen, "Política y vivienda en México, 1910–1952."

21. Bloque Revolucionario de Colonos del Distrito Federal to Lázaro Cárdenas, October 24, 1940, AGN, LCR, file 545.2/4.

22. Insofar as the Reglamento de Colonias ordered that resident associations were "licensed" by the state and awarded them a "monopoly" over the representation of residents, it can be considered an archetypal corporatist law. I am following Schmitter's definition of corporatism in "Still the Century of Corporatism?" (93–94) as "a system of interest representation in which the constituent units are organized into a limited number of singular, compulsory, noncompetitive, hierarchically ordered and functionally differentiated categories, recognized or licensed (if not created) by the state and granted a deliberate representational monopoly within their respective categories in exchange for observing certain controls on their selection of leaders and articulation of demands and supports."

23. Article 16. Family patrimony was regulated in the 1928 Civil Code (Título XII, Capítulo Único, Libro Primero). See Azuela, "El marco jurídico de la vivienda," 43.

24. "Un hogar intocable para la familia," *Gaceta Oficial del Departamento del Distrito Federal*, June 16, 1941.

25. Bloque Nacional de Colonos Revolucionarios to Manuel Ávila Camacho, March 20, 1941, AGN, MAC, box 759, file 545.2/69.

26. Azuela and Cruz, "La institucionalización de las colonias populares y la política urbana en la Ciudad de México (1940–1946)."

27. The existence of a land market in colonias proletarias in defiance of these regulations has been amply documented. See INV, *Características, problemas y programa de acción en beneficio de las colonias proletarias*; and Ward, "The Practice and Potential of Self-Help Housing in Mexico City."

28. "Reglamento sobre fraccionamientos de terreno en el Distrito Federal," *Diario Oficial*, December 31, 1941.

29. INV, *Características, problemas y programa de acción en beneficio de las colonias proletarias*, 1. The existence of this dual regime was proposed by Azuela and Cruz, "La institucionalización de las colonias populares y la política urbana en la Ciudad de México (1940–1946)."

30. The decree is cited in Cymet Lerer and Ortiz Flores, *El problema de las colonias proletarias, Ciudad de México*, 1: "Artículo 1. Se declara de utilidad pública el fomento y mejoría de las habitaciones para las clases pobres."

31. For the reluctance of planners to locate colonias proletarias in wealthy and middle-class areas, see "Comisión Reguladora del Crecimiento de la Ciudad," October 2, 1946, AHCDMX, Planoteca, box 258, file 4. Planners expressed concern about the establishment of a colonia proletaria in Colonia Nápoles, given the prospect of the land increasing in value over time.

32. Perló Cohen, "Política y vivienda en México, 1910–1952," 796, citing *El Universal*, February 25, 1951.

33. Perló Cohen, "Política y vivienda en México," 796, citing *El Universal*, February 25, 1951.

34. From the viewpoint of the municipal government, this arrangement was anomalous because it gave the Oficina de Colonias (part of the Secretaría de Gobernación)

a key role in handling urbanization. The anomaly was noted in DDF, *Gobierno del Distrito Federal, sexenio 1940-1946*, 29. According to a government report, the Oficina de Colonias handled "social and demographic data" in colonias proletarias, whereas the distribution of urban services and the planning, sewage disposal, and policing of colonias proletarias were undertaken by other offices. AHCDMX, OP, box 658, bundle 1.

35. When the DDF created colonias proletarias, it ordered that lot purchasers would contribute to "obras de urbanización" following the Ley de Hacienda del Distrito Federal. But how much would be paid and for which urban services was a matter of continuous negotiation. The arbitrary nature of urban services payments is further evidenced by such initiatives as the Colonias Proletarias Award created in 1945 by the Oficina de Colonias. The prize was municipal services provided to the neighborhood that had made the biggest efforts toward "improving" its housing conditions. AHCDMX, OP, box 248, bundle 1.

36. For instance, the 1946 Ley de Ingresos ordered that colonias proletarias would pay a lower property tax, negotiated with the Oficina de Colonias. See "Ley de Ingresos del Distrito Federal para el ejercicio fiscal de 1946," *Gaceta Oficial del Departamento del Distrito Federal* 6, no. 167, February 10, 1946. See also Oldman et al. *Financing Urban Development in Mexico City*, 51.

37. Cited in INV, *Características, problemas y programa de acción en beneficio de las colonias proletarias*, 9.

38. Ramírez, "El problema de la habitación y los niveles de vida," 335.

39. Benítez Zenteno, "Habitación, comercio, industria, educación, culto y diversiones en la Ciudad de México," 309.

40. Connolly, "Uncontrolled Settlements and Self-Build," 147–149; Duhau, *Habitat popular y política urbana*, 136–137.

41. Lewis's books do not provide the real names of the characters and the neighborhoods where they lived, but his transcripts do contain this information. El Dorado, the site of Sánchez's first house, is identified as La Esmeralda or Casas Alemán (neighboring colonias); both Iztapalapa and Iztacalco (delegaciones adjacent to each other) are mentioned as the location of the second house. Oscar Lewis Archive, box 53, "Santos Hernández Story—Spanish."

42. Lewis, *Five Families*, 214.

43. I delve into these questions in chapters 5 and 6.

44. The Department of Public Works assembled information on the following categories: (1) neighborhood name; (2) location; (3) area (in square meters); (4) number of lots; (5) land value; (6) population; (7) owner (publicly or privately owned); (8) topographic characteristics; (9) date of establishment; (10) existence of a neighborhood association; (11) urban services; (12) existence of an official blueprint.

45. The city cadaster was completed in 1945 but did not encompass delegaciones, where most colonias proletarias were located. Sánchez Mejorada, *Rezagos de la modernidad*, 118–119. See also "Decreto que fija normas a que deberán sujetarse las traslaciones de dominio de bienes inmuebles en el Distrito Federal," *Gaceta Oficial del Departamento del Distrito Federal* 2, no. 59, February 10, 1943.

46. My calculation is based on the list of 279 neighborhoods included in Cymet Lerer and Ortiz Flores, *El problema de las colonias proletarias, Ciudad de México*, 68–73.

47. In a typical case in Colonia Carrera Lardizabal, for example, dozens of families were dispossessed when the official blueprint was approved. These families were

waiting for the government to provide new lots once work in the neighborhood was completed. "Carrera Lardizabal," AHCDMX, OP, box 471, bundle 2.

48. The city government reported in 1949 that it was in the process of completing a Padrón General de Colonos (General Census of Settlers) that would allow it to "identify settlers in possession of government-granted lots, preventing these settlers from accumulating multiple lots." DDF, *Resumen de actividades* (1949), 198.

49. "Ex–Escuela de Tiro," AHCDMX, OP, box 658, bundle 1.

50. A list of the correspondence between Public Works and the Oficina de Colonias can be found in "Relaciones, relativas a la correspondencia recibida de enero de 1941 hasta el 30 de abril de 1945," AHCDMX, Planoteca, box 194, bundle 1.

51. Cornejo Cabrera, "La colonia proletaria Escuadrón 201," 167.

52. In 1942 the Oficina de Colonias replaced the Oficina de Cooperación, whose goal had been to organize and establish colonias proletarias. See DDF, *Memoria del Departamento del Distrito Federal* (1941), 73. In 1972 the Oficina de Colonias was replaced by the Procuraduría de Colonias Populares. Cisneros Sosa, *La ciudad que construimos*, 198.

53. See articles 6, 12, 13, and 15 of the Reglamento de Asociaciones. In a 1955 article praising the office, Alfredo Félix Díaz Escobar described—among its many actions—avoiding illegal invasions, tranferring lots, eliminating brokers, moralizing the leadership of neighborhoods, distributing construction materials, and contributing to such public works as water provision, pavements, and schools. "Colonias proletarias," *El Universal*, June 25, 1955.

54. DDF, *Memoria del gobierno del Distrito Federal* (1945), 5.

55. A partial list of the heads of the Oficina de Colonias includes José Garibay Centeno (ca. 1942–1945); Rodolfo Encizo Ponce (ca. 1947); Juan Reyes (active in October 1947); Francisco Linares (active in December 1947); Carlos Zapata Vela (ca. 1950–1951); and Rafael Suárez Ocaña (ca. 1953).

56. See, for example, the work of José Garibay Centeno in securing lots for residents of Colonia Ampliación Niños Héroes, in AGN, MAC, box 771, file 545.22.

57. Rafael Suárez Ocaña to Lino Gómez, Nicolás Hurtado et al., April 17, 1956, AHCDMX, OP, box 471, bundle 2.

58. See the case of Colonia Ajusco, the subject of a lengthy investigation. Alonso, *Lucha urbana y acumulación de capital*, 303–321.

59. Cornelius, *Politics and the Migrant Poor in Mexico City*, 136–154. On the 1970s, see also Eckstein, "The State and the Urban Poor."

60. "Atropello de un lider de colonos," *La Prensa*, July 30, 1954; "Esquilman a los colonos pobres, cinco liderzuelos," *El Popular*, April 15, 1955. I tell the story of this neighborhood in chapter 5.

61. Paz, *El ogro filantrópico*; Escalante Gonzalbo, *México: el peso del pasado*.

62. Sánchez Mejorada, *Rezagos de la modernidad*, 61–75.

63. On the rent-control decree, see Sánchez Mejorada, *Rezagos de la modernidad*, 216–225. On the war years, see Niblo, *Mexico in the 1940s*, 115–124.

64. Federación de Organizaciones Populares del Distrito Federal, "Primer Consejo General Ordinario: conclusiones y recomendaciones," July 20, 1944, AGN, DGG, box 2712, 2/331.9(29)/158, 18–19.

65. This group formed the Comité Directivo de la Federación de Colonias Proletarias (Steering Committee of the Federation of Proletarian Neighborhoods). See

"Toma de posesión de las directivas de las sociedades de colonos del Distrito Federal, en Bellas Artes," in *Historia Documental de la CNOP, 1943–1959*, 147.

66. "Toma de posesión de las directivas de las sociedades de colonos del Distrito Federal, en Bellas Artes," in *Historia Documental de la CNOP, 1943–1959*, 145, 147.

67. José Muñoz Cota to Lázaro Cárdenas, October 10, 1938, AGN, LCR, box 883, file 545.2/4.

68. According to Jiménez Muñoz in *La traza del poder* (255–259), the others were the Federación de Organizaciones del Distrito Federal, Frente Único de Colonos de la República, and Confederación de Colonos de México.

69. Invitations to the event in AGN, MAC, box 759, file 545.2/69, bundle 1. At the time, the coalition was led by Nicanor Sánchez Vilches as secretary general, while Salvador Flores was secretary of the interior.

70. Coalición de Colonos to Manuel Ávila Camacho, October 8, 1945, AGN, MAC, box 759, file 545.2/69, bundle 1.

71. Salvador Flores to Luis Viñals Carsi, August 4, 1945, AGN, MAC, box 759, file 545.2/69, bundle 2.

72. These neighborhoods are mentioned in Coalición de Colonos to Miguel Alemán Valdés, February 17, 1947, AGN, MAV, file 418.2/1.

73. Coalición de Colonos to Miguel Alemán Valdés, February 17, 1947, AGN, MAV, file 418.2/1.

74. On the Unidad Modelo project, see de Anda Alanís, *Vivienda colectiva de la modernidad en México*, 227–232; and Gómez Mayorga, "El problema de la habitación en México."

75. Gómez Mayorga, "El problema de la habitación en México," 77.

76. Salvador Flores to Manuel Ávila Camacho, April 8, 1946, AGN, MAC, box 759, file 545.2/69 (2). On the coalition's rejection of housing projects, see also Coalition de Colonos to Miguel Alemán Valdés, February 17, 1947, AGN, MAV, file 418.2/1.

77. "Carta abierta de los colonos de Américas Unidas," AGN, ARC, file 418.2/84.

78. MX$8.50 per square meter. "Carta abierta de los colonos de Américas Unidas," AGN, ARC, file 418.2/84.

79. Adalberto Pliego and Mario Chávez to Javier Rojo Gómez, February 3, 1944, AGN, MAC, 418.2/167.

80. "Carta abierta de los colonos de Américas Unidas," AGN, ARC, file 418.2/84.

81. "[Concepción de Hoth] ha azuzado a las personas que tienen escrituras en sus manos . . . y estas personas que tienen escrituras compraron sus lotes a sabiendas que nosotros teníamos posesión cincos o seis años atrás." AGN, ARC, file 418.2/84.

82. For police violence, see Salvador Flores, June 25, 1944, AGN, MAC, file 418.2/167.

83. "El señor Flores y socios buscando adictos que no sabemos con qué fines hace falsas promesas a compañeros faltos de preparación y niega el PLANO que siendo aprobado fue entregado a las directivas de Américas Unidas y Amp. Niños Héroes." Adalberto Pliego and Mario Chávez to President Manuel Ávila Camacho, February 3, 1944, AGN, MAC, file 418.2/167.

84. "Dicho señor Flores carece de escrúpulos y de solvencia moral y . . . lo único que ha venido pretendiendo es desorientar a la colonia y crear un estado permanente

de agitación perjudicial para nosotros." Adalberto Pliego and Mario Chávez to President Manuel Ávila Camacho, February 3, 1944, AGN, MAC, file 418.2/167.

85. Adalberto Souza to President Manuel Ávila Camacho, August 26, 1946, AGN, MAC, file 418.2/167.

86. Salvador Flores to President Miguel Alemán, February 17, 1947, AGN, MAV, box 281, 418.2/1.

87. Trapp E. Ador, "Escoba y Recogedor," *El Nacional*, February 22, 1950. The citation comes from *trascendidos* (leaks), unsigned messages that still abound in the Mexican press.

88. Javier Piña y Palacios [Dirección de Servicios Legales, Oficina Jurídica] to Director de Obras Públicas, July 2, 1952, AHCDMX, OP, box 359, bundle 1.

89. Salvador Flores to President Adolfo Ruiz Cortines, September 3, 1953, AGN, ARC, file 418.2/84.

90. Jesús González Valencia and Mario Coquet to Lamberto Ortega, June 16, 1949, AGN, DGIPS, box 103, file 1.

91. Jesús González Valencia and Mario Coquet to Lamberto Ortega, June 16, 1949, AGN, DGIPS, box 112, file 4.

92. Cornejo Cabrera, "La colonia proletaria Escuadrón 201," 171.

93. "Carta abierta del Señor Vidal Alonso, al C. Presidente de la República en relación con la Colonia Escuadrón 201," AGN, DGIPS, box 112, file 4.

94. Undated press clipping in AGN, DGIPS, box 112, file 4.

95. "Carta abierta del Señor Vidal Alonso, al C. Presidente de la República en relación con la Colonia Escuadrón 201," AGN, DGIPS, box 112, file 4.

96. Cornejo Cabrera, "La colonia proletaria Escuadrón 201," 173.

97. Memorandum to Lamberto Ortega, August 30, 1948, AGN, DGIPS, box 112, file 4.

98. Cornejo Cabrera, "La colonia proletaria Escuadrón 201," 172–173.

99. I have seen evidence of Flores's involvement in Gertrudis Sánchez, Gabriel Ramos Millán, Ampliación Niños Héroes, Atlampa, and Modelo, among other neighborhoods.

100. "La ciudad," *El Universal*, August 20, 1950.

101. Coalición de Colonos to Miguel Alemán Valdés, August 14, 1948, AGN, MAV, box 281, file 418.2/1.

102. Jesús González Valencia and Mario Coquet to Lamberto Ortega, June 16, 1949, DGIPS, box 103, file 1.

103. "Nosotros tratamos de exponer a usted, el problema del Colono en posesión de su lote y de su casa construida con ímprobos sacrificios, de ninguna manera del paracaidista contumaz, que a diario plantea problemas a su Gobierno, ese paracaidista no es el ciudadano que trata de dar hogar a su familia, sino el instrumento de vivales que han hecho un suculento negocio con lo más caro del Pueblo (su necesidad); los Colonos que representamos son el nervio mismo de nuestra ciudadanía." Abel Boza Alemán and Rubén Rodríguez Lozano to Miguel Alemán Valdés, April 5, 1949, AGN, MAV, box 281, file 418.2/1.

104. In 1947 the Unión de Colonos de Tecpan petitioned for his liberation from prison. Isidro Quintanar to Miguel Alemán Valdés, September 1, 1947, AGN, MAV, box 548, file 542.2/72. See also Cisneros Sosa, *La ciudad que construimos*, 101.

105. "Fue sepultado el Srio General de la Coalición de Colonos," *El Nacional*, December 23, 1953.

106. Historians disagree regarding the nature of this relationship. Sánchez Mejorada has written that the coalition was part of the PRI (*Rezagos de la modernidad*, 245), but Cisneros Sosa claimed the opposite (*La ciudad que construimos*).

107. Flores's maneuvers are recorded in AGN, MAC, box 433, file 433/500.

108. Clodomiro Morales Camacho to Lamberto Ortega, June 9, 1949, AGN, DGIPS box 112, file 4.

109. Cornelius, *Politics and the Migrant Poor in Mexico City*.

110. See note 39 in the introduction.

111. Some of the coalition's official documents note its membership in the CNOP, but the significance of this membership is dubious. I have found no evidence that the coalition was following any party line.

112. I am borrowing the words of Abrams, in his well-known demystification of the state: "Notes on the Difficulty of Studying the State," 82.

Chapter 5: From Proletarian to Marginal Neighborhoods

1. Monsiváis, "Los hermanos Mayo," 92.

2. "La ciudad perdida desapareció y sus moradores tienen nuevo hogar," *El Nacional*, December 26, 1950; "Traslado de los colonos del Rancho del Charro," *El Nacional*, December 18, 1950.

3. A sample voucher can be accessed in AHCDMX, DDF, Fondo Gobernación, box 162.

4. The 1955 calculation was made by Cymet Lerer and Ortiz Flores, *El problema de las colonias proletarias, Ciudad de México*, 71. Colonia Ramos Millán had been divided into two sections (Tlacotal and Bramadero) by 1960, adding up to 49,599 residents. México: Dirección General de Estadística, *8° censo general de población: 1960*, 67. The population of Iztacalco increased from 33,945 in 1950 to 198,904 in 1960. According to Mexico City's Oficina de Colonias, Colonia Ramos Millán had 5,970 lots in 1955. See "Relación de colonias proletarias," AHCDMX, DDF, Fondo Gobernación, box 323.

5. Jiménez y Castilla, "Bramadero."

6. DDF, *Atlas general del Distrito Federal*, 297. On Iztacalco's history, see Instituto Nacional de Antropología e Historia, *Catálogo nacional, monumentos históricos*.

7. Álvarez, "Tercer circuito pro-turismo," 209.

8. González Castillo, "Los parásitos intestinales en Santa Anita, Distrito Federal."

9. "Se informa sobre la situación legal de los poblados de Colonia Independencia, Ixtacalco, San Juanico Mextipa, y Mexicaltzingo," April 3, 1945, AGA, Ixtacalco, 23/910, bundle 5.

10. "Se informa sobre la situación legal de los poblados de Colonia Independencia, Ixtacalco, San Juanico Mextipa, y Mexicaltzingo," April 3, 1945, AGA, Ixtacalco, 23/910, bundle 5. See also the letter from Ing. Joaquín Madrazo (Delegado Agrario en el DF) to C. Jefe del Departamento Agrario, July 25, 1945, AGA, Ixtacalco, 29/910, bundle 13.

11. Azuela and Saavedra, "Uso, desgaste y reuso de la expropiación en la Ciudad de México." On the expropriation of the ejido lands to create the Universidad Nacional, see Mack, "De ejidos urbanos a Ciudad Universitaria."

12. "Escrito del arquitecto Enrique Guerrero registrado en la Oficialía de Partes con el número 1675 anexando en dicho oficio proyecto para proceder a fraccionar para fines industriales los predios del Rancho de Tlacotal, ubicado en la Delegación Ixtacalco, D.F.," September 23, 1942, AHCDMX, DDF, OP, box 161, bundle 1. Mexico City's municipal archive has an unsigned and undated blueprint that could be Guerrero's. "Fraccionamiento Tlacotal," AHCDMX, Planoteca, box 78, bundle 4.

13. "Decreto que declara zona industrial la comprendida al oriente de la Ciudad de México, dentro de la Delegación de Ixtacalco, D.F.," *Diario Oficial*, November 24, 1944.

14. "Dictamen que presenta la consultoría #4, a cargo del C. Ing. Jesús Molina Urquidez, en el expediente de restitución de ejidos al poblado de Ixtacalco, delegación de Ixtacalco, del Distrito Federal," September 29, 1945, AGA, Ixtacalco, 24/910, bundle 15.

15. "Solución al problema de las habitaciones," *El Universal*, May 10, 1949. The total value of the 1,300,000 square meters was MX$4,330,725.75, which the government planned to recover after selling the land to proletarian settlers. The details of the sale can be read in "Libro de registro de acuerdos y decretos presidenciales años 1941–1950," AHCDMX, OP, box 248, bundle 2.

16. A blueprint of the "Unidad de Vivienda 2 y 3. Tlacotal y Bramadero" can be found in AGN, CL, box 49, file 233; BNHOP, *Memoria de las conferencias de habitación popular organizadas por el Banco Nacional Hipotecario Urbano y de Obras Públicas*, 175–176.

17. Gómez Mayorga, "El problema de la habitación en México."

18. Sánchez Mejorada, *Rezagos de la modernidad*, 72–82; Perló Cohen, "Política y vivienda en México, 1910–1952," 826.

19. Rodríguez Kuri, "Ciudad oficial, 1930–1970," 442–443.

20. Tercer Consejo General de la Coalición Popular de Colonos del Distrito Federal, June 16, 1949, AGN, DGIPS, box 103, file 1.

21. Salvador Flores to Miguel Alemán Valdés, February 25, 1948, AGN, MAV, file 418.2/116.

22. "'La ciudad perdida' desapareció y sus moradores tienen nuevo hogar," *El Nacional*, December 26, 1950.

23. "La ciudad perdida ha sido recuperada," *El Nacional*, January 2, 1951.

24. "Ejidatarios que se muestran," *El Universal*, March 6, 1951.

25. "Noticiario del Distrito Federal," *El Nacional*, June 6, 1951; "30,000 colonos de Ixtacalco, D.F., recibieron en emotivo acto sus títulos de propiedad," *El Nacional*, August 20, 1951.

26. "Fraccionamientos: Gabriel Ramos Millán," AHCDMX, OP, box 471, bundle 2.

27. "Monografía de la Colonia Gabriel Ramos Millán: sección Bramadero," AHCDMX, OP, box 471, bundle 2, On the places of origin of settlers, see also "Bello acto de solidaridad humana y social de colonos de la 'Gabriel Ramos Millán,'" *El Nacional*, October 24, 1951.

28. On the birthplace of the residents, see Jiménez y Castilla, "Bramadero."

29. His authority was recorded in a letter from the neighborhood association to President Miguel Alemán, published in *El Nacional*, September 21, 1951

30. Vicenta Martínez de González to Adolfo Ruiz Cortines, September 21, 1954, AGN, ARC, file 418.2/13.

31. Erasto Castillo to Adolfo Ruiz Cortines, AGN, ARC, file 418.2/13.

32. Lauro O. Gorocica Concha to Adolfo Ruiz Cortines, July 28, 1956, AGN, ARC, file 418.2/13.

33. INV, *Características, problemas y programa de acción en beneficio de las colonias proletarias*; Ward, "The Practice and Potential of Self-Help Housing in Mexico City."

34. Jiménez y Castilla, "Bramadero."

35. "Atropello de un lider de colonos," *La Prensa*, July 30, 1954; "Ciudades perdidas a granel," *La Prensa*, December 16, 1954; "Esquilman a los colonos pobres, cinco liderzuelos," *El Popular*, April 15, 1955.

36. "Fraccionamientos: Colonia Gabriel Ramos Millán," AHCDMX, OP, box 471, file 2.

37. For instance, in July 1954 the Coalición de Colonos asked the DDF for a number of lots in Ramos Millán. This request was then sent to Rafael Suárez Ocaña, who answered that the census of lots in the neighborhood was being revised. "Fraccionamientos: Colonia Gabriel Ramos Millán," AHCDMX, OP, box 471, file 2.

38. Roque Plata Belmont to Adolfo Ruiz Cortines, AGN, ARC, file 418.2/232.

39. Asociación Mexicana de la Cruz Roja to Ernesto P. Uruchurtu, August 8, 1954, "Fraccionamientos: Atlampa," AHCDMX, OP, box 471, bundle 2.

40. Rafael Suárez Ocaña to Ernesto P. Uruchurtu, December 18, 1953, "Fraccionamientos: Atlampa," AHCDMX, OP, box 471, bundle 2.

41. Roque Plata Belmont to Presidencia, June 14, 1954, "Fraccionamientos: Atlampa," AHCDMX, OP, box 471, bundle 2.

42. Conrado Mercado to Lic. Enrique Rodríguez Cano, secretario del Presidente de la República, June 23, 1953, AGN, ARC, file 418.2/13.

43. Directivos de la Colonia Ramos Millán to Ernesto P. Uruchurtu, June 6, 1952, AGN, ARC, file 418.2/13.

44. Colonos de Gabriel Ramos Millán to Adolfo Ruiz Cortines, no date, AGN, ARC, file 418.2/13.

45. Conrado Mercado to Adolfo Ruiz Cortines, AGN, ARC, file 418.2/23.

46. "Fraccionamientos: Colonia Gabriel Ramos Millán," AHCDMX, OP, box 71, bundle 2.

47. "Monografía de la Colonia Gabriel Ramos Millán: sección Bramadero," AHCDMX, OP, box 471, file 2.

48. "Monografía de la Colonia Gabriel Ramos Millán: sección Bramadero," AHCDMX, OP, box 471, file 2.

49. The historiography on this period has rapidly grown over the last decade. This section is informed by the work of Perló Cohen, *Uruchurtu*; Davis, *Urban Leviathan*; Novoa, "México como visión de la ciudad ideal"; Kram Villarreal, "Gladiolas for the Children of Sánchez"; Jordan, "Flowers and Iron Fists"; and Rodríguez Kuri, "Ciudad oficial, 1930–1970."

50. Davis, *Urban Leviathan*, 126.

51. "Proyecto de Historia Oral: entrevista realizada a Teodoro González de León, realizada por Graciela de Garay, el día 15 de agosto de 1991 en la Ciudad de México," Archivo de la Palabra del Instituto de Investigaciones Dr. José María Luis Mora.

52. Cited in Novoa, "México como visión de la ciudad ideal," 255.

53. A small sample of works from the decade includes Luis Buñuel's *Los olvidados* (1950, screened in the United States as *The Young and the Damned*), Carlos Fuentes's *La region más transparente del aire* (1958), Mauricio Gómez Mayorga's *¿Qué hacer por la Ciudad de México?* (1957), and Oscar Lewis's *Five Families* (1959, published in Mexico as *Antropología de la pobreza*).

54. Fifty-five neighborhoods were authorized by Uruchurtu, according to Novoa, "México como visión de la ciudad ideal," 316.

55. Perló Cohen, *Uruchurtu*, 1:240–243; Davis, *Urban Leviathan*, 132–133. Uruchurtu did support the construction of two large-scale housing projects for workers: San Juan de Aragón and Santa Cruz Mayehualco, which I describe in the following chapter.

56. Evidence of the (illegal and highly organized) subdivision and sale of lots in the pueblo of Santa Úrsula de Coapa, as well as the unsuccessful efforts of Public Works to stop it, can be found in Ingeniero Campuzano and Arturo Barcena Betana, "De los trabajos de fraccionamiento que se están ejecutando en el poblado de Santa Ursula de Coapa Coyoacán, D.F.," September 30, 1953, AHCDMX, OP, box 85, bundle 1.

57. Sánchez Mejorada, *Rezagos de la modernidad*, 229.

58. Different versions of the law are found in AHCDMX, DDF, Fondo Gobernación, box 175. This box contains several files with annotated versions of the law.

59. These policies were proposed at Tercer Consejo General de la Coalición Popular de Colonos del Distrito Federal, June 16, 1949, AGN, DGIPS, box 103, file 1. See chapter 4.

60. Azuela and Meneses Reyes, "The Everyday Formation of Public Space," 175.

61. Azuela and Saavedra, "Uso, desgaste y reuso de la expropiación en la Ciudad de México."

62. *Diario Oficial de la Federación*, December 31, 1951.

63. "Pero es la falta de un instrumento jurídico que proporcione los medios eficaces para que la función del Estado se desarrolle en forma proteccionista . . . la capacidad del pueblo humilde para poder resolver por sí el problema de habitación." *Diario Oficial de la Federación*, December 31, 1951.

64. "Realista advertencia formula el Lic. Uruchurtu a los capitalinos," *El Universal*, October 3, 1953. Cited in Perló Cohen, *Uruchurtu*, 1:240.

65. "Proyecto de Ley de Colonización Proletaria," Diputado Enrique Rangel to Adolfo Ruiz Cortines, February 24, 1952; and "Problema de las Colonias del Distrito Federal," Unión Mexicanista Revolucionaria to Adolfo Ruiz Cortines, July 1, 1952, both in AHCDMX, OP, box 617, file 3.

66. These environmental warnings were included in a diagnosis of the city sent to Ruiz Cortines by political officials and urban experts in the summer of 1953. See Gonzalo Blanco Macías, "Urbanismo patológico"; and Carlos Contreras, "Sugestiones para formular el programa de política urbana a seguir para lograr la solución del problema del Valle de México," both in AHCDMX, OP, box 617, file 3.

67. The environmental history of the city is a growing historiographic topic. See Vitz, *A City on a Lake*; and Miranda Pacheco, "El Frankenstein urbano." On hydraulic engineering in the city after the Porfirian period, see Chahim, "Flood Control Politics"; and de Coss-Corzo, "The Infrastructure of Internal Colonialism."

68. Vitz, *A City on a Lake*, 228. Vitz is interpreting the ideas of Guillermo Zárraga, another environmentalist from this period. On the ideas of these experts and their disagreements, see Miranda Pacheco, "El Frankenstein urbano."

69. Architects and planners had criticized the law's predecessor (Contreras's Planning Law of 1936) because it lacked the legal force to curtail the expansion of the city. Cuevas et al., "Sugestiones que hace la Sociedad de Arquitectos Mexicanos a la Dirección de Obras Públicas del Gobierno del Distrito Federal para la formulación de la nueva Ley de Planificación y Zonificación del D.F."

70. "Bases para la celebración de convenios que se encuentran suspendidos," May 11, 1954, AHCDMX, OP, box 258, file 1. For further evidence on Uruchurtu's firm stance on neighborhoods requesting exemptions from legal obligations, see "Agrupaciones que han venido gestionando se les exima del cumplimiento de todas o algunas de las obligaciones que se han mencionado," April 29, 1955, AHCDMX, Gobernación, box 217. As these measures suggest, Uruchurtu was highly successful in expanding the city's tax base. Rodríguez Kuri, "Ciudad official, 1930–1970," 446–447.

71. Perló Cohen, *Uruchurtu*, 1:216.

72. Eduardo Molina to Ángela Alessio Robles, September 12, 1954, AHCDMX, OP, box 86, bundle 1.

73. "Se informa sobre el fraccionamiento Agrícola Pantitlán," March 2, 1962, AHCDMX, OP, box 590, bundle 2. For more examples of the denial of urban services to "clandestine neighborhoods," see AHCDMX, OP, box 86, bundle 1.

74. "Sociedad Civil Fraternidad y Cooperación 'FyC' Pro-Habitación del Maestro" to Ernesto P. Uruchurtu, July 22, 1955, AHCDMX, OP, box 258, bundle 1.

75. "Agrupaciones que han venido gestionando se les exima del cumplimiento de todas o algunas de la obligaciones que se han mencionado," April 29, 1955, AHCDMX, Fondo Gobernación, box 323. The same box contains several petitions from neighborhoods requesting water payment exemptions. Two well-connected neighborhoods (Colonia Urbana Marte and Reforma Iztaccíhuatl, "sponsored" by powerful members of the armed forces) had long and harsh negotiations about the drainage and water grid, as described in Novoa, "México como visión de la ciudad ideal," 321–322.

76. Benigno Prado Valencia and Samuel Suárez Yañez, *La cuchilla del tesoro: ante la ley y la razón* (n.p., 1965), no page number. The pamphlet, along with other materials regarding the case, can be found in AHCDMX, Gobernación, box 325, Comisión de Límites.

77. Jiménez y Castilla, "Bramadero." Her thesis was part of a much larger research project led by demographer Raúl Benítez Zenteno and supported by the Escuela Nacional de Ciencias Políticas y Sociales of the UNAM and the New York–based Population Council.

78. Gorelik, *La ciudad latinoamericana*.

79. Rodríguez Kuri makes this point in "Secretos de la idiosincrasia."

80. Hauser, *Urbanization in Latin America*. On the role played by Mexico City in these transnational debates, see de Antuñano, "Mexico City as an Urban Laboratory."

81. My argument on the "local" character of colonias proletarias is inspired by Fischer's arguments about Brazilian favelas in "A Century in Present Tense."

82. Jiménez y Castilla, "Bramadero," 96.

83. As noted in the 1950s by Lewis in "Urbanization without Breakdown."

84. Evidence of this participation in the labor market and national culture can be seen in Jiménez y Castilla, "Bramadero," 47. On the urban popular culture of this period, see Joseph, Rubinstein, and Zolov, *Fragments of a Golden Age*.

85. Perlman, *The Myth of Marginality*. See also Mangin, "Latin American Squatter Settlements."

86. Jorge Stanford, "A propósito de la creación del Instituto Nacional de la Vivienda: este es el problema," *Mañana*, June 11, 1955. Article clipping in AGN, INV, box 12.

87. Alfredo Félix Díaz Escobar, "Colonias Proletarias," *El Universal*, June 25, 1955.

88. Ward, "Una comparación entre colonias paracaidistas y ciudades perdidas de la Ciudad de México," 102, fn. 2.

89. Loyo, *Notas sobre la evolución demográfica de la Ciudad de México*.

90. "El pavoroso problema de la habitación," *La Prensa*, October 16, 1955.

91. Gómez Mayorga, *¿Qué hacer por la Ciudad de México?*, 21–22.

92. "Se deben al hecho elemental de no haber entendido a los grupos sociales a los que se quería redimir, y al haber supuesto gratuita—y marxistamente—que el fenómeno era de índole puramente económica . . . no prodiguemos tanto la expresión 'justicia social,' porque puede ser que estemos simplificando lastimosamente las cosas y que no entendemos que la gente vive, no sólo como puede, sino como quiere." Gómez Mayorga and Fischlowitz, *La superurbanización caótica*, 28–29.

93. "Monografía de la Colonia Gabriel Ramos Millán: sección Bramadero," AHCDMX, OP, box 471, file 2.

94. "Monografía de la Colonia Gabriel Ramos Millán: sección Bramadero," AHCDMX, OP, box 471, file 2. Police reports can be seen in AHCDMX, DDF, Gobernación, box 162, "Policía Ixtacalco 1955."

95. The same duality—a so-called marginal neighborhood in the midst of a process of improvement with the support of the government—is visible in many other assessments of colonias proletarias. For contemporary examples, see Cornejo Cabrera, "La colonia proletaria Escuadrón 201"; and Acosta and López Bermúdez, "La ciudad, sus áreas representativas y un programa de bienestar social urbano."

96. Schulte-Sasse, *Nacida entre chinampas*. I thank Leonardo Novoa for sharing this source with me.

97. DDF, *La Ciudad de México*.

98. Dirección de Salubridad en el DF, "Informe narrativo de las labores desarrolladas por las diversas dependencias de la Dirección de Salubridad en el D.F., del día 1º de septiembre al 31 de diciembre de 1953," AHSS, SubSyA, box 45, file 1. See also Schers, "The Popular Sector of the Mexican PRI," 82–90.

99. "Informe de María Luisa Flores sobre el 6º Centro de Bienestar Social Urbano Benito Juárez," AHSS, SubSyA, box 32, file 4.

100. Enrique Villa Michel to Raúl Salinas Lozano, "Proyecto de programa de inversiones en las colonias proletarias," July 17, 1957, AGN, INV, box 1.

101. The participation of working-class youth in the student movement of 1968 has been documented by Rodríguez Kuri, *Museo del universo*. My conversations with residents from Colonia Ramos Millán confirm Rodríguez Kuri's arguments about the social and geographical diversity of the movement.

102. Anaya Monroy, "El ministerio público y su función social en el medio urbano," 403–404.

Chapter 6: The Housing Problem in the Era of Modernization

1. In the latter part of this period, between 1963 and 1971, the economy expanded at a yearly rate of 7 percent, with a Gross Domestic Product per capita growth rate of

more than 3 percent and a low inflation rate of 2.8 percent per year. Loaeza, "Modernización autoritaria a la sombre de la superpotencia, 1944–1968," 683–684.

2. My reading of the decade is inspired by Rodríguez Kuri, *Museo del universo*; and Castañeda, *Spectacular Mexico*.

3. Perló Cohen, *Uruchurtu*, 2:16.

4. De Antuñano, "Mexico City as an Urban Laboratory"; Freije, *Citizens of Scandal*, chapter 1.

5. Unsurprisingly, this was a key trope in a largely optimistic depiction of the city in the mass media published as a special issue of the weekly *Mañana*, no. 1044, August 31, 1963.

6. "Los problemas que plantea el desarrollo urbano tienen dos sentidos: el extensivo hacia afuera, y el intensivo o interno . . . la renovación." Vila, "Conjunto urbano Tlatelolco," 79.

7. I reviewed this change in chapter 5. See also Duhau, *Hábitat popular y política urbana*, 198–200.

8. Yee, *Informal Metropolis*.

9. Agostoni, *Monuments of Progress*; Piccato, *City of Suspects*.

10. A 1938 editorial from *Excelsiór* noted: "Racial negligence produced the *cuarto redondo* where families were born, grew, and died at the margins of civilization." "El Instituto Internacional de Urbanismo," *Excelsiór*, August 19, 1938.

11. For critiques of the term, see Mayne, *Slums*; Roy, "Slumdog Cities"; and Massidda, "Slums, *Villas Miseria*, and *Barriadas*."

12. Lewis, *The Children of Sánchez*, xxv, xxvii.

13. Pani often used "slum" in English to refer to the herradura de tugurios. Gómez Mayorga, "El problema de la habitación en México: una conversación con el arquitecto Mario Pani," 74.

14. "The Attraction of Repulsion" is chapter 2 in Mayne, *Slums*. On Mexico City's slummers, see Tenorio Trillo, *I Speak of the City*; and González Rodríguez, *Los bajos fondos*.

15. "El problema de la habitación en la Ciudad de México," *Estudios* 6 (1952): iii, 4.

16. Adolfo Zamora, "Memorandum," April 23, 1936, AGN, CL, box 89, file 8.

17. Sánchez, "La realidad mexicana y las nuevas concepciones arquitectónicas urbanísticas en material de habitación popular," 48.

18. Alanís de Anda, *Vivienda colectiva de la modernidad en México*.

19. BNHOP, *Memoria de las conferencias sobre habitación popular organizadas por el Banco Nacional Hipotecario Urbano y de Obras Públicas*, 19. See also "La habitación: por la casa popular," *El Universal*, September 10, 1950.

20. However, the survey added two transitional categories: *jacales* (shacks or huts) and *zonas decadentes* (decaying areas). Located on the outskirts of the city and lacking public services, shacks were provisional homes built with improvised materials. Decaying areas, usually adjacent to slums, were better off but were in a process of deterioration. The unstated assumption was that with time they would eventually become slums. BNHOP, *Memoria de las conferencias sobre habitación popular organizadas por el Banco Nacional Hipotecario Urbano y de Obras Públicas*, 139.

21. A similar deflection of attention took place in many cities across the world, where turn-of-century tenements close to the city center continued to be considered the epicenter of the housing problem decades after their population had plummeted

relative to the city total. For a similar observation, regarding Buenos Aires, see Moya, *Cousins and Strangers*, chapter 4, "Settling in the City."

22. Hayner, "Mexico City."

23. Hayner's statistical and cartographic data were provided by the BNHOP. He was aided by Adolfo Zamora, Félix Sánchez, and sociologist Lucio Mendieta y Nuñez.

24. Hayner, *New Patterns in Old Mexico*, 61–62.

25. Hayner, "La Ciudad de México."

26. "El problema de la habitación obrera," AGN, INV, box 1.

27. The survey was published as a special issue of *Estudios*, the journal of the BNHOP.

28. BNHOP, "Proyecto de estudio de la Ciudad de México"; BNHOP, "El problema de la habitación en la Ciudad de México": special issue of *Estudios* 6 (1952).

29. BNHOP, "El problema de la habitación en la Ciudad de México," 17, 187.

30. Connolly, "Uncontrolled Settlements and Self-Build," 150; Miranda Pacheco, "La vivienda popular del Milagro mexicano en la Ciudad de México."

31. BNHOP, "El problema de la habitación en la Ciudad de México," 49.

32. Ortiz and Villaseñor, "Desarrollo de las colonias proletarias de la Ciudad de México."

33. BNHOP, "El problema de la habitación en la Ciudad de México," 40.

34. BNHOP, "El problema de la habitación en la Ciudad de México," 15.

35. BNHOP, "Proyecto de estudio de la Ciudad de México," 104.

36. A different critique was made by architect Alberto T. Arai, who argued that the study focused on the built environment but not on its residents. Arai, "Conocerse para mejorarse," no pagination.

37. "Entrevista realizada a Mario Pani, realizada por Graciela de Garay, el día 11 de julio de 1990 en la Ciudad de México," Archivo de la Palabra del Instituto de Investigaciones Dr. José María Luis Mora.

38. See Lewis, *Five Families*, *The Children of Sánchez*, and "Urbanization without Breakdown."

39. The censuses of the neighborhood assembled by Lewis and his students are located in Lewis's archive: ORLP, box 124, file 105.

40. De Antuñano, "Mexico City as an Urban Laboratory."

41. Monsiváis, *Dias de guardar*, 288.

42. "Investigación social en el centro urbano 'Presidente Juárez,'" ORLP, box 123. Lewis also conducted research in these neighborhoods and had little good to say of them: families spent long evenings watching TV, with little drama. The middle classes, Lewis concluded, were extremely boring, as cited in Rigdon, *The Cultural Façade*, 53.

43. Eckstein, *The Poverty of Revolution*, 52–53. Over the last three decades, the popular neighborhoods surrounding the city's historical core have lost many of their low-income residents, displaced by a process of gentrification driven by tourism. See Moctezuma, *El desvanecimiento de lo popular*.

44. "Herradura tugurios Jamaica Merced," AGN, INV, box 1.

45. "Herradura tugurios Jamaica Merced," AGN, INV, box 1.

46. "El tugurio . . . amerita un tratamiento radical de eliminación y substitución por nuevas habitaciones." "Herradura de tugurios Jamaica Merced," AGN, INV, box 1.

47. "[N]o lleva una vida higiénica . . . en la parte emotiva domina sus instintos. . . . Posee relativa emotividad y sólo creada por la fantasía. A veces con estados depresivos

en lo intelectual. Toma por rutina su oficio, sin encontrar placer en él. Es desordenada en lo intelectual y en lo económico, porque no persigue una meta, por falta de idea de superación; porque su posición social es casi nula; en lo social, no cumple con sus deberes, desatiende su persona y su familia; en lo moral, escasean los principios y en lo espiritual, posee pocas tendencias idealistas, menos artísticas y casi nada de científicas . . . está constantemente expuesto a ser engañando por merolicos, tenderos, líderes, etc." "Herradura tugurios Jamaica Merced," AGN, INV, box 1. See also Valencia, *La Merced*.

48. Valencia, *La Merced*, 9, 352.

49. "Estudios diversos sobre vivienda urbana," AGN, INV, box 1, (n.d.).

50. Moses's bright light, however, would soon dim. In 1961 Jacobs recast Moses as an authoritarian, Moloch-like destroyer of urban communities, a reputation cemented in later works by Robert Caro and Marshall Berman. On the waning of urban renewal, see Klemek, *The Transatlantic Collapse of Urban Renewal*.

51. Azuela, "Trasplantes complicados."

52. Warman et al., *De eso que llaman la antropología mexicana*; Bonfil Batalla, *México Profundo*.

53. While Bonfil Batalla (the anthropologist critic of the developmentalist state) and Moses (the powerful New York City parks commissioner) are certainly an unlikely pair, I do not want to overstress the connection. Bonfil Batalla was in his twenties, and I have found little evidence of further participation with the INV.

54. INV, *La vivienda popular*, 39.

55. "Entrevista realizada a Reinaldo Pérez Rayón, realizada por Graciela de Garay, el día 2 de octubre de 1991 en la Ciudad de México," Archivo de la Palabra del Instituto de Investigaciones Dr. José María Luis Mora.

56. "Entrevista realizada a Reinaldo Pérez Rayón, realizada por Graciela de Garay, el día 5 de noviembre de 1991 en la Ciudad de México," Archivo de la Palabra del Instituto de Investigaciones Dr. José María Luis Mora. See also Drago Quaglia, "Doctrina Lazo."

57. Cymet Lerer and Ortiz Flores, *El problema de las colonias proletarias, Ciudad de México*, 12.

58. Cymet Lerer and Ortiz Flores, *El problema de las colonias proletarias, Ciudad de México*, 33, 63.

59. Cymet Lerer and Ortiz Flores, *El problema de las colonias proletarias, Ciudad de México*, 66.

60. Guillermo Ortiz Flores, "La vivienda popular," AGN, INV, box 12.

61. The colonias proletarias team was led by Cymet Lerer, Ortiz Flores, and José María Gutiérrez Trujillo. It included economists, anthropologists, sociologists, and social workers. INV, *Colonias proletarias*.

62. "Equipo técnico: colonias proletarias," AGN, INV, box 1.

63. This same contrast is clearly offered by Eckstein in *The Poverty of Revolution*, 62–63.

64. INV, *Colonias proletarias*, 20, 10.

65. Wakeman, *Practicing Utopia*, 51–52.

66. INV, *Colonias proletarias*, 13, 11.

67. Frieden, "The Search for Housing Policy in Mexico City," 91; Adrián García Cortez, "Cartilla de la Vivienda," *El Universal*, May 16, 1957.

68. Cornelius referenced these policies in *Politics and the Migrant Poor in Mexico City*.

69. "Plan de mejoramiento integral de la Colonia Agrícola Oriental," AGN, INV, box 1.

70. Gilbert and Ward, *Housing, the State, and the Poor*, 12–13.

71. Frieden, "The Search for Housing Policy in Mexico City," 81.

72. Gyger, *Improvised Cities*, 17.

73. Mangin, "Latin American Squatter Settlements," 65.

74. Turner, "Barriers and Channels for Housing Development in Modernizing Countries."

75. Roy, "Transnational Trespassings," 308. My application of the myth of the urban frontier to the urban margins is also informed by Brown, "Gridded Lives."

76. Félix Sánchez, "Planificación urbana," *Espacios* 14 (1953): no pagination.

77. Gómez Mayorga, "El problema de la habitación en México," 74.

78. Pani, *Nonoalco-Tlatelolco*, no pagination.

79. As sociologist René Coulomb explains, bulldozer policies expelled more than 150,000 residents from the city center between 1950 and 1980. The largest urban renewal was Nonoalco-Tlatelolco, but families were displaced from many other colonias, including Morelos, Doctores, and Candelaria de los Patos. Coulomb, "Políticas urbanas en la ciudad central del área metropolitana de la Ciudad de México (1958–1983)," 38–40.

80. Vila, "Conjunto urbano Tlatelolco," 94, 92.

81. Sotomayor, *El México en donde nací*, 338.

82. Tlatelolco featured in other Mexican and international journals, including *L'Architecture d'Aujourd'hui* and *Architectural Digest*. Jácome Moreno, "Las construcciones de la imagen," 94. In making these arguments I am inspired by the work of Castañeda, *Spectacular Mexico*; Rodríguez Kuri, *Museo del Universo*; and Flaherty, *Hotel Mexico*.

83. Jácome Moreno, "Las construcciones de la imagen," 90.

84. Cited in Agostoni, *Monuments of Progress*, 74.

85. Julio Scherer García, "Costará mil millones de pesos y ocupará más de cien hectáreas," *Excelsiór*, no date. Newspaper clipping in "Expediente de la Colonia Prolongación Guerrero," AHCDMX, OP, box 658.

86. Agustín Barrios Gómez, "Muy pronto será una realidad el proyecto Nonoalco-Tlatelolco," *Novedades*, April 29, 1960. Newspaper clipping in "Expediente de la Colonia Prolongación Guerrero," AHCDMX, OP, box 658.

87. Freije, *Citizens of Scandal*.

88. Pani, *Nonoalco-Tlatelolco*, plates 11 and 14.

89. "Tres mil colonos de quejaron de despojo," *Diario de la Tarde*, March 1, 1960. Newspaper clipping in "Expediente de la Colonia Prolongación Guerrero," AHCDMX, OP, box 658.

90. They formed a neighborhood association (Junta de Mejoras Materiales) to make contributions for a school, a kindergarten, sidewalks, and other public facilities.

91. "Expediente de la Colonia Prolongación Guerrero," AHCDMX, OP, box 658.

92. "Habían invadido lo que fue la Terminal del Mexicano" (undated clipping from unnamed newspaper), located in "Expediente de la Colonia Prolongación Guerrero," AHCDMX, AHCDMX, OP, box 658.

93. "Extraña forma de plantear la planificación de una colonia" (undated clipping from unnamed newspaper), located in "Expediente de la Colonia Prolongación Guerrero," AHCDMX, AHCDMX, OP, box 658.

94. For an analysis of the expansion of Reforma Avenue, see Zenteno Martínez, "El ordenamiento vial de la Ciudad de México y los proyectos de regeneración urbana del gobierno federal."

95. My analysis is based on a session from the Comisión Mixta de Planificación, April 19, 1961. AHCDMX, OP, box 658, bundle 1.

96. Manuel Moreno Cárdenas to Ernesto P. Uruchurtu, December 20, 1960, AHCDMX, OP, box 658, bundle 1.

97. "Entrevista realizada a Mario Pani, realizada por Graciela de Garay, el día 11 de julio de 1990 en la Ciudad de México." Archivo de la Palabra del Instituto de Investigaciones Dr. José María Luis Mora.

98. Luna Elizarrarás, "Ordenar el habitar popular," 7–8. For slightly larger numbers, see Ruiz, "¿Quién habita Sta. Cruz Mayehualco?"

99. These housing requests can be found in AHCDMX, OP, box 617, bundle 2. I owe the reference to Luna Elizarrarás, "Ordenar el habitar popular."

100. The project merited a brief mention in *Arquitectos de México* as a humble "experiment" with low-cost materials. Valenzuela and Rojas, "Unidad de Habitación Santa Cruz Mayehualco," 48.

101. Analyses of the project include Cisneros Sosa, *La ciudad que construimos*; Yee, *Informal Metropolis*; Perló Cohen, *Uruchurtu*; Novoa, "México como visión de la ciudad ideal"; and Escudero, "Conjunto urbano San Juan de Aragón."

102. On the middle-class population of Tlatelolco, see Franco de los Reyes, "Vecinos de la modernidad." On the residents of San Juan de Aragón and Santa Cruz Mayehualco, see Ruiz, "¿Quién habita Sta. Cruz Mayehualco?"; Velázquez, "¿Dónde vives?"; and Cornelius, *Politics and the Migrant Poor in Mexico City*, 51.

103. Novoa, "México como visión de la ciudad ideal," 296–308.

104. The differences between the two men are cited by Perló Cohen, *Uruchurtu*, 2:145–146.

105. Cervantes Sánchez was recommended by Argentinean historian and architect Jorge Hardoy. Novoa, "México como visión de la ciudad ideal," 299.

106. Velázquez, "¿Dónde vives?," 13.

107. Wakeman, *Practicing Utopia*.

108. Based on a random sampling of the neighborhood contracts, historian David Yee calculated that "32 percent of the new residents were categorized as *obreros* (workers), 29 percent as federal employees, and 10 percent as *albañiles*" (construction workers) in *Informal Metropolis*, 36.

109. Velázquez, "¿Dónde vives?," 15.

110. The reference to the Cerro de Tepeyac is included in Escudero, "Conjunto urbano San Juan de Aragón," 190. Other residents hailed from Guerrero, Santa María La Redonda, Morelos, Peralvillo, and Candelaria de los Patos. See Perló Cohen, *Uruchurtu*, 2:148; Velázquez, "¿Dónde vives?," 10; and Novoa, "México como visión de la ciudad ideal," 298.

111. Velázquez, "¿Dónde vives?," 13. These words referred to the housing projects designed by Juan Legarreta in the 1930s, analyzed in chapter 2.

112. "Solicitud para comprar una casa en la zona de habitación popular del Conjunto Urbano 'Peñón de San Juan de Aragón,'" AHCDMX, OP, box 96, file 3. The same regulations were enacted in Santa Cruz Mayehualco. See Luna Elizarrarás, "Ordenar el habitar popular," 12. See also AGN, INV, Box 10.

113. Teresa María Careaga de Moreno to Edmundo Arguelles, December 4, 1964, AGN, INV, box 10.

114. Luna Elizarrarás, "Ordenar el habitar popular." For examples of these social programs, see also AGN, INV, box 10.

115. Leidenberger, "Colonias proletarias y conjuntos habitacionales," 252–253. On the limits of the formal/informal dichotomy, see also Landa, "Overflowing Architecture."

116. Zamorano Villarreal, *Vivienda mínima obrera en el México posrevolucionario*, 141–146.

117. Carlos Schutte to Jorge Heredia Ferráez, October 5, 1964, AGN, INV, box 10. On tenancy conflicts in San Juan de Aragón, see AGN, INV, box 8.

118. Teresa María Careaga de Moreno to Edmundo Arguelles, February 4, 1965, AGN, INV, box 10.

119. Following the death of Salvador Flores, for example, Roque Plata Belmont led the Coalición de Colonos and pressured the DDF to provide lots in Ramos Millán to residents of Atlampa. Roque Plata Belmont to Adolfo Ruiz Cortines, July 14, 1955, AGN, ARC, file 418.2/232.

120. Duhau, *Hábitat popular y política urbana*, 199.

121. Juan Toledo, president of the Federación de Colonias Proletarias, participated in the sale of lots. Calvo Isaza, *Urbanización y revolución en América Latina*, 320.

122. Perló Cohen, *Uruchurtu*, 2:268–277.

Conclusion

1. "Entrevista realizada a Pedro Ramírez Vazquez, realizada por Graciela de Garay, el día 6 de junio de 1994 en la Ciudad de México," Archivo de la Palabra del Instituto de Investigaciones Dr. José María Luis Mora.

2. Numbers from 1980 through 2020 in Schteingart, Sobrino, and Ugalde, *Mexico City*, chapter 1.

3. The quip is from journalist Emiliano Ruiz Parra, in reference to the neighborhood of Golondrinas. Ricardo Raphael, "Las golondrinas," *Milenio*, July 2, 2022. "Day without . . . *mexiquenses*" refers to Sergio Arau's film *A Day Without a Mexican* (2004), which imagines a day in Los Angeles without Mexican workers. See also Ruiz Parra, *Golondrinas*.

4. The federation was led by PRI congressman Alberto Briseño Ruiz. For reports on the Congress, see AGN, DGIPS, box 1656 C, file 9.

5. See Cornelius, *Politics and the Migrant Poor in Mexico City*; Eckstein, *The Poverty of Revolution*; Vélez-Ibáñez, *Rituals of Marginality*; and Schers, "The Popular Sector of the Mexican PRI." Tellingly, the data on colonias proletarias that Cornelius used were not provided by the DDF but by the PRI, an indication of the party's role in urban governance.

6. For a general interpretation of the erosion of the PRI in Mexico City, see Loaeza, "Perspectivas para una historia política del Distrito Federal en el siglo XX." The historiography on radical settler associations has expanded during the last decade. See Calvo Isaza, *Urbanización y revolución*; Yee, *Informal Metropolis*; and Puma, "The Nazas-Aguanaval Group."

7. Gilbert and Ward, *Housing, the State and the Poor*, 190. On Echeverría's housing policy, see COPEVI, *Investigación sobre vivienda: las políticas habitacionales del estado mexicano*; and Buchanan, "Working for the Workers?"

8. Varley, "¿Clientalismo o tecnocracia?," 150; Gilbert and Ward, *Housing, the State and the Poor*, 188–196; Cisneros Sosa, *La ciudad que construimos*, chapter 9.

9. Ward, *Mexico City*, 204.

10. Azuela, *La ciudad, la propiedad privada y el derecho*, 117.

11. Yee, *Informal Metropolis.*

12. "[E]l problema más grave del Distrito Federal: la irregularidad en la tenencia de la tierra," *El Día*, March 2, 1977. Untitled newspaper clipping in AGN, DGIPS, box 1670 B, file 7.

13. The tendency to minimize the problem of informality before 1970, particularly the government response to it, is common in excellent scholarly works by urban scholars. See, for instance, Gilbert and Ward, *Housing, the State and the Poor*; Ward, *Mexico City*, 197; COPEVI, *Las políticas habitacionales del estado mexicano*; and Varley, "¿Clientalismo o tecnocracia?"

14. I have explored this change of emphasis in more detail in Azuela and de Antuñano, "Four Regimes of Informality."

15. Ward, *Mexico City*, 202 (emphasis in the original).

16. On the importance of land titles for settlers, see Varley, "¿Clientelismo o tecnocracia?," 138–139.

17. Many of the leaders of the MRC of Ciudad Netzahualcóyotl became affiliated with the PRI and profited handsomely from sponsoring land invasions.

18. Ramírez Saiz, *El movimiento urbano popular en México*; Alonso, *Los movimientos sociales en el Valle de México.*

19. Moctezuma Barragán, "La Coordinadora Nacional del Movimiento Urbano Popular en el Valle de México."

20. For useful accounts of the crisis, see Walker, *Waking from the Dream*; Lomnitz, "Times of Crisis"; and Ramírez de Garay, "El sismo de 1985 en la Ciudad de México."

21. Ramírez de Garay, "El sismo de 1985 en la Ciudad de México"; Eckstein, "Poor People versus the State and Capital."

22. For a revisionist history of the earthquake, see Ramírez de Garay, "El sismo de 1985 en la Ciudad de México." The metanarrative of the "transition to democracy" has been criticized as overly teleological. See Escalante, *Si persisten las molestias.*

23. Sociologist Pedro Moctezuma Barragán is perhaps the best-known participant in the movement who also wrote about it: see *Despertares.* See also Moctezuma Barragán and Navarro, *La urbanización popular en la Ciudad de México*

24. Haber, "La migración del Movimiento Urbano Popular a la política de partido en el México contemporáneo."

25. Inklings of this history can be found in Marván, "De la ciudad del presidente al gobierno propio, 1970–2000"; Ramírez de Garay, "El sismo de 1985 en la Ciudad de México"; and Yee, *Informal Metropolis.*

26. Ortega Alcázar, *Autoconstrucción de vivienda, espacio y vida familiar en la Ciudad de México*, 10.

27. Schteingart, Sobrino, and Ugalde, *Mexico City*, chapter 4.

28. When ethnographer Susan Eckstein returned to the field in the 1990s, she found out that the communities that she had studied twenty or thirty years earlier had deteriorated, largely because of the economic crisis. Once again flipping the orthodoxy, Eckstein entitled her revision of her earlier work "Urbanization Revisited: Inner-City Slum of Hope and Squatter Settlement of Despair." The same shift was analyzed by anthropologist Mercedes de la Rocha, who reassessed her own research on Guadalajara after two decades of neoliberalism in "From the Resources of Poverty to the Poverty of Resources?"

29. An estimated 20 million people moved into these neighborhoods between 2001 and 2012. Richard Marosi, "A Failed Vision," *Los Angeles Times*, November 26, 2017. For analyses of this policy, see Gónzalez Escobar, "From Inclusive Informality to Alienating Inclusion"; and Hartman, "Homes with Value."

30. Azuela and de Antuñano, "Four Regimes of Informality."

31. Jill Wigle, "The 'Graying' of 'Green' Zones."

Bibliography

Archives

Mexico

Archivo de la Palabra del Instituto de Investigaciones Dr. José María Luis Mora, Mexico City

Archivo General Agrario (AGA), Mexico City

Archivo General de la Nación (AGN), Mexico City
- Fondo Adolfo Ruiz Cortines (ARC)
- Fondo Carlos Lazo (CL)
- Fondo Dirección General de Gobierno (DGG)
- Fondo Dirección General de Investigaciones Políticas y Sociales (DGIPS)
- Fondo Gonzalo Robles (GR)
- Fondo Hermanos Mayo (HM)
- Fondo Instituto Nacional de la Vivienda (INV)
- Fondo Lázaro Cárdenas del Río (LCR)
- Fondo Miguel Alemán Valdés (MAV)
- Fondo Miguel Ávila Camacho (MAC)
- Fondo Plutarco Elías Calles (O/C)

Archivo Histórico de la Ciudad de México (AHCDMX), Mexico City
- Departamento de Obras Públicas (OP)
- Fondo Ayuntamiento
- Planos y Proyectos
- Planoteca
- Secretaría de Gobernación (SG)

Archivo Histórico de la Secretaría de Salud (AHSS), Mexico City
- Fondo Secretaría de Salubridad y Asistencia (SSyA)

Centro de Estudios de Historia de México (CARSO), Mexico City
- Fondo Luis Montes de Oca

Mapoteca Orozco y Berra, Mexico City

United States

Environmental Design Library, University of California, Berkeley
Francis Violich Papers (FVP)
Nettie Lee Benson Latin American Collection, University of Texas Libraries, Austin
University of Illinois Archives, Urbana
Oscar and Ruth Lewis Papers (ORLP)

Journals, Newspapers, Official Publications

El Arquitecto
Arquitectos de México
Arquitectura/México
Arquitectura y lo Demás
Asistencia (Órgano de la Secretaría de Asistencia Pública)
Boletín del Departamento de Salubridad Pública
Diario de Debates de la Cámara de Diputados
Diario Oficial de la Federación
Estudios (Órgano Bimestral del Banco Nacional Hipotecario y de Obras Públicas)
Estudios Sociológicos
Excelsiór
Gaceta del Departamento del Distrito Federal
Mañana
Memorias del Departamento del Distrito Federal
Obras Públicas
Planificación
El Popular
Problemas Agrícolas e Industriales de México
Revista Mexicana de Ingeniería y Arquitectura
Salubridad y Asistencia
Semanario Hispanoamericano de la Vida y la Verdad
Siempre
El Universal

Printed Sources

Abbott, Andrew. *The System of Professions*. Chicago: University of Chicago Press, 1988.

Aboites, Luis. *El agua de la nación: una historia política de México*. Mexico City: CIESAS, 1988.

Abrams, Philip. "Notes on the Difficulty of Studying the State (1977)." *Journal of Historical Sociology* 1, no. 1 (1988): 58–89.

Acosta, Francisca, and Antonio López Bermúdez. "La ciudad, sus áreas representativas y un programa de bienestar social urbano." *Estudios Sociológicos* 2 (1956): 151–165.

Agostoni, Claudia. *Monuments of Progress: Modernization and Public Health in Mexico City, 1876–1910*. Calgary: University of Calgary Press, 2003.

Aguirre, Enrique C. "Plazas públicas para deportes en el Distrito Federal." *Obras Públicas* 2 (February 1930): 115–120.

Ai Camp, Roderic. *Mexican Political Biographies, 1935–1993*. 3rd ed. Austin: University of Texas Press, 1995.

Alanís de Anda, Enrique X. *La arquitectura de la revolución mexicana: corrientes y estilos en la década de los veinte*. Mexico City: UNAM, 2008.

Alanís de Anda, Enrique X. *Vivienda colectiva de la modernidad en México: los multifamiliares durante el periodo presidencial de Miguel Alemán (1946–1952)*. Mexico City: UNAM, 2011.

Alexander, Anna Rose. *City on Fire: Technology, Social Change, and the Hazards of Progress in Mexico City, 1860–1910*. Pittsburgh: University of Pittsburgh Press, 2016.

Almada, Vicente G. "Ideas sobre la organización conveniente de la Dirección de Obras Públicas del Distrito Federal." *Obras Públicas* 1 (January 1930): 1–10.

Almandoz, Arturo. "Urbanization and Urbanism in Latin America: From Haussman to CIAM." In *Planning Latin America's Capital Cities*, edited by Arturo Almandoz, 13–44. London: Routledge, 2002.

Almandoz, Arturo. "Urban Planning and Historiography in Latin America." *Progress in Planning* 65 (2006): 81–123.

Alonso, Jorge, ed. *Lucha urbana y acumulación de capital*. Mexico City: Centro de Investigaciones Superiores del INAH, 1980.

Alonso, Jorge, ed. *Los movimientos sociales en el Valle de México*. Mexico City: SEP, 1986.

Álvarez, Roberto J. "Tercer circuito pro-turismo." *Obras Públicas* 2, no. 10–11 (October–November 1930): 206–230.

Anaya Monroy, Fernando. "El ministerio público y su función social en el medio urbano." *Estudios Sociológicos* 2 (1956): 403–404.

"Anteproyecto de las terminales ferroviarias de México." *Arquitectura y lo Demás* 3, no. 13 (January–August 1949): n.p.

Antúnez Echegaray, Francisco. "La foto-topografía aérea y sus aplicaciones prácticas." *Planificación* 1, no. 5 (1927): 18–20.

Arai, Alberto T. "Conocerse para mejorarse." *Espacios* 29 (1956): n.p.

Aréchiga Córdoba, Ernesto. "De acueductos, acequias y atarjeas: obra hidraúlica para la Ciudad de México (1770–1912)." In *Problemas de la urbanización en el Valle de México, 1810–1910*, edited by Mario Barbosa and Salomón González, 193–225. Mexico City: Universidad Autónoma Metropolitana, 2009.

Aréchiga Córdoba, Ernesto. "Saneamiento e higiene pública en la Ciudad de México." PhD diss., El Colegio de México, 2017.

Aréchiga Córdoba, Ernesto. *Tepito: del antiguo barrio de indios al arrabal*. Mexico City: Unidad Obrera y Socialista, 2003.

Auyero, Javier. *Poor People's Politics: Peronist Survival Networks and the Legacy of Evita*. Durham, NC: Duke University Press, 2000.

Ayala Alonso, Enrique, and Gerardo Álvarez Montes. *El espacio habitacional en la arquitectura moderna: colonias, fraccionamientos*. Mexico City: UAM/CONACYT, 2013.

Azuela, Antonio. "Avatares de un cronotopo: el ejido en el fin del orden posrevolucionario." In *Si persisten las molestias*, edited by Fernando Escalante, 53–88. Mexico City: Cal y Arena, 2018

Azuela, Antonio. *La ciudad, la propiedad privada y el derecho*. Mexico City: El Colegio de México, 1989.

Azuela, Antonio. *El derecho en movimiento: once ensayos de sociología jurídica*. Mexico City: Tirant lo Blanch, 2019.

Azuela, Antonio. "El marco jurídico de la vivienda." In *Procesos habitacionales de la Ciudad de México*, edited by Marco A. Michel, 43–62. Mexico City: UAM, 1988.

Azuela, Antonio. "Mexico City: The City and Its Law in Eight Episodes, 1940–2005." In *Law and the City*, edited by Andreas Philippopoulos-Mihaloupoulos, 153–170. New York: Routledge-Cavendish, 2007.

Azuela, Antonio. "Trasplantes complicados: Nueva York en el urbanismo de la Ciudad de México." *Estudios Demográficos y Urbanos* 38, no. 3 (2023): 683–714.

Azuela, Antonio, and Emilio de Antuñano. "Four Regimes of Informality: Legal Practices and Revolutionary Politics in 20th-Century Mexico City." In *Informal Cities: History, Power, and Precarity in Latin Europe, Latin America, and Colonial North Africa*, edited by Brodwyn Fischer and Charlotte Vorms, 27–52. Chicago: University of Chicago Press, 2025.

Azuela, Antonio, and María Soledad Cruz. "La institucionalización de las colonias populares y la política urbana en la Ciudad de México (1940–1946)." *Sociológica* 4, no. 9 (1989): 111–133.

Azuela, Antonio, and Rodrigo Meneses Reyes. "The Everyday Formation of Urban Space: Law and Poverty in Mexico City." In *The Expanding Spaces of Law*, edited by Irus Braverman, Nicholas Blomley, David Delaney, and Alexandre Kedar, 167–189. Stanford, CA: Stanford University Press, 2014.

Azuela, Antonio, and Camilo Saavedra. "Uso, desgaste y reuso de la expropiación en la Ciudad de México." In *Expropiación y conflicto social en cinco metrópolis latinoamericanas*, edited by Antonio Azuela, 409–454. Mexico City: UNAM/Lincoln Institute of Land Policy, 2013.

Babb, Sarah. *Managing Mexico: Economists from Nationalism to Neoliberalism*. Princeton, NJ: Princeton University Press, 2004.

Banco Nacional Hipotecario y de Obras Públicas (BNHOP). *Memoria de las conferencias sobre habitación popular organizadas por el Banco Nacional Hipotecario Urbano y de Obras Públicas, S.A.* Mexico City: BNHOP, 1950.

Banco Nacional Hipotecario y de Obras Públicas (BNHOP). "El problema de la habitación en la Ciudad de México." Special issue of *Estudios* 6 (1952).

Banco Nacional Hipotecario y de Obras Públicas (BNHOP). "Proyecto de estudio de la Ciudad de México." *Estudios* 2 (1952): 101–104.

Barbosa, Mario, and Salomón González. *Problemas de la urbanización en el Valle de México: un homenaje visual en la celebración de los centenarios*. Mexico City: Universidad Autónoma Metropolitana, 2009.

Barona, Miguel. "Realidad económica y social en México." *Arquitectos de México* 19–20 (1963): 26–27.

Bataillon, Claude. *La ciudad y el campo en el México central*. Mexico City: Siglo XXI, 1972.

Bataillon, Claude. "Mexico: capital métis." *Caravelle* 3, no. 1 (1964): 159–191.

Bataillon, Claude. *Las zonas suburbanas de la Ciudad de México*. Mexico City: UNAM, 1968.

Benítez Zenteno, Raúl. "Habitación, comercio, industria, educación, culto y diversiones en la Ciudad de México." *Estudios Sociológicos* 2 (1956): 293–311.

Berman, Marshall. *All That Is Solid Melts into Air: The Experience of Modernity*. New York: Simon & Schuster, 1982.

Berra, Erika. "La expansión de la Ciudad de México y los conflictos urbanos, 1900–1930." PhD diss., El Colegio de México, 1983.

Bleynat, Ingrid. *Vendors' Capitalism: A Political Economy of Public Markets in Mexico City*. Stanford, CA: Stanford University Press, 2021.

Bliss, Katherine Elaine. *Compromised Positions: Prostitution, Public Health, and Gender Politics in Revolutionary Mexico City*. University Park: Pennsylvania State University Press, 2001.

Boils, Guillermo. "Segunda modernidad y las colonias proletarias al oriente de la Ciudad de México: Colonia Diez de Mayo." In *El espacio habitacional en la arquitectura moderna: colonias, fraccionamientos*, edited by Enrique Ayala Alonso and Gerardo Álvarez Montes, 63–85. Mexico City: UAM/CONACYT, 2013.

Boils, Guillermo. "Urbanización popular en la Ciudad de México de los años cuarenta (colonias proletarias en los márgenes del Gran Canal del Desagüe)." In *Aproximaciones a la historia del urbanismo popular*, edited by Héctor Quiroz Rothe, 209–235. Mexico City: UNAM, 2014.

Bonfil Batalla, Guillermo. *México Profundo: Reclaiming a Civilization*. Translated by Philip A. Dennis. Translations from Latin America Series. Austin: University of Texas Press, 1996.

Born, Esther. *The New Architecture in Mexico*. New York: Architectural Record/William Morrow, 1937.

Bribiesca, Juan. *Memoria del H. Ayuntamiento en 1908*. Mexico City: Imprenta Dirigida por J. Aguilar Vera, 1910.

Briseño, Lilián. *Candil de la calle, oscuridad de la casa: la iluminacion en la Ciudad de Mexico durante el porfiriato*. Mexico City: Instituto Mora/Miguel Ángel Porrúa, 2008.

Brown, Kate. "Gridded Lives: Why Kazakhstan and Montana are Nearly the Same Place." In *Dispatches from Dystopia: Histories of Places Not Yet Forgotten*, 97–133. Chicago: University of Chicago Press, 2015.

Brubaker, Rogers, and Frederick Cooper. "Beyond 'Identity.'" *Theory and Society* 29, no. 1 (2000): 1–47.

Buchanan, Jordan. "Working for the Workers? Infonavit's Creation and Its Foundational Motivations, 1972–1976." *Journal of Urban History* (2024): 00961442241288520.

Buffington, Robert, and Pablo Piccato. *True Stories of Crime in Modern Mexico*. Albuquerque: University of New Mexico Press, 2009.

Calderón Cockburn, Julio. *La ciudad ilegal: Lima en el siglo XX*. Lima: Fondo Editorial de la Facultad de Ciencias Sociales UNMSM, 2005.

Calvo Isaza, Óscar. *Urbanización y revolución en América Latina: Santiago de Chile, Buenos Aires y Ciudad de México (1950–1980)*. Mexico City: El Colegio de México/Universidad Nacional de Colombia, 2023.

Candelario Galicia, Tatiana Carolina. "Industrial Vallejo: una historia económica, urbana y política de la industrialización en la Ciudad de México, 1940–1982." PhD diss., El Colegio de México, 2019.

Candiani, Vera. *Dreaming of Dry Land: Environmental Transformation in Colonial Mexico City*. Stanford, CA: Stanford University Press, 2014.

Carranza, Luis E. *Architecture as Revolution: Episodes in the Forming of Modern Mexico*. Austin: University of Texas Press, 2010.

Castañeda, Luis. *Spectacular Mexico: Design, Propaganda, and the 1968 Olympics*. Minneapolis: University of Minnesota Press, 2014.

Castells, Manuel. *The City and the Grassroots: A Cross-cultural Theory of Urban Social Movements*. Berkeley: University of California Press, 1983.

Castells, Manuel. *La cuestión urbana*. Madrid: Siglo XXI, 1974.

Centro Operacional de Vivienda y Poblamiento (COPEVI). *Investigación sobre vivienda: las políticas habitacionales del estado mexicano*. Vol. 3. Mexico City: Centro Operacional de Vivienda y Poblamiento, 1977.

Cervantes de Salazar, Francisco. *Life in the Imperial and Loyal City of Mexico in New Spain and the Royal and Pontifical University of Mexico: As Described in the Dialogues for the Study of the Latin Language* (1554). Translated by Minnie Lee Barrett Shepard. With an introduction and notes by Carlos Eduardo Castañeda. Austin: University of Texas Press, 1953.

Chahim, Dean. "Flood Control Politics: Engineering, Urban Growth, and Disaster in Mexico City." PhD diss., Stanford University, 2021.

Chakrabarty, Dipesh. *Provincializing Europe: Postcolonial Thought and Historical Difference*. Princeton, NJ: Princeton University Press, 2000.

Chaterjee, Partha. *The Politics of the Governed*. New York: Columbia University Press, 2004.

Choay, Françoise. *The Modern City: Planning in the 19th Century*. Translated by Marguerite Hugo and George R. Collins. New York: George Braziller, 1969.

Cisneros Sosa, Armando. *La ciudad que construimos: registro de la expansión de la Ciudad de México*. Mexico City: UAM, 1993.

Connolly, Priscilla. "La ciudad y el hábitat popular: paradigma latinoamericano." In *Teorías sobre la ciudad en América Latina*, edited by Blanca Rebeca Ramírez Velázquez and Emilio Pradilla Cobos, 505–562. Mexico City: UAM, 2013.

Connolly, Priscilla. "Latin American Informal Urbanism: Contexts, Concepts, and Contributions with Specific Reference to Mexico." In *Marginal Urbanisms: Informal and Formal Development in Cities in Latin America*, edited by Felipe Hernández and Axel Becerra, 22–47. Newcastle, UK: Cambridge Scholars Publishing, 2017.

Connolly, Priscilla. "Observing the Evolution of Irregular Settlements: Mexico City's *Colonias Populares*, 1990 to 2005." *International Development Planning Review* 31, no. 1 (2009): 1–35.

Connolly, Priscilla. "Uncontrolled Settlements and Self-Build: What Kind of Solution? The Mexico City Case." In *Self-Help Housing: A Critique*, edited by Peter Ward, 141–174. London: Mansell, 1982.

Connolly, Priscilla. "Vaivenes tempranos del urbanismo popular en América Latina." In *Aproximaciones a la historia del urbanismo popular: una mirada desde México*, edited by Héctor Quiroz, 35–67. Mexico City: Universidad Nacional Autónoma de México.

Connolly, Priscilla, and Jill Wigle. "(Re)constructing Informality and 'Doing Regularization' in the Conservation Zone of Mexico City." *Planning Theory & Practice* 18, no. 2 (2017): 183–201.

Consejo Superior de Salubridad. *Informes rendidos por los inspectores sanitarios de cuartel y los de distrito al Consejo Superior de Salubridad*. Mexico City: Imprenta de Gobierno en el Ex-Arzobispado, 1895 (HathiTrust).

Contreras, Carlos. "Comité del Plano Regional de la Ciudad de México y sus Alrededores." *Planificación* 7 (March 1928): 21–23.

Contreras, Carlos. *Informe final del XVI Congreso Internacional de Planificación y de la Habitación*. Mexico City: Congreso Internacional de Planificación, 1939.

Contreras, Carlos. "National Planning Project for the Republic of Mexico." *City Planning* 1, no. 1 (July 1925): 97–109.

Contreras, Carlos. "Plan Development of Mexico City." In *The New Architecture in Mexico*, edited by Esther Born, 4–7. New York: Architectural Record/William Morrow, 1937.

Contreras, Carlos. *El plano regulador*. Mexico City: n.p., 1933.

Contreras, Carlos. *Planos reguladores 1946–1953*. Mexico City: UAM/UNAM, 2008.

Contreras, Carlos. "¿Qué cosa es la planificación de ciudades y regiones?" *Planificación* 1 (September 1927): 4–5.

Contreras, Carlos, José A. Cuevas, and Carlos Tarditi, eds. *International Glossary of Technical Terms Used in Housing and Town Planning*. Mexico City: XVI Congreso Internacional de Planificación y de la Habitación, 1938.

Cornejo Cabrera, Ezequiel. "La colonia proletaria Escuadrón 201." *Estudios Sociológicos* 2 (1956): 167-181.

Cornelius, Wayne A. *Politics and the Migrant Poor in Mexico City*. Stanford, CA: Stanford University Press, 1975.

Cossio, José Lorenzo. "Algunas noticias sobre las colonias de esta capital." *Boletín de la Sociedad Mexicana de Geografía y Estadística* 47, no. 1 (1937): 5–41.

Cossío Díaz, José Ramón, and Ricardo A. Ortega Soriano. *La herencia del constitucionalismo social mexicano y sus desafíos*. Mexico City: Suprema Corte de Justicia de la Nación, 2017.

Coulomb, René. "Políticas urbanas en la ciudad central del área metropolitana de la Ciudad de México (1958–1983)." *Iztapalapa: Revista de Ciencias Sociales y Humanidades* 9 (1983): 35–50.

Craib, Raymond B. *Cartographic Mexico: A History of State Fixations and Fugitive Landscapes*. Durham, NC: Duke University Press, 2004.

Cross, John C. *Informal Politics: Street Vendors and the State in Mexico City*. Stanford, CA: Stanford University Press, 1998.

Crossa, Verónica. *Luchando por un espacio en la Ciudad de México: comerciantes ambulantes y el espacio público*. Mexico City: El Colegio de México, 2018.

Cruz Rodríguez, María Soledad. *Crecimiento urbano y procesos sociales en el Distrito Federal (1920–1928)*. Mexico City: UAM, 1994.

Cruz Rodríguez, María Soledad. *Propiedad, poblamiento y periferia rural en la zona metropolitana de la Ciudad de México*. Mexico City: Programa Editorial de la Red de Investigación Urbana, 2001.

Cuevas, José Luis, Carlos Contreras, Vicente Urquiaga, Enrique Guerrero, and Carlos Tarditti. "Sugestiones que hace la Sociedad de Arquitectos Mexicanos a la Dirección de Obras Públicas del Gobierno del Distrito Federal para la formulación de la nueva Ley de Planificación y Zonificación del D.F." *Arquitectura y lo Demás* 8 (1946): 12–13.

Cymet Lerer, David, and Guillermo Ortiz Flores. *El problema de las colonias proletarias, Ciudad de México*. Mexico City: Escuela Superior de Ingeniería y Arquitectura/IPN, 1955.

Dávalos, Marcela. *Los letrados interpretan la ciudad: los barrios de indios en el umbral de la Independencia*. Mexico City: Instituto Nacional de Antropología e Historia, 2018.

Davis, Diane. "The Social Construction of Mexico City: Political Conflict and Urban Development." *Journal of Urban History* 24, no. 3 (1998): 364–415.

Davis, Diane. *Urban Leviathan: Mexico City in the Twentieth Century*. Philadelphia: Temple University Press, 1994.

Davis, Mike. *Planet of Slums*. New York: Verso, 2006.

de Anda Alanís, Enrique. *La arquitectura de la revolución mexicana: corrientes y estilos en la década de los veinte*. Mexico City: UNAM, 2008.

de Anda Alanís, Enrique. *Vivienda colectiva de la modernidad en México: los multifamiliares durante el periodo presidencial de Miguel Alemán (1946–1952)*. Mexico City: UNAM, 2011.

de Antuñano, Emilio. "Mexico City as an Urban Laboratory: Oscar Lewis, the 'Culture of Poverty' and the Transnational History of the Slum." *Journal of Urban History* 45, no. 4 (2019): 813–830.

de Caldeira, Teresa. "Peripheral Urbanization: Autoconstruction, Transversal Logics, and Politics in Cities of the Global South." *Environment and Planning D: Society and Space* 35, no. 1 (2017): 3–20.

de Coss-Corzo, Alejandro. "The Infrastructures of Internal Colonialism: State, Environment, and Race in Lerma, Mexico." *Antipode* 55, no. 3 (2023): 810–829.

de Gortari, Hira, and Regina Hernández Franyuti. *La Ciudad de México y el Distrito Federal: una historia compartida*. 4 vols. Mexico City: DDF/Instituto de Investigaciones Dr. José María Luis Mora, 1989.

de la Rocha, Mercedes. "From the Resources of Poverty to the Poverty of Resources? The Erosion of a Survival Model." *Latin American Perspectives* 28, no. 4 (2001): 72–100.

de la Rocha, Mercedes. *Los recursos de la pobreza: familias de bajos ingresos en Guadalajara*. Guadalajara: Colegio de Jalisco-CIESAS, 1986.

Delgado Aguilar, Francisco Javier. "La demanda de alumbrado y la formación de la esfera pública: Aguascalientes en la primera mitad del siglo XX." In *Ciudades mexicanas del siglo XX: seis estudios históricos*, edited by Ariel Rodríguez Kuri and Carlos Lira Vásquez, 217–254. Mexico City: El Colegio de México/UAM/CONACYT, 2009.

del Paso, Fernando. *José Trigo*. Mexico City: Siglo XXI, 1966.

"Demoliciones gratis por el enemigo público." *Arquitectura y lo Demás* 1, no. 1 (May 945): 22.

de Murga, Gonzalo. "Atisbos sociológicos: el fraccionamiento de tierras, las habitaciones baratas." *Boletín de la Sociedad Mexicana de Geografía y Estadística*, 5th series, 6 (1913): 485–497.

Departamento del Distrito Federal (DDF). *Atlas general del Distrito Federal* (1930). Reprint, Mexico City: CONDUMEX, 1992.

Departamento del Distrito Federal (DDF). *La Ciudad de México: Departamento del Distrito Federal, 1952–1964*. Mexico City: Imprenta Nuevo Mundo, 1964.

Departamento del Distrito Federal (DDF). *El Departamento del Distrito Federal y la habitación para empleados y obreros*. Mexico City: Imprenta Mundial, 1934.

Departamento del Distrito Federal (DDF). *Gobierno del Distrito Federal: sexenio 1940–1946*. Mexico City: DDF, 1947.

Departamento del Distrito Federal (DDF). *Informe presidencial: memoria del Departamento del Distrito Federal que rinde el C. Jefe del Mismo, Lic. Aarón Sáenz por el periodo administrativo entre el 1 de julio de 1932 y el 30 de junio de 1933*. Mexico City: DDF, 1933.

Departamento del Distrito Federal (DDF). *Informe que rinde el C. Jefe del Distrito Federal de la obra realizada durante el año de 1934.* Mexico City: Talleres Tipolinográficos del Depto. del DF, 1934.

Departamento del Distrito Federal (DDF). *Memoria del Departamento del Distrito Federal, del 1 de septiembre de 1937 al 30 de agosto de 1938.* Mexico City: DAPP, 1938.

Departamento del Distrito Federal (DDF). *Memoria del Departamento del Distrito Federal, del 1 de septiembre de 1938 al 31 de agosto de 1939.* Mexico City: Talleres Gráficos de la Penitenciaría, 1939.

Departamento del Distrito Federal (DDF). *Memoria del Departamento del Distrito Federal, del 1 de septiembre de 1939 al 31 de agosto de 1940.* Mexico City: DDF, 1940.

Departamento del Distrito Federal (DDF). *Memoria del Departamento del Distrito Federal, del 1 de septiembre de 1940 al 31 de agosto de 1941.* Mexico City: DDF, 1941.

Departamento del Distrito Federal (DDF). *Memoria del Departamento del Distrito Federal, del 1 de septiembre de 1942 al 31 de agosto de 1943.* Mexico City: DDF, 1943.

Departamento del Distrito Federal (DDF). *Memoria del Departamento del Distrito Federal, presentada por el C. Jefe del mismo, al Heroico Congreso de la Unión.* Mexico City: DDF, 1935.

Departamento del Distrito Federal (DDF). *Memoria del Departamento del Distrito Federal que rinde el C. Jefe del mismo, Lic. Aarón Sáenz, por el periodo administrativo comprendido entre el 1 de julio de 1932 y el 30 de junio de 1933.* Mexico City: DDF, 1933.

Departamento del Distrito Federal (DDF). *Memoria del gobierno del Distrito Federal, del 1 de septiembre de 1944 al 31 de agosto de 1945.* Mexico City: DDF, 1945.

Departamento del Distrito Federal (DDF). *México a través de los informes presidenciales: la Ciudad de México.* Vol. 16. Mexico City: Departamento del Distrito Federal/ Secretaría de la Presidencia, 1976.

Departamento del Distrito Federal (DDF). *Resumen de actividades.* Mexico City: DDF, 1947.

Departamento del Distrito Federal (DDF). *Resumen de actividades.* Mexico City: DDF, 1948.

Departamento del Distrito Federal (DDF). *Resumen de actividades.* Mexico City: Turanzas del Valle, 1949.

de Soto, Hernando. *The Other Path.* New York: Harper & Row, 1989.

de Sousa Santos, Boaventura. "Law: A Map of Misreading, toward a Postmodern Conception of Law." *Journal of Law and Society* 14 (1987): 279–302.

Díaz y Díaz, Martín. *Ensayos sobre la propiedad.* Mexico City: UNAM/Instituto de Investigaciones Jurídicas, 2014.

Dotson, Floyd, and Lilian Ota Dotson. "La estructura ecológica de las ciudades mexicanas." *Revista Mexicana de Sociología* 19, no. 1 (1957): 39–66.

Drago Quaglia, Elisa. "Doctrina Lazo: política de planificación integral." In *Segunda modernidad urbano arquitectónica*, edited by Enrique Ayala Alonso and Gerardo Álvarez Montes, 95–115. Mexico City: UAM/CONACYT, 2013.

Duhau, Emilio. *Habitat popular y política urbana.* Mexico City: UAM/Porrúa, 1998.

Duhau, Emilio. "The Informal City: An Enduring Slum or a Progressive Habitat?" In *Cities from Scratch: Poverty and Informality in Urban Latin America*, edited by Brodwyn Fischer, Brian McCann, and Javier Auyero, 150–169. Durham, NC: Duke University Press, 2014.

Duhau, Emilio. "La urbanización popular en América Latina: ¿Institucionalización o pactos sociales implícitos?" In *Procesos habitacionales de la Ciudad de México*, edited by Marco A. Michel, 19–30. Mexico City: UAM, 1988.

Duhau, Emilio, and Ángela Giglia. *Las reglas del desorden: habitar la metrópoli*. Mexico City: Siglo XXI, 2008.

Durand, Jorge. *La ciudad invade al ejido: proletarización, urbanización y lucha política en el Cerro del Judío, D.F.* Mexico City: CIESAS, 1983.

Eckstein, Susan. "Poor People versus the State and Capital: Anatomy of a Successful Community Mobilization for Housing in Mexico City." *International Journal of Urban & Regional Research* 14, no. 2 (1990): 274–296.

Eckstein, Susan. *The Poverty of Revolution: The State and the Urban Poor in Mexico*. Princeton, NJ: Princeton University Press, 1977.

Eckstein, Susan. "The State and the Urban Poor." In *Authoritarianism in Mexico*, edited by José Luis Reyna and Richard S. Weinert, 23–46. Philadelphia: Institute for the Study of Human Issues, 1977.

Eckstein, Susan. "Urbanization Revisited: Inner-City Slum of Hope and Squatter Settlement of Despair." *World Development* 18, no. 2 (1990): 165–181.

Escalante Gonzalbo, Fernando. *Ciudadanos imaginarios*. Mexico City: El Colegio de México, 1992.

Escalante Gonzalbo, Fernando. *Estampas de Liliput: bosquejos para una sociología de México*. Mexico City: FCE, 2006.

Escalante Gonzalbo, Fernando. *México: el peso del pasado: ensayo de interpretación*. Mexico City: Cal y Arena, 2023.

Escalante Gonzalbo, Fernando, ed. *Si persisten las molestias (Noticias de algunos casos de ceguera ilustrada)*. Mexico City: Cal y Arena, 2018.

Escalante Gonzalbo, Pablo, and Alejandro Alcántara Gallegos. "La Ciudad de México desde su fundación hasta la conquista española." In *Historia política de la Ciudad de México*, edited by Ariel Rodríguez Kuri, 19–66. Mexico City: El Colegio de México, 2012.

Escobar, Arturo. *Encountering Development: The Making and the Unmaking of the Third World*. Princeton, NJ: Princeton University Press, 2011.

Escudero, Alejandrina. *Una ciudad noble y lógica*. Mexico City: UNAM, 2018.

Escudero, Alejandrina. "La ciudad posrevolucionaria en tres planos." *Anales del Instituto de Investigaciones Estéticas* 93 (2008): 103–136.

Escudero, Alejandrina. "Conjunto urbano San Juan de Aragón." In *El espacio habitacional en la arquitectura moderna: colonias, fraccionamientos, unidades habitacionales, equipamiento urbano y protagonistas*, edited by Enrique Ayala Alonso and Gerardo Álvarez Montes, 187–202. Mexico City: UAM/CONACY, 2013.

Estrada Berg, Ricardo, and Domingo Quijano. "Comité del Plano Regional de la Ciudad de México y sus Alrededores." *Planificación* 1, no. 7 (March 1928): 21–23.

Fischer, Brodwyn. "A Century in Present Tense: Crisis, Politics, and Intellectual History of Brazil's Informal Cities." In *Cities from Scratch: Poverty and Informality in Latin America*, edited by Brodwyn Fischer, Javier Auyero, and Bryan McCann, 9–67. Durham, NC: Duke University Press, 2014.

Fischer, Brodwyn. "Historicising Informal Governance in 20th Century Brazil." *Contemporary Social Science* 17, no. 3 (2022): 205–221.

Fischer, Brodwyn. *A Poverty of Rights: Citizenship and Inequality in Twentieth-Century Rio de Janeiro*. Stanford, CA: Stanford University Press, 2008.

Fischer, Brodwyn, and Charlotte Vorms. "Introduction: Informal Urbanism as History." In *Informal Cities: History, Power, and Precarity in Latin Europe, Latin America, and Colonial North Africa*, edited by Charlotte Vorms and Brodwyn Fischer, 1–24. Chicago: University of Chicago Press, 2025.

Fishmann, Robert. *Urban Utopias in the Twentieth Century: Ebenezer Howard, Frank Lloyd Wright, Le Corbusier*. New York: Basic Books, 1978.

Flaherty, George F. *Hotel Mexico: Dwelling on the '68 Movement*. Berkeley: University of California Press, 2016.

Franco de los Reyes, Diego Antonio. "Vecinos de la modernidad: la Colonia Guerrero ante el conjunto urbano Nonoalco Tlatelolco, 1942–1972." MA thesis, Instituto Mora, 2018.

Freije, Vanessa. *Citizens of Scandal: Journalism, Secrecy, and the Politics of Reckoning in Mexico*. Durham, NC: Duke University Press, 2020.

Frieden, Bernard. "The Search for Housing Policy in Mexico City." *Town Planning Review* 36, no. 2 (July 1965): 75–94.

Fuentes, Carlos. *La región más transparente del aire*. 1958. Reprint, Mexico City: Alfaguara, 2008.

Galindo y Villa, Jesús. *Historia sumaria de la Ciudad de México*. Mexico City: Editorial Cultura, 1925.

García Cortés, Adrián. *La reforma urbana de México: crónicas de la Comisión de Planificación del Distrito Federal*. Mexico City: Bay Gráfica y Ediciones, 1972.

García Cubas, Antonio. *Geografía e historia del Distrito Federal*. Mexico City: Antigua Imprenta de E. Murguía, 1884.

Garza, Gustavo. *El proceso de industrialización de la Ciudad de México (1821–1970)*. Mexico City: El Colegio de México, 1985.

Garza, Gustavo. *La urbanización de México en el siglo XX*. Mexico City: El Colegio de México, 2003.

Gauss, Susan. *Made in Mexico: Regions, Nation, and the State in the Rise of Mexican Industrialism*. University Park: Pennsylvania State University Press, 2010.

Gerlof, Bob. *Monstrous Politics: Geography, Rights, and the Urban Revolution in Mexico City*. Nashville: Vanderbilt University Press, 2023.

Gilbert, Alan. *In Search of a Home: Rental and Shared Housing in Latin America*. Tucson: University of Arizona Press, 1993.

Gilbert, Alan. "The Return of the Slum: Does Language Matter?" *International Journal of Urban and Regional Research* 31 (2007): 697–713.

Gilbert, Alan, and Peter M. Ward. *Housing, the State and the Poor: Policy and Practice in Three Latin American Cities*. Cambridge: Cambridge University Press, 1985.

Gilbert, Liette, and Feike de Jong. "Entanglements of Periphery and Informality in Mexico City." *International Journal of Urban and Regional Research* (2015): 518–532.

Gillingham, Paul, and Benjamin T. Smith, eds. *Dictablanda: Politics, Work, and Culture in Mexico, 1938–1968*. Durham, NC: Duke University Press, 2014.

Gilly, Adolfo. *El Cardenismo: una utopía mexicana*. Mexico City: Cal y Arena, 1994.

Gómez, Lilia, and Miguel Ángel de Quevedo, eds. *Testimonios vivos: 20 arquitectos*. Mexico City: Secretaría de Educación Pública, INBA, 1981.

Gómez Mayorga, Mauricio. "El plano de la ciudad." *Arquitectura y lo Demás* 11 (1947–1948): 16.

Gómez Mayorga, Mauricio. "El problema de la habitación en México (una conversación con el arquitecto Mario Pani)." *Arquitectura México* 27 (April 1949): 67–74.

Gómez Mayorga, Mauricio. *¿Qué hacer por la Ciudad de México?* Mexico City: B. Costa-Amic, 1957.

Gómez Mayorga, Mauricio, and Estanislau Fischlowitz. *La superurbanización caótica.* Mexico City: Centro de Estudios y Documentación Sociales, AC, 1963.

González Castillo, Longines. "Los parásitos intestinales en Santa Anita, Distrito Federal." BA thesis, Universidad Nacional Autónoma de México, 1947.

González Escobar, Inés. "From Inclusive Informality to Alienating Inclusion: The Rise of Mexico's Debtfare Society on the Urban Fringes of Guadalajara." *Critical Historical Studies* 9, no. 2 (2022): 161–193.

González Navarro, Moisés. *Población y sociedad en México.* Vol. 1. Mexico City: UNAM, 1974.

González Rodríguez, Sergio. *Los bajos fondos: el antro, la bohemia, el café.* Mexico City: Cal y Arena, 1990.

Gorelik, Adrián. *La ciudad latinoamericana: una figura de la imaginación social del siglo XX.* Buenos Aires: Siglo XXI, 2022.

Gorelik, Adrián. "Pan-American Routes: A Continental Planning Journey between Reformism and the Cultural Cold War." *Planning Perspectives* 32, no. 1 (2017): 47–66.

Granados, Luis Fernando. "Cosmopolitan Indians and Mesoamerican Barrios in Bourbon Mexico City." PhD diss., Georgetown University, 2008.

Granados, Luis Fernando. "De la ciudad capitalista a la ciudad colonial: dinámica histórica y segregación socioespecial en *El derecho a la ciudad.*" In *Uso y valor de Henri Lefebvre: siete ensayos a propósito de "El derecho a la ciudad,"* edited by Luis Fernando Granados, 105–150. Xalapa: Universidad Veracruzana, 2022.

Granados, Luis Fernando. "Nuestra urbe." *El Presente del Pasado*, May 15, 2017. https://elpresentedelpasado.com/2017/05/15/nuestra-urbe-1-de-2 (accessed November 13, 2025).

Granados, Luis Fernando. "Tres *civitates* y una sola *urbs* verdadera: Tenochtitlán, Tlatelolco, y la Ciudad de México en el siglo XVI." Paper presented at the XIV Reunión Internacional de Historiadores de México, Chicago, September 19, 2014.

Granados, Luis Fernando, ed. *Uso y valor de Henri Lefebvre: siete ensayos a propósito de "El derecho a la ciudad."* Xalapa: Universidad Veracruzana, 2022.

Guerrero, Enrique. "Urbanismo oficial." *Arquitectura y lo Demás* (1945): 16–22.

Guerrero, Julio. *La génesis del crimen en México.* Mexico City: Librería de la V. de Ch. Bouret, 1901.

Gyger, Helen. *Improvised Cities: Architecture, Urbanization and Innovation in Peru.* Pittsburgh: University of Pittsburgh Press, 2019.

Haber, Paul. "La migración del Movimiento Urbano Popular a la política de partido en el México contemporáneo." *Revista Mexicana de Sociología* 71, no. 2 (2009): 213–245.

Hall, Peter. *Cities of Tomorrow.* Cambridge, UK: Blackwell, 1995.

Hannerz, Ulf. *Exploring the City: Inquiries toward an Urban Anthropology.* New York: Columbia University Press, 1980.

Hardoy, Jorge E. "Theory and Practice of Urban Planning in Europe, 1850–1930." In *Rethinking the Latin American City*, edited by Richard Morse, 20–49. Baltimore: Johns Hopkins University Press, 1992.

Hart, Keith. "Informal Income Opportunities and Urban Employment in Ghana." *Journal of Modern African Studies* 11 (1973): 61–89.

Harth-Deneke, Jorge Alberto. "The Colonias Proletarias of Mexico City: Low Income Settlements at the Urban Fringe." PhD diss., MIT, 1966.

Hartman, Georgia. "'Homes with Value': Mortgage Finance and the Reconfiguration of Home Value in Urban Mexico." *City & Society* 33, no. 1 (2021): 17–39.

Hauser, Philip, ed. *Urbanization in Latin America.* New York: International Documents Service, 1961.

Hayner, Norman S. "La Ciudad de México: su estructura ecológica latinoamericana." *Revista Mexicana de Sociología* 26, no. 1 (1964): 221–231.

Hayner, Norman S. "Differential Social Change in a Mexican Town." *Social Forces* 36 (May 1948): 381–390.

Hayner, Norman S. "Mexico City: Its Growth and Configuration." *American Journal of Sociology* 50 (January 1945): 295–304.

Hayner, Norman S. *New Patterns in Old Mexico.* New Haven, CT: College & University Press, 1966.

Hernández, Felipe, and Peter Kellett. "Chapter 1. Introduction: Reimagining the Informal in Latin America." In *Rethinking the Informal City: Critical Perspectives from Latin America*, edited by Felipe Hernández, Peter Kellett, and Lea K. Allen, 1–20. New York: Berghahn Books, 2010.

Hernández, Felipe, Peter Kellett, and Lea K. Allen, eds. *Rethinking the Informal City: Critical Perspectives from Latin America.* New York: Berghahn Books, 2010.

Hernández Rodríguez, Rogelio. *Historia mínima del PRI.* Mexico City: El Colegio de México, 2016.

Herrera-Martín, Carlos Reynaldo. "Judicial Review of Expropriation: The Case of Mexico." PhD diss., University College London, 2014.

Holston, James. *Insurgent Citizenship: Disjunctures of Democracy and Modernity in Brazil.* Princeton, NJ: Princeton University Press, 2008.

Holston, James. *The Modernist City: An Anthropological Critique of Brasilia.* Chicago: University of Chicago Press, 1989.

House, Jim. "Urban Risk? Constructing Shantytowns as a Problem of Colonial Governance in Algiers and Casablanca, 1919–1962." In *Informal Cities: History, Power, and Precarity in Latin Europe, Latin America, and Colonial North Africa*, edited by Charlotte Vorms and Brodwyn Fischer, 245–268. Chicago: University of Chicago Press, 2025.

Ibargüengoitia, Jorge. *La casa de usted y otros viajes.* Mexico City: Joaquín Mortiz, 1991.

"Informe que rinde el Comité del Plano Regulador integrado por el arquitecto Carlos Contreras, ingeniero José A. Cuevas y arquitecto Carlos Tarditi, a la Comisión de Planificiación del Distrito Federal." *Planificación* 3, nos. 3–6 (March–December 1935): 59–72.

Instituto Nacional de Antropología e Historia. *Catálogo nacional, monumentos históricos: inmuebles y muebles, Iztacalco D.F.* Mexico City: INAH, 1992.

Instituto Nacional de la Vivienda (INV). *Características, problemas y programa de acción en beneficio de las colonias proletarias.* Mexico City: INV, 1957.

Instituto Nacional de la Vivienda (INV). *Una ciudad perdida*. Mexico City: INV, 1968.
Instituto Nacional de la Vivienda (INV). *Colonias proletarias: problemas y soluciones*. Mexico City: INV, 1958.
Instituto Nacional de la Vivienda (INV). *Herradura de tugurios: problemas y soluciones*. Mexico City: INV, 1958.
Instituto Nacional de la Vivienda (INV). *Tacubaya: problemas y soluciones*. Mexico City: INV, 1958.
Instituto Nacional de la Vivienda (INV). *La vivienda popular: problemas y soluciones*. Mexico City: INV, 1958.
Jackson, Kenneth T. *Crabgrass Frontier: The Suburbanization of the United States*. Oxford: Oxford University Press, 1985.
Jacobs, Jane. *The Death and Life of Great American Cities*. New York: Random House, 1961.
Jácome Moreno, Cristóbal Andrés. "Las construcciones de la imagen: la serie del Conjunto Urbano Nonoalco-Tlatelolco de Armando Salas Portugal." *Anales del Instituto de Investigaciones Estéticas* 31, no. 95 (2009): 85–118.
Jiménez, Cristina. *Making an Urban Public: Popular Claims to the City in Mexico*. Pittsburgh: University of Pittsburgh Press, 2019.
Jiménez Muñoz, Jorge H. *La traza del poder: historia de la política y los negocios urbanos en el Distrito Federal: de sus orígenes a la desaparición del Ayuntamiento (1824–1928)*. Mexico City: Secretaría de Cultura del Distrito Federal/UACM, 2012.
Jiménez y Castilla, Martha Regina. "Bramadero: un caso ilustrativo de población marginal." BA thesis, UNAM, 1963.
Johnson, David. *Planning the Great Metropolis: The 1929 Regional Plan of New York and Its Environs*. London: Chapman & Hall, 1996.
Jordan, Robert M. "Flowers and Iron Fists: Ernesto P. Uruchurtu and the Contested Modernization of Mexico City." PhD diss., University of Nebraska, 2013.
Joseph, Gilbert M., Anne Rubinstein, and Eric Zolov, eds. *Fragments of a Golden Age*. Durham, NC: Duke University Press, 2001.
Kagan, Richard L. *Urban Images of the Hispanic World, 1493–1794*. New Haven, NJ: Yale University Press, 2000.
Keiser, Thorten. "Social Conceptions of Property and Labour: Private Law in the Aftermath of the Mexican Revolution and European Legal Science." *Journal of the Max Planck Institute for European Legal History* 20 (2012): 258–273.
Kennedy, Duncan. "Two Globalizations of Law & Legal Thought: 1850–1968." *Suffolk University Law Review* 36 (2003): 631–679.
Klemek, Christopher. *The Transatlantic Collapse of Urban Renewal: Postwar Urbanism from New York to Berlin*. Chicago: University of Chicago Press, 2011.
Knight, Alan. "Racism, Revolution, and Indigenismo: Mexico, 1910–1940." In *The Idea of Race in Latin America, 1870–1940*, edited by Richard Graham, 71–114. Austin: University of Texas Press, 1990.
Konove, Andrew. *Black Market Capital: Urban Politics and the Shadow Economy in Mexico City*. Berkeley: University of California Press, 2018.
Konove, Andrew. "Making a Modern Barrio: Infrastructure and Progress in Mexico City, 1900–1903." *Journal of Urban History* 46, no. 3 (2020): 516–540.
Kourí, Emilio, ed. *En busca de Molina Enríquez: cien años de "Los grandes problemas nacionales."* Mexico City: El Colegio de México/Katz Center for Mexican Studies, 2009.

Kourí, Emilio. "Interpreting the Expropriation of Indian Pueblo Lands in Porfirian Mexico: The Unexamined Legacies of Andrés Molina Enríquez." *Hispanic American Historical Review* 82, no. 1 (2002): 69–117.

Kram Villarreal, Rachel. "Gladiolas for the Children of Sánchez: Ernesto P. Uruchurtu's Mexico City, 1950–1968." PhD diss., University of Arizona, 2008.

Kuecker, Glenn David, and Alejandro Puga. *Mapping the Megalopolis: Order and Disorder in Mexico City*. Lanham, MD: Lexington Books, 2018.

Kuntz Fischer, Sandra, and Elisa Speckman Guerra. "El Porfiriato." In *Nueva historia general de México*, 487–536. Mexico City: El Colegio de México, 2010.

Kwak, Nancy. "California Formalising: A Story of Deliberately Designed Inequality." *Architectural Review*, December 17, 2020. https://www.architectural-review.com/essays/california-formalising-a-story-of-deliberately-designed-inequality.

Landa, Pablo. "Overflowing Architecture: Home, Neighborhood, and Nation in Mexico's Modern Experience." PhD diss., Princeton University, 2015.

Leal, Alejandra. "'You Cannot Be Here': The Urban Poor and the Specter of the Indian in Neoliberal Mexico." *Journal of Latin American and Caribbean Anthropology* 21, no. 3 (2016): 539–559.

Lear, John. "Mexico City: Popular Classes and Revolutionary Politics." In *Cities of Hope: People, Protests, and Progress in Urbanizing Latin America, 1870–1930*, edited by Ronn Pineo and James A. Baer, 53–87. Boulder, CO: Westview Press, 1998.

Lear, John. *Workers, Neighbors, and Citizens: The Revolution in Mexico City*. Lincoln: University of Nebraska Press, 2001.

Leidenberger, Georg. "Colonias proletarias y conjuntos habitacionales: reflexiones sobre la vivienda del estado mexicano a mediados del siglo veinte." In *Estudios de la forma urbana: análisis contemporáneo en México*, edited by Gabriela Lee Alardín, 250–267. Mexico City: Universidad Iberoamericana, 2019.

Leidenberger, Georg. "Las 'pláticas' de los arquitectos de 1933 y el giro racionalista y social en el México posrevolucionario." In *Polémicas intelectuales del México moderno*, edited by Carlos Illades and Georg Leidenberger, 187–225. Mexico City: CONACULTA/UAM, 2008.

Leidenberger, Georg. "Todo aquí es *Vulkanisch*: el arquitecto Hannes Meyer en México, 1938 a 1949." In *México a la luz de sus revoluciones*, edited by Laura Rojas and Susan Deeds, 499–540. Vol. 2. Mexico City: El Colegio de México, 2014.

Lepenies, Wolf. *Between Literature and Science: The Rise of Sociology*. Cambridge: Cambridge University Press, 1988.

Lewis, Oscar. *Anthropological Essays*. New York: Random House, 1970.

Lewis, Oscar. *The Children of Sánchez: Autobiography of a Mexican Family*. New York: Random House, 1961.

Lewis, Oscar. *Five Families: Mexican Case Studies in the Culture of Poverty*. New York: Basic Books, 1959.

Lewis, Oscar. "Urbanization without Breakdown: A Case Study." *Scientific Monthly* 75, no. 1 (1952): 31–41.

Lindner, Rolf. *The Reportage of Urban Culture: Robert Park and the Chicago School*. Translated by Adrian Morris. Cambridge: Cambridge University Press, 1996.

Lira, Andrés. *Comunidades indígenas frente a la Ciudad de México: Tenochtitlán y Tlatelolco, sus pueblos y barrios, 1812–1919*. Mexico City: El Colegio de México/El Colegio de Michoacán, 1983.

Loaeza, Soledad. "Modernización autoritaria a la sombra de la superpotencia, 1944–1968." In *Nueva historia general de México*, 653–698. Mexico City: El Colegio de México, 2010.

Loaeza, Soledad. "Perspectivas para una historia política del Distrito Federal en el siglo XX." *Historia Mexicana* 45, no. 1 (1996): 99–158.

Lomnitz, Claudio. "Modes of Citizenship in Mexico." *Public Culture* 11, no. 1 (1999): 269–293.

Lomnitz, Claudio. "Times of Crisis: Historicity, Sacrifice, and the Spectacle of Debacle in Mexico City." *Public Culture* 15, no. 1 (2003): 127–147.

Lomnitz, Larissa Adler de. *¿Cómo sobreviven los marginados?* Mexico City: Siglo Veintiuno Editores, 1993.

López Caballero, Paula. *Indígenas de la nación: etnografía histórica de la alteridad en México (Milpa Alta, siglos XVII–XXI)*. Mexico City: FCE, 2012.

López Rangel, Rafael. "Carlos Contreras en la historia de la planificación urbana." In *Planificación y urbanismo visionarios de Carlos Contreras: escritos de 1925 a 1938*, 25–34. Mexico City: UNAM, 2003.

López Rangel, Rafael. *La planificación y la Ciudad de México, 1900–1940*. Mexico City: UAM, 1993.

López Romero, Paulo César. "Un espacio para acceder a la ciudad: las colonias agrícolas de Xalapa, 1924–1937." In *Uso y valor de Henri Lefebvre: siete ensayos a propósito de "El derecho a la ciudad,"* edited by L. Fernando Granados, 151–182. Xalapa: Universidad Veracruzana, 2022.

Loyo, Gilberto. *Notas sobre la evolución demográfica de la Ciudad de México*. Mexico City: n.p., 1936.

Loyo, Gilberto. "Una oficina municipal de estadística e investigación." *Planificación* 2, no. 3 (1934): 24–29.

Lozano, Irma. *De la opinión a la noticia*. Mexico City: Kiosko, 1992.

Luna Elizarrarás, Sara Minerva. "Ordenar el habitar popular: apuntes en torno a la Unidad Habitacional Santa María Cruz Mayehualco (1963)." Paper presented at the III Congreso de la Asociación Iberoamericana de Historia Urbana, Madrid, Spain, November 25, 2022.

Macedo, Miguel. *La criminalidad en México: medios de combatirla, discurso pronunciado por el Sr. Licenciado Miguel M. Macedo*. Mexico City: Oficina Tip. de la Secretaría de Fomento, 1897.

Mack, Jessica. "De ejidos urbanos a Ciudad Universitaria: expropiación, ciudadanía y modernización en la Ciudad de México, 1943–1972." Paper presented at the XVI Reunión Internacional de Historiadores de México, Austin, TX, November 2, 2022.

Maffitt, Kenneth. "From the Ashes of the Poet Kings: Exodus, Identity Formation, and the New Politics of Place in Mexico City's Industrial Suburbs, 1948–1975." *International Labor and Working-Class History* 64 (2003): 74–90.

Mangin, William. "Latin American Squatter Settlements: A Problem and a Solution." *Latin American Research Review* 2, no. 3 (1967): 65–98.

Marino, Daniela. "Institucionalización de la Reforma Agraria (1915–1937): revolución y modernización jurídica en México." In *Derecho privado y modernización: América Latina y Europa en la primera mitad del siglo XX*, edited by María Rosario Polotto, Thorsten Keiser, and Thomas Duve, 153–178. Frankfurt: Max Planck Institute for European Legal History, 2015.

Martin, Percy Alvin, ed. *Who's Who in Latin America: A Biographical Dictionary of the Outstanding Living Men and Women of Spanish America and Brazil.* Stanford, CA: Stanford University Press, 1935.

Martínez Delgado, Gerardo. *La experiencia urbana: Aguascalientes y su abasto en el siglo XX.* Mexico City: Instituto de Investigaciones Dr. José María Luis Mora/CONACYT/Universidad Autónoma de Aguascalientes/Universidad Autónoma de Guanajuato, 2017.

Marván, Ignacio. "De la ciudad del presidente al gobierno propio, 1970–2000." In *Historia política de la Ciudad de México*, edited by Ariel Rodríguez Kuri, 483–563. Mexico City: El Colegio de México, 2012.

Massidda, Adriana. "Slums, *Villas Miseria*, and *Barriadas*: Why Terms Matter." *Journal of Urban History* 49, no. 3 (2023): 552–570.

Mayne, Alan. *Slums: The History of a Global Injustice.* Chicago: University of Chicago Press, 2017.

McMichael, Carol. "The Urban Development of Mexico City, 1850–1930." In *Planning Latin America's Capital Cities*, edited by Arturo Almandoz, 139–159. London: Routledge, 2002.

Mendiola, Sandra C. *Street Democracy: Vendors, Violence, and Public Space in Late Twentieth-Century Mexico City.* Lincoln: University of Nebraska Press, 2017.

Meneses Reyes, Rodrigo. "Los efectos materiales del constitucionalismo mexicano: una perspectiva de la sociología del derecho." In *La herencia del constitucionalismo mexicano y sus desafíos*, 301–329. Mexico City: Suprema Corte de Justicia de la Nación, 2017.

Mercado Revilla, Leslie Teresa. "Colonia Obrera." In *El territorio excluido: historia y patrimonio culturas de las colonias al norte del Río de La Piedad*, edited by María Eugenia Herrera, 167–194. Mexico City: Palabra de Clío, 2015.

México: Dirección General de Estadística. *6º censo general de población: 1940.* Mexico City: Talleres Gráficos de la Nación, 1941.

México: Dirección General de Estadística. *8º censo general de población: 1960.* Mexico City: Secretaría de la Economía Nacional, Dirección General de Estadística, México, 1963.

México: Secretaría de Gobernación. *Código civil para el Distrito y territorios federales.* Mexico City: Talleres Gráficos de la Nación, 1928.

Meyer, Hannes. "La Ciudad de México: fragmentos de un estudio urbanístico." *Arquitectura/México* 12 (1942): 96–109.

Miranda Pacheco, Sergio. *La creación del Departamento del Distrito Federal: urbanización, política y cambio institucional.* Mexico City: UNAM, 2008.

Miranda Pacheco, Sergio. "El Frankenstein urbano: ecólogos, urbanistas e ingenieros frente a la crisis hidrológica de la Ciudad de México a mitad del siglo XX." *HALAC: Historia Ambiental, Latinoamericana y Caribeña* 10, no. 2 (2020): 162–202.

Miranda Pacheco, Sergio. *Tacubaya: de suburbio veraniego a ciudad.* Mexico City: UNAM, 2007.

Miranda Pacheco, Sergio. "Urbe inmunda: poder y prejuicios sociales en la urbanización y desagüe de la Ciudad y el Valle de México en el siglo XIX." In *De olfato: aproximaciones a los olores en la historia de México*, edited by Élodie Dupey García and Guadalupe Pinzón Ríos, 193–250. Mexico City: Secretaría de Cultura/FCE/UNAM, 2020.

Miranda Pacheco, Sergio. "La vivienda popular del milagro mexicano en la Ciudad de México: notas para su historia." In *Aproximaciones a la historia del urbanismo popular*, edited by Héctor Quiroz Rothe, 111–124. Mexico City: UNAM, 2014.

Mitchell, Timothy. *Rule of Experts: Egypt, Techno-Politics, Modernity*. Berkeley: University of California Press, 2002.

Moctezuma, Vicente. *El desvanecimiento de lo popular: gentrificación en el centro histórico de la Ciudad de México*. Mexico City: El Colegio de México, 2021.

Moctezuma Barragán, Pedro. "La Coordinadora Nacional del Movimiento Urbano Popular en el Valle de México." In *Los movimientos sociales en el Valle de México*, edited by Jorge Alonso, 199–264. Vol. 1. Mexico City: CIESAS, 1986.

Moctezuma Barragán, Pedro. *Despertares: comunidad y organización urbano popular en México*. Mexico City: UAM/Universidad Iberoamericana, 1999.

Moctezuma Barragán, Pedro, and Bernardo Navarro. *La urbanización popular en la Ciudad de México*. Mexico City: UNAM/Instituto de Investigaciones Económicas, 1989.

Monsiváis, Carlos. *Días de guardar*. Mexico City: ERA, 1970.

Monsiváis, Carlos. "Los Hermanos Mayo: las variedades de la experiencia histórica." In *Maravillas que son, sombras que fueron: la fotografía en México*, 91–99. Mexico City: CONACULTA/ERA/Museo del Estanquillo, 2012.

Monsiváis, Carlos. *Los rituales del caos*. Mexico City: ERA, 1995.

Montaño, Diana. *Electrifying Mexico: Technology and the Transformation of a Modern City*. Austin: University of Texas Press, 2021.

Montaño, María Cristina. *La tierra de Ixtapalapa: luchas sociales desde las chinampas hasta la transformación urbana*. Mexico City: UAM, 1984.

Morales, María Dolores. "La expansión de la Ciudad de México en el siglo XIX: el caso de los fraccionamientos." In *Ciudad de México: ensayo de construcción de una historia*, edited by Alejandra Moreno Toscano and Carlos Aguirre, 71–96. Mexico City: Secretaría de Educación Pública, 1978.

Morales, María Dolores, and María Gayón Córdova. "Casas y viviendas de la Ciudad de México: espejos de las transformaciones urbanas, 1848–1882." *Scripta Nova: Revista Electrónica de Geografía y Ciencias Sociales* 7 (2003). https://www.ub.edu/geocrit/sn/sn-146(016).htm (accessed November 13, 2025).

Moreno Toscano, Alejandra. "A propósito del crecimiento anárquico." *Revista Habitación* no. 2/3 (April–September 1981): 3–5.

Morse, Richard. "Cities as People." In *Rethinking the Latin American City*, edited by Richard M. Morse and Jorge Hardoy, 3–19. Washington, DC: Woodrow Wilson Center Press/Johns Hopkins University Press, 1992.

Moya, José. *Cousins and Strangers: Spanish Immigrants in Buenos Aires, 1850–1930*. Berkeley: University of California Press, 1998.

Mraz, John. "Close-up: An Interview with the Hermanos Mayo (May Day Brothers); Spanish-American Photojournalists, 1930s–Present." *Studies in Latin American Popular Culture* 11 (1992): 195–218.

Mumford, Lewis. *The Culture of Cities*. New York: Harcourt, Brace, 1938.

Mundy, Barbara E. *The Death of Aztec Tenochtitlan, the Life of Mexico City*. Austin: University of Texas Press, 2015.

Muñoz, Antonio. "Control arquitectónico del desarrollo urbano." *Obras Públicas* 12 (December 1930): 284–289.

Navarrete, Federico. "Blanquitud vs. blancura, mestizaje y privilegio en México de los siglos XIX a XXI: una propuesta de interpretación." *Estudios Sociológicos* 40 (February 2022): 127–162.

Niblo, Stephen. *Mexico in the 1940s: Modernity, Politics, and Corruption.* Wilmington, DE: Scholarly Resources, 1999.

Nightingale, Carl H. *Segregation: A Global History of Divided Cities.* Chicago: University of Chicago Press, 2012.

Noelle, Louise, ed. *Mario Pani.* Mexico City: UNAM-IIE, 2008.

Novoa, Leonardo. "México como visión de la ciudad ideal: implicaciones de la regencia de Ernesto P. Uruchurtu." PhD diss., UNAM, 2021.

Ochoa, Enrique C., and Jaime Pensado. *Mexico beyond 1968; Revolutionaries, Radicals, and Repression during the Global Sixties and the Subversive Seventies.* Tucson: University of Arizona Press, 2018.

O'Gorman, Edmundo. "Reflexiones sobre la distribución colonial de la Ciudad de México" (1938). In *Seis estudios históricos de tema mexicano,* 11–40. Xalapa: Universidad Veracuzana, 1960.

O'Hara, Matthew D. *A Flock Divided: Race, Religion, and Politics in Mexico, 1749–1857.* Durham, NC: Duke University Press, 2009.

Oldman, Oliver, Henry J. Aaron, Richard M. Bird, and Stephen L. Kass. *Financing Urban Development in Mexico City.* Cambridge, MA: Harvard University Press, 1967.

Olsen, Patrice Elizabeth. *Artifacts of Revolution: Architecture, Society, and Politics, 1920–1940.* Lanham, MD: Rowman & Littlefield, 2008.

O'Rourke, Kathryn E. *Modern Architecture in Mexico City: History, Representation, and the Shaping of a Capital.* Pittsburgh: Pittsburgh University Press, 2016.

Orozco y Berra, Manuel. *Memoria para el plano de la Ciudad de México: formada de orden del ministerio de fomento.* Mexico City: Ministerio de Fomento, Colonización e Industria, 1867.

Ortega Alcázar, Iliana. *Autoconstrucción de vivienda, espacio y vida familiar en la Ciudad de México.* Mexico City: Programa Universitario de Estudios Sobre la Ciudad, 2016.

Ortiz, Guillermo. "La vivienda popular." *Boletín de la Sociedad Mexicana de Urbanismo* 1 (1962): 32–42.

Ortiz, Guillermo, and Carlos Villaseñor. "Desarrollo de las colonias proletarias de la Ciudad de México." *Boletín de la Sociedad Mexicana de Urbanismo* 2 (1962): 23–27.

Ortiz Escamilla, Juan. "Política y poder en una época revolucionaria: Ciudad de México (1800–1824)." In *Historia política de la Ciudad de México,* edited by Ariel Rodríguez Kuri, 159–220. Mexico City: El Colegio de México, 2012.

Ortiz Mena, Antonio. *La legislación sobre planificación en la República Mexicana.* Mexico City: DDF/Congreso Internacional de Planificación, 1938.

Ortiz Molina, Luis G. *Prontuario: codificación de acuerdos, bandos, circulares, decretos, leyes, reglamentos y demás disposiciones vigentes de la Secretaría de Gobernación y sus dependencias.* Mexico City: Imprenta del Gobierno Federal, 1911.

Palafox, Silvano. "El reglamento de construcciones de la Ciudad de México." *Obras Públicas* 2 (February 1930): 79–80.

Pallares, Alfonso. "Lo que significa el fraccionamiento de Hipódromo de la Condesa." In *Cultura arquitectónica de la modernidad mexicana: antología de textos 1922–1963,* edited by Enrique X. de Anda Alanís and Salvador Lizárraga Sánchez, 41–45. Mexico City: UNAM/Instituto de Investigaciones Estéticas, 2010.

Pani, Alberto J. *La higiene en México.* Mexico City: Imprenta de J. Ballescá, 1916.

Pani, Mario. *Los multifamiliares de pensiones.* Mexico City: Editorial Arquitectura, 1952.

Pani, Mario. *Nonoalco-Tlatelolco Urban Development Scheme: The Urban Regeneration of Mexico City.* Mexico City: BNHOP, 1961.

Pani, Mario. "Zonificación urbana." *Arquitectura/México* 16, no. 71 (September 1960): 122–135.

Parra, Manuel Germán. *La industrialización en México.* Mexico City: Imprenta Universitaria, 1954.

Partido Revolucionario Institucional. *Historia documental de la CNOP, 1943–1959.* Mexico City: PRI, 1984.

Paz, Octavio. *El ogro filantrópico: historia y política, 1971–1978.* Mexico City: Joaquín Mortiz, 1978.

Peraza Guzmán, Marco Tulio, and Lourdes Cruz González Franco, eds. *Segunda modernidad urbano arquitectónica: proyectos y obras.* Mexico City: UAM-CONACYT, 2014.

Pérez Toledo, Sonia. "Formas de gobierno local, modelos constitucionales y cuerpo electoral, 1824–1867." In *Historia política de la Ciudad de México*, edited by Ariel Rodríguez Kuri, 221–286. Mexico City: El Colegio de México, 2012.

Perlman, Janice. *Favela: Four Decades of Living on the Edge in Rio de Janeiro.* Oxford: Oxford University Press, 2010.

Perlman, Janice. *The Myth of Marginality: Urban Poverty and Politics in Rio de Janeiro.* Berkeley: University of California Press, 1976.

Perló Cohen, Manuel. *Estado, vivienda y estructura urbana en el cardenismo.* Mexico City: Instituto de Investigaciones Sociales/UNAM, 1981.

Perló Cohen, Manuel. *El paradigma porfiriano: historia del desagüe del Valle de México.* Mexico City: Porrúa, 1999.

Perló Cohen, Manuel. "Política y vivienda en México, 1910–1952." *Revista Mexicana de Sociología* 41, no. 3 (1979): 769–835.

Perló Cohen, Manuel. *Uruchurtu: el regente de hierro.* 2 vols. Mexico City: UNAM, 2023.

Piccato, Pablo. *City of Suspects: Crime in Mexico City, 1900–1931.* Durham, NC: Duke University Press, 2001.

Piccato, Pablo. *Historia mínima de la violencia en México.* Mexico City: El Colegio de México, 2022.

Pineo, Ronn F., and James A. Baer, eds. *Cities of Hope: People, Protests, and Progress in Urbanizing Latin America, 1870-1930.* New York: Routledge, 1998.

Platt, Harold L. *Shock Cities: The Environmental Transformation and Reform of Manchester and Chicago.* Chicago: University of Chicago Press, 2005.

Pradilla, Emilio. "Notas acerca del problema de la vivienda." *Ideología y Sociedad* (Bogotá) 16 (January–March 1976): 70–107.

Prantl, Adolfo, and José Grosso. *La Ciudad de México: novísima guía universal de la capital de la república.* Mexico City: Juan Buxó y Compañía y Librería Madrileña, 1901.

Puig Casauranc, José Manuel. "Por qué y en qué extensión faltan los servicios de urbanización en el Distrito Federal." *Obras Públicas* 4 (April 1930): 225–231.

Puma, Jorge. "The Nazas-Aguanaval Group: Radical Priests, Catholic Networks, and Maoist Politics in Northern Mexico." *Americas* 79, no. 2 (2022): 291–320.

Quirarte, Vicente. *Elogio de la calle: biografía literaria de la Ciudad de México*. Mexico City: Cal y Arena, 2001.

Quiroz Rothe, Héctor, ed. *Aproximaciones a la historia del urbanismo popular*. Mexico City: UNAM, 2014.

Quiroz Rothe, Héctor. "Introducción." In *Aproximaciones a la historia del urbanismo popular*, 11–31. Mexico City: UNAM, 2014.

Rama, Ángel. *La ciudad letrada*. Montevideo: Fundación Internacional Ángel Rama, 1984.

Ramírez, Ramón. "El problema de la habitación y los niveles de vida." *Investigación Económica* 13, no. 3 (1953): 323–377.

Ramírez de Garay, Iván. *Entre el abuso de poder y la intermediación: las expropiaciones en la Ciudad de México tras el sismo de 1985*. Mexico City: Centro de Estudios Espinosa Yglesias, 2022.

Ramírez de Garay, Iván. "El sismo de 1985 en la Ciudad de México: una historia política." PhD diss., El Colegio de México, 2021.

Ramírez Saiz, Juan Manuel. *El movimiento urbano popular en México*. Mexico City: Siglo XXI, 1986.

Redfield, Robert. "The Folk Society." *American Journal of Sociology* 52, no. 4 (January 1947): 293–308.

Reyna, José Luis, and Richard S. Weinert, eds. *Authoritarianism in Mexico*. Philadelphia: Institute for the Study of Human Issues, 1977.

Rigdon, Susan. *The Cultural Façade: Art, Science, and Politics in the Work of Oscar Lewis*. Urbana: University of Illinois Press, 1988.

Robinet, Romain. "¿Los orígenes trasnacionales del 'corporativismo mexicano'? Una historia intelectual de la 'democracia funcional' en América Latina." *Historia Mexicana* 74, no. 2 (2024): 605–654.

Robinson, Jennifer. *Ordinary Cities: Between Modernity and Development*. London: Routledge, 2005.

Robles Pezuela, Luis. *Memoria presentada a S. M. el Emperador por el ministro de fomento Luis Robles Pezuela de los trabajos ejecutados en su ramo en el año de 1865*. Mexico City: Imprenta de Andrade y Escalante, 1866.

Rodgers, Daniel T. "In Search of Progressivism." *Reviews in American History* 10, no. 4 (1982): 113–132.

Rodríguez Kuri, Ariel. "Ciudad oficial, 1930–1970." In *Historia política de la Ciudad de México*, edited by Ariel Rodríguez Kuri, 417–482. Mexico City: El Colegio de México, 2012.

Rodríguez Kuri, Ariel. *La experiencia olvidada: el Ayuntamiento de México: política y gobierno, 1876–1912*. Mexico City: UAM-COLMEX, 1996.

Rodríguez Kuri, Ariel. "Hacia México 68: Pedro Ramírez Vázquez y el proyecto olímpico." *Secuencia: Revista de Historia y Ciencias Sociales* 56 (2003): 35–74.

Rodríguez Kuri, Ariel. *Historia del desasosiego: la revolución en la Ciudad de México, 1911–1922*. Mexico City: El Colegio de México, 2010.

Rodríguez Kuri, Ariel, ed. *Historia política de la Ciudad de México*. Mexico City: El Colegio de México, 2012.

Rodríguez Kuri, Ariel. *Museo del universo: los juegos olímpicos y el movimiento estudiantil de 1968*. Mexico City: El Colegio de México, 2019.

Rodríguez Kuri, Ariel. "Secretos de la idiosincrasia: urbanización y cambio cultural en México, 1950–1970." In *Ciudades mexicanas del siglo XX: siete estudios históricos*, edited by Carlos Lira Vásquez and Ariel Rodríguez Kuri, 19–57. Mexico City: El Colegio de México/UAM/CONACYT, 2009.

Rodríguez Kuri, Ariel. "Urbanización y secularización en México: temas y problemas historiográficos (ca. 1960s–1970s)." In *México en tres momentos: 1810–1910–2010, hacia la conmemoración de la Independencia y del Centenario de la Revolución Mexicana: retos y perspectivas*, edited by Alicia Mayer, 107–120. Vol. 1. Mexico City: UNAM, 2007.

Rolland, Modesto C. *El desastre municipal en la República Mexicana*. Mexico City: self-published, 1939.

Romero, José Luis. *Latinoamérica: las ciudades y las ideas*. Mexico City: Siglo XXI, 1976.

Ronda, Stéphanie, and Vicente Ugalde. "Planeación urbana en la Ciudad de México en los cincuenta: controversias y debates en la Comisión de Planificación del Distrito Federal." *Secuencia* 70 (2008): 69–100.

Rosemblatt, Karin Alejandra. *The Science and Politics of Race in Mexico and the United States, 1910–1950*. Chapel Hill: University of North Carolina Press, 2018.

Roy, Ananya. *City Requiem, Calcutta: Gender and the Politics of Poverty*. Minneapolis: University of Minnesota Press, 2003.

Roy, Ananya. "Slumdog Cities: Rethinking Subaltern Urbanism." *International Journal of Urban and Regional Research* 35, no. 2 (2011): 224–225.

Roy, Ananya. "Transnational Trespassings: The Geopolitics of Urban Informality." In *Urban Informality: Transnational Perspectives from the Middle East, Latin America, and South Asia*, edited by Ananya Roy and Nezar AlSayyad, 289–317. Lanham, MD: Lexington Books, 2004.

Roy, Ananya. "Urban Informality: The Production of Space and the Practice of Planning." In *The Oxford Handbook of Urban Planning*, edited by Rachel Weber and Randall Crane, 691–705. Oxford: Oxford University Press, 2012.

Roy, Ananya. "Urban Informality: Towards an Epistemology of Planning." *Journal of the American Planning Association* 71, 2 (2005): 147–158.

Roy, Ananya. "Why India Cannot Plan Its Cities: Informality, Insurgence and the Idiom of Urbanization." *Sage Journals* 8, no. 1 (2009). https://doi.org/10.1177/1473095208099299.

Roy, Ananya, and Nezar AlSayyad, eds. *Urban Informality: Transnational Perspectives from the Middle East, Latin America, and South Asia*. Lanham, MD: Lexington Books, 2004.

Ruiz, Ana Esther. "¿Quién habita Sta. Cruz Mayehualco?" *Calli* 15 (January–February 1965): 6–7.

Ruiz Parra, Emiliano. *Golondrinas: un barrio marginal del tamaño del mundo*. Mexico City: Debate, 2022.

Salazar, Clara, and Ann Varley. "La urbanización del ejido: de los asentamientos irregulares a los conjuntos urbanos." Paper presented at the international conference "El Siglo del Ejido: Una Revisión," Chicago, October 24, 2015.

Sánchez, Félix. "La realidad mexicana y las nuevas concepciones arquitectónicas urbanísticas en material de habitación popular." *Estudios* 1 (1952): 43–50.

Sánchez de Tagle, Esteban. *Los dueños de la calle: una historia de la vía pública en la época colonial*. Mexico City: INAH, 1997.

Sánchez Mejorada, Cristina. *Rezagos de la modernidad: memorias de una ciudad presente*. Mexico City: UAM, 2005.

Sánchez Mejorada, Javier. "Discurso leído por el señor ingeniero Javier Sánchez Mejorada, secretario de comunicaciones y obras públicas, en la sesión de apertura del Primer Congreso Nacional de Planificación." *Obras Públicas* 2 (February 1930): 76–78.

Sánchez Ruiz, Gerardo G. "El contexto que rodeó a las propuestas de planificación del arquitecto Carlos Contreras." In *Planificación y urbanismo visionarios de Carlos Contreras: escritos de 1925 a 1938*, 9–24. Mexico City: UNAM/UAM/Universidad Autónoma de San Luis Potosí, 2003.

Sánchez Ruiz, Gerardo G. *Planificación y urbanismo de la revolución mexicana: los sustentos de una nueva modernidad en la Ciudad de México*. Mexico City: UAM, 2002.

Sánchez Ruiz, Gerardo G. *Planificación y urbanismo visionarios de Carlos Contreras: escritos de 1925 a 1938*. Mexico City: UNAM/UAM/Universidad Autónoma de San Luis Potosí, 2003.

Schers, David. "The Popular Sector of the Mexican PRI." PhD diss., University of New Mexico, 1972.

Schmitter, Philip. "Still the Century of Corporatism?" *Review of Politics* 36, no. 1 (1974): 85–131.

Schteingart, Martha. "Prácticas de producción y reproducción en el sector informal en México" (1990). In *Desarrollo urbano-ambiental, políticas sociales y vivienda: treinta y cinco años de investigación*, 149–166. Mexico City: El Colegio de México, 2015.

Schteingart, Martha. "Sector inmobiliario capitalista y formas de apropiación del suelo urbano: el caso de México." *Demografía y Economía* 13, no. 4 (1979): 449–466.

Schteingart, Martha, Jaime Sobrino, and Vicente Ugalde. *Mexico City*. Newcastle upon Tyne, UK: Agenda Publishing, 2023 (ProQuest Ebook Central).

Schulte-Sasse, Josef, ed. *Nacida entre chinampas: historia de la Colonia Gabriel Ramos Millán–Tlacotal en la Delegación Iztacalco*. Mexico City: Casa de Cultura Las Jarillas/Gobierno del Distrito Federal, Misereor, 2010.

Schulz, Enrique. "Breve reseña acerca de los trabajos relacionados con la planificación de la Ciudad de México." *Planificación* 2, no. 5 (November 1934): 34–37.

Scott, James. *Seeing Like a State*. New Haven, CT: Yale University Press, 1998.

Selvidge, Sarah. "Modernism and Miracles: Architecture, Housing, and the State in Mexico, 1930–1970." PhD diss., University of California, Berkeley, 2015.

Senorio, Alberto F. "Lo social como contenido del derecho." *Revista Mexicana de Sociología* 1, no. 1 (March–April 1939): 80–87.

Sheridan, Guillermo. *Lugar a dudas*. Mexico City: Tusquets, 2000.

Silva, Sergio. "Forking Paths: Authoritarianism, Population Growth and Economic Performance in Mexico and Spain, 1934–2000." PhD diss., Harvard University, 2009.

Snitcofsky, Valeria. *Historia de las villas en la ciudad de Buenos Aires*. Buenos Aires: Tejido Urbano, 2021.

Soares Gonçalves, Rafael. *Favelas do Rio de Janeiro: história e direito*. Rio de Janeiro: Editora PUC-Rio, 2018.

Sotomayor, Arturo. *El México en donde nací*. Mexico City: Porrúa, 1968.

Speckman Guerra, Elisa. *Crimen y castigo: legislación penal, interpretaciones de la criminalidad y administración de justicia (Ciudad de México, 1872–1910)*. Mexico City: COLMEX/UNAM, 2002.

Tenorio Trillo, Mauricio. *Elogio de la impureza: promiscuidad e historia en Norteamérica*. Mexico City: Siglo XXI, 2023.

Tenorio Trillo, Mauricio. *I Speak of the City: Mexico City at the Turn of the Twentieth Century*. Chicago: University of Chicago Press, 2012.

Tenorio Trillo, Mauricio. *Latin America: The Allure and Power of an Idea*. Chicago: University of Chicago Press, 2017.

Torres-Mazuera, Gabriela, and Kirsten Appendini, eds. *La regulación imposible: (i)legalidad e (i)legitimidad en los mercados de tierra en México al inicio del siglo XXI*. Mexico City: El Colegio de México, 2020.

Torres Puga, Gabriel. "La ciudad novohispana: ensayo sobre su vida política." In *Historia política de la Ciudad de México*, edited by Ariel Rodríguez Kuri, 112–143. Mexico City: El Colegio de México, 2012.

Touissant, Manuel. *Planos de la Ciudad de México, siglos XVI y XVII: estudio histórico, urbanístico y bibliográfico*. 1938. Reprint, Mexico City: CONDUMEX, 1990.

Townsend, Camilla. *Fifth Sun: A New History of the Aztecs*. Oxford: Oxford University Press, 2019.

Turner, J. C. "Barriers and Channels for Housing Development in Modernizing Countries." *Journal of the American Institute of Planners* 33, no. 3 (1967): 167–181.

Tutino, John. *The Mexican Heartland: How Communities Shaped Capitalism, a Nation, and World History, 1500–2000*. Princeton, NJ: Princeton University Press, 2018.

Unikel, Luis. *El desarrollo urbano de México*. Mexico City: El Colegio de México, 1976.

United Nations–Habitat. *The Challenge of Slums: Global Report on Human Settlements 2003*. London: Earthscan Publications, 2003.

"Urbanismo oficial." *Arquitectura y lo Demás* 1, no. 3 (1945): 21.

Urbina Martínez, Gilberto. "Algunas formas de negociación de los sectores populares ante los juzgados civiles de la Ciudad de México en las primeras décadas del siglo XX." *Trashumante: Revista Americana de Historia Social* 6 (2015): 82–103.

Urbina Martínez, Gilberto. "Años veinte, organización vecinal y desarrollo urbano." *Legajos* 1 (July–September 2009): 27–43.

Urbina Martínez, Gilberto. "Los colonos se organizan: aproximaciones a un posible mecanismo de interlocución entre habitantes y autoridades en la Ciudad de México (años veinte y treinta)." In *Actores y cambio social en la revolución mexicana*, edited by Nicolás Cárdenas García and Enrique Guerra Manzo, 165–192. Mexico City: Universidad Autónoma Metropolitana, 2014.

Urbina Martínez, Gilberto. "De discursos y realidades: los habitantes de algunas colonias populares al norte de la Ciudad de México (1875–1929)." PhD diss., El Colegio de México, 2012.

Valencia, Enrique. *La Merced: estudio ecológico y social de una zona de la Ciudad de México*. Mexico City: INAH, 1965.

Valenzuela, Gilberto, and Jorge Rojas. "Unidad de Habitación Santa Cruz Mayehualco." *Arquitectos de México: Cinco Años de Arquitectura Social en México* 19–20 (September 1963): 48.

Valenzuela Aguilera, Alfonso. *Urbanistas y visionarios: la planeación de la Ciudad de México en la primera mitad del siglo XX*. Cuernavaca: Universidad Autónoma del Estado de Morelos, 2014.

Valladares, Licia. *A invenção da favela: do mito de origem a favela.com*. Rio de Janeiro: Editora FGV, 2005.

Valverde, Mariana. "Seeing Like a City: The Dialectic of Modern and Premodern Ways of Seeing in Urban Governance." *Law and Society Review* 25, no. 2 (2011): 277–312.

Vargas Salgero, Ramón, Amaya Larrucea, and Carlos Chanfón Olmos, eds. *Arquitectura de la revolución y revolución de la arquitectura*. Vol. 4 of *Historia de la arquitectura y el urbanismo mexicanos*. Mexico City: FCE, 2009.

Varley, Ann. "¿Clientalismo o tecnocracia? La lógica política de la regularización de la tierra urbana." *Revista Mexicana de Sociología* 56, no. 4 (1994): 135–164.

Varley, Ann. "Postcolonialising Informality?" *Environment and Planning D: Society and Space* 31 (2013): 4–22.

Varley, Ann. "¿Propiedad de la revolución? Los ejidos en el crecimiento de la Ciudad de México." *Revista Interamericana de la Planificación* 22 (1985): 125–155.

Varley, Ann. "Urbanization and Agrarian Law: The Case of Mexico City." *Bulletin of Latin American Research Review* 4, no. 1 (1988): 1–16.

Varley, Ann, and Clara Salazar. "The Impact of Mexico's Land Reform on Periurban Housing Production: Neoliberal or Neocorporatist?" *International Journal of Urban and Regional Research* 45, no. 6 (2021): 964–984.

Vázquez Ramírez, Esther Martina. *Organización y resistencia popular en la Ciudad de México durante la crisis de 1929–1932*. Mexico City: Instituto Nacional de Estudios Históricos de la Revolución Mexicana, 1998.

Velázquez, Héctor. "¿Dónde vives? Conjunto urbano Peñón San Juan de Aragón." *Calli* 15 (January–February 1965): 9–16.

Vélez-Ibañez, Carlos G. *Rituals of Marginality: Politics, Process, and Culture Change in Urban Central Mexico, 1969–1974*. Berkeley: University of California Press, 1983.

Vila, Víctor. "Conjunto urbano Tlatelolco: aspectos urbanísticos." *Arquitectura/México* 94–95 (1966): 73–105.

Violich, Francis. *Cities of Latin America: Housing and Planning to the South*. New York: Reinhold Publishing, 1944.

Viqueira, Juan Pedro. *¿Relajados o reprimidos? Diversiones públicas y vida social en la Ciudad de México durante el siglo de las luces*. Mexico City: Fondo de Cultura Económica, 1987.

Vitz, Matthew. *A City on a Lake: Urban Political Ecology and the Growth of Mexico City, 1880–1950*. Durham, NC: Duke University Press, 2018.

Vitz, Matthew. *Globalizing Urban Environmental History*. Cambridge: Cambridge University Press, 2024.

Vitz, Matthew. "A Social History of Urban Expertise: Between Technobureaucratic Rule and the Right to the City in Twentieth-Century Mexico." In *Technocratic Visions: Engineers, Technology, and Society in Mexico*, edited by J. Justin Castro and James A. Garza, 181–204. Pittsburgh: Pittsburgh University Press, 2022.

Voekel, Pamela. "Peeing on the Palace: Bodily Resistance to Bourbon Reforms in Mexico City." *Journal of Historical Sociology* 5, no. 2 (2006): 183–208.

Vorms, Charlotte, and Brodwyn Fischer, eds. *Informal Cities: Histories of Governance and Inequality in Latin Europe, Latin America, and Colonial North Africa*. Chicago: University of Chicago Press, 2025.

Wakeman, Rosemary. *Practicing Utopia: An Intellectual History of the New Town Movement*. Chicago: University of Chicago Press, 2016.

Walker, Louise. *Waking from the Dream: Mexico's Middle Classes after 1968*. Stanford, CA: Stanford University Press, 2013.

Ward, Peter M. *Colonias and Public Policy in Mexico and Texas: Urbanization by Stealth*. Austin: University of Texas Press, 1999.

Ward, Peter M. "Una comparación entre colonias paracaidistas y ciudades perdidas de la Ciudad de México: hacia una nueva política." *Investigaciones Geográficas* 8 (1977): 101–121.

Ward, Peter M. *Mexico City: The Production and Reproduction of an Urban Environment*. 2nd ed. New York: John Wiley, 1998.

Ward, Peter M. "The Practice and Potential of Self-Help Housing in Mexico City." In *Self-Help Housing: A Critique*, edited by Peter M. Ward, 175–209. London: Mansell, 1982.

Ward, Peter M., ed. *Self-Help Housing: A Critique*. London: Mansell, 1982.

Ward, Peter M. "Self-Help Housing in Mexico City: Social and Economic Determinants of Success." *Town Planning Review* 49, no. 1 (January 1978): 38–50.

Ward, Peter M. *Welfare Politics in Mexico: Papering Over the Cracks*. London: Allen & Unwin, 1986.

Warman, Arturo, Guillermo Bonfil Batalla, Margarita Nolasco, Mercedes Olivera, and Enrique Valencia. *De eso que llaman la antropología mexicana*. Mexico City: Editorial Nuestro Tiempo, SA, 1970.

Weber, Jonathan M. *Death Is All around Us: Corpses, Chaos, and Public Health in Porfirian Mexico City*. Lincoln: University of Nebraska Press, 2019.

Wigle, Jill. "The 'Graying' of 'Green' Zones: Spatial Governance and Irregular Settlement in Xochimilco, Mexico City." *International Journal of Urban and Regional Research* 38, no. 2 (2014): 573–589.

Wood, Andrew Grant. "*Viva la Revolución Social!* Postrevolutionary Tenant Protest and State Housing Reform in Veracruz, Mexico." In *Cities of Hope: People, Protests, and Progress in Urbanizing Latin America, 1870–1930*, edited by Ronn F. Pineo and James A. Baer, 88–128. Boulder, CO: Westview Press, 1998.

Yee, David. *Informal Metropolis: Life on the Edge of Mexico City, 1940–1976*. Lincoln: University of Nebraska Press, 2024.

Yiftachel, Oren. "Theoretical Notes on 'Gray Cities': The Coming of Urban Apartheid?" *Planning Theory* 8, no. 1 (2009): 88–100.

Yúdico, Juan. "Las colonias de la capital." In *Memoria del H. Ayuntamiento de México correspondiente a 1908*, 291–302. Mexico City: Imprenta dirigida por J. Aguilar Vera, 1910.

Zamora, Adolfo. "Situación y estructura del Banco Nacional Hipotecario Urbano y de Obras Públicas." *Trimestre Económico* 13 (1946): 271–305.

Zamorano Villarreal, Claudia C. *Vivienda mínima obrera en el México posrevolucionario: aportaciones de una utopía urbana (1932–2004)*. Mexico City: CIESAS / Publicaciones de la Casa Chata, 2013.

Zenteno Martínez, Carlota. "La Comisión Mixta de Planificación: un organismo clave en el ordenamiento urbano de la Ciudad de México durante la regencia de Ernesto P. Uruchurtu." *Anuario de Espacios Urbanos* 28 (2021): 19–41.

Zenteno Martínez, Carlota. "El ordenamiento vial de la Ciudad de México y los proyectos de regeneración urbana del gobierno federal: el caso de la prolongación del Paseo de la Reforma y la propuesta de ampliación de varias calles de la Colonia Guerrero, 1958–1964." *Meyibó* 25 (2023): 13–44.

Ziccardi, Alicia. "La Sociedad Cooperativa 'Plutarco Elías Calles' S.C.L., colonizadora y urbanizadora de los terrenos de la colonia Ex–Hipódromo Peralvillo." *Habitación* 5 (1982): 32–38.

Index

Note: Page numbers in *italics* indicate figures and tables. Abbreviations have been used for Department of Public Works (DPW) and neighborhood associations (NAs).

www.ingramcontent.com/pod-product-compliance
Lightning Source LLC
LaVergne TN
LVHW092159290826
846720LV00004B/57